6TH EDITION

Wanted TO BUY

A listing of serious buyers paying CASH for everything collectible!

COLLECTOR BOOKS
A Division of Schroeder Publishing Co., Inc.

The current values in this book should be used only as a guide. They are not intended to set prices, which vary from one section of the country to another. Auction prices as well as dealer prices vary greatly and are affected by condition as well as demand. Neither the Editors nor the Publisher assumes responsibility for any losses that might be incurred as a result of consulting this guide.

Searching for a Publisher?

We are always looking for knowledgeable people considered to be experts within their fields. If you feel that there is a real need for a book on your collectible subject and have a large comprehensive collection, contact Collector Books.

Cover Design: Beth Summers
Book Design: Donna Ballard

Introduction

This book was compiled to help put serious buyers in contact with the non-collecting sellers all over the country. Most of us have accumulated things that are not particularly valuable to us but could very well be of interest to one of the buyers in this book. Not only does this book list the prices that collectors are willing to pay on thousands of items, it also lists hundreds of interested buyers along with the type of material each is buying. *Wanted to Buy* is very easy to use. The listings are alphabetically arranged by subject, with the interested buyer's name and address preceding each group of listings. In the back of the book, we have included a special section which lists the names and addresses of over 250 buyers along with the categories that they are interested in. When you correspond with these buyers, be sure to enclose a self-addressed, stamped envelope if you want a reply. If you wish to sell your material, quote the price that you want or send a list. Ask if there are an items on the list that they might be interested in and the price that they would be willing to pay. If you want the list back, be sure to send a SASE large enough for it to be returned.

Packing and Shipping Instructions

Special care must be exercised in shipping fragile items in the mail or UPS Double boxing is a must when shipping glass and china pieces. It is extremely important that each item be wrapped in several layers of newspaper. First, put a four-inch layer of wadded newspaper in the bottom of the box. Secondly, start placing the well-wrapped items on top of the crushed newspaper, making certain that each piece of glass or china is separated from the others. Make sure that there are at least four inches of cushioning newspaper or foam between each item. When the box is nearly full, place more cushioning material on top of the contents and then seal the box.

Finally, place this box and contents in a large box cushioned again with a at least four inches of newspaper on all four sides, top and bottom. This double boxing is very important. Our Postal Service and United Parcel Service are efficient; however, we must pack well just in case there is undue bumping in handling.

When shipping coins and precious metals, be sure to register your shipment and request a return slip so that you will know that the buyer received the goods, as well as the date that they were delivered. All material should be insured for full value. Remember, always use strong boxes, lots of packing, and good shipping tape.

Adding Machines

Collector seeks **antique adding machines and calculators**, catalogs, stocks, advertising leaflets, and instruction booklets (no cut outs). Some machines were sold in huge numbers; therefore, **I do not buy machines manufactured by Burroughs, Lightning, and Monroe.** Paying top dollar for machines in mint condition but will also buy items in need of repair or restoration. Description should include any information you can find on the machine, such as manufacturer, patent dates, serial numbers, and condition. Willing to pay finder's fee. Other wants include **typewriters, sewing machines, pencil sharpening machines, hand-powered vacuum cleaners (bellows type), knitting machines, radios (pre-1935), and television sets (pre-1948).** Please call 1-800-942-8968 for immediate cash. The machines listed here are just a few, there are many more, call for complete list of machines wanted.

Peter Frei
P.O. Box 500
Brimfield, MA 01010-0500
800-942-8968 or fax 413-245-6079

We Pay

Baldwin Arithometer 1874	600.00
Baldwin 1875	750.00
Bouchet 1883	1,600.00
Calcumeter, The Standard Desk Calcumeter	200.00
Comptograph, w/wooden frame	1,000.00
Comptometer, w/wooden frame	450.00
Contostyle, Arithstyle	180.00
Diera	600.00
Gab-Ka	2,000.00
GEM, w/wooden frame	250.00
Grant	1,500.00
Midget	1,000.00
Millionaire	600.00
Peerless	400.00
Rapid Computer Adding Machine 1893	200.00
Saxonia, in wood case	600.00
Smith 1881	650.00
Spalding	750.00
Thomas Arithmometre	1,300.00
Weeb's	140.00

Nobody pays more! For world's leading collection, I am buying single items or entire collections for top prices! I am especially looking for **early typewriters, ribbon tins, telephones, telegraphs, copying machines, pencil sharpeners, and postcards about the old office**. Also see my listing in this book under **Typewriters**.

Uwe H Breker
6731 Ashley Ct.
Sarasota, FL 34241
941-925-0385 or fax 941-925-0487

Calculators   We Pay

Arithmaurel, 1849	**25,000.00**
Babbage's, 1812-1880	**50,000.00**
Baldwin, 1875	**20,000.00**
Edmondson, 1885	**20,000.00**
Grant, 1877	**25,000.00**
Stanhope, 1777	**75,000.00**

Advertising

We buy old advertising. Prices for items are based on excellent condition or better as well as rarity. Soda fountain items, general store, drug store, gas and automotive, hardware and lumber company, and railroad items are wanted. Pre-1920s Texas examples (other states wanted also), beer items, porcelain signs, flanges, door pushes, thermometers, Dan Patch, 1906 World Famous Pacer, and Dr. Daniel's veterinary items are sought. Other items include: soft drink, gum, and cigar items; small 5¢ coin-operated machines; and advertising glass and wood counter top display cases. No large items or machines or no magazine ads are wanted. All items bought must be in excellent or better condition and guaranteed authentic with full return rights, if not so.

Mark and Jeri Devers
1610 Madera
Garland, TX 75040
214-276-5875

We Pay

Advertising Pot Scrapers, colorful graphics on 1 side	**up to 75.00+**
Advertising Pot Scrapers, colorful graphics on 2 sides	**up to 100.00+**

Advertising

Shoe Horns, colorful graphics ....**up to 50.00+**
Counter-Top Display Case, wood & glass w/gum advertising.......**up to 250.00+**
Tip Trays, soda, beer, cigars, etc...**up to75.00+**
Clocks, soda, beer, cigar, auto, railroad, etc. ....**up to 100.00+**
Thermometers, glass face, soda, beer, cigars, etc. ....**up to 75.00+**

We buy **advertising items of almost any kind**: Campbell Kids, Coke, Elsie the Cow, Esso, Howard Johnsons, Pepsi, Planters Peanuts, Reddy Kilowatt, Speedy Alka-Seltzer, NYC Stork Club, Coney Island-related items, Freedom-land, lighted advertising clocks, door push plates, advertising and/or figural radios, vinyl figural advertising characters. Also wanted are airline memora-bilia, plates and dishes with logos from any of the previously mentioned cate-gories or anything similar. Country store collectibles are of interest. Planters Peanuts is our specialty (we hosted the 1995 National Convention). We have spent top dollar for old advertising of all kinds. We are always looking for rare and hard-to-find items. If you are not sure if the item is new or old, please call. We reimburse actual UPS and insurance charges.

Marty Blank
P.O. Box 405
Fresh Meadows, NY 11365
516-485-8071 (6:30-9:30 pm EST)

We Pay

Campbell Kids Salt & Pepper Shakers...**20.00**
Coke Figural Cooler Radio, ca 1950s ....**200.00+**
Col. Sanders Bobbin' Head, plastic **30.00**
Elsie the Cow Clock, lighted...**50.00+**
Elsie the Cow Cookie Jar...**70.00+**
Esso Oil Man Drop Bank...**25.00+**
Heinz Talking Clock **50.00**
Michelin Man Figural Tire Ashtray **20.00**
Pan Am Airlines Memorabilia..**Call**
Piel's Bert & Harry Salt & Pepper Shakers **50.00**
Pepsi Can Radio **15.00**
Planters Peanuts, **Our Specialty — We Pay Highest** ....**Call**
Mr Peanut Vendor Bank **150.00-250.00**
Reddy Kilowatt Advertising Figure ....**100.00+**
Reddy Kilowatt Zippo Lighter..**20.00**
Snap, Crackle, Pop Vinyl Dolls **30.00**
Stork Club Items..**Call**

I am interested in **any items with Horlick on them**. The items can be glass, pottery, metal, paper, beaters, hand mixers, tins (including small to large sizes), wooden boxes, and so on. I prefer items that have only the location of Wisconsin but will buy those that show Wisconsin and England. The items should be in excellent to mint condition other than paper products, wooden boxes, and tins. I will pay UPS actual charges including any additional insurance. Listed below is only a sampling of items I would like.

Susan N. Cox
237 E Main St.
El Cajon, CA 92020
fax 619-447-0185

We Pay

Postcard, any design **7.00**
Tin, beige w/blue writing, 2x3" **16.00**
Beater, glass w/cast iron top & mechanism, Horlick on top.....................**375.00**
Mixer, glass w/red on blue Horlick on glass, no lid..................................**12.00**
Mirror, round w/Horlick, woman & cow on reverse, sm **50.00**
Pen light, metal w/Horlick, w/cardboard box **75.00**
Box, wood, no lid, 12" long, 3" tall...**25.00**

We collect, buy, and trade **glass jars and trays many companies supplied their vendors**. These had a company logo or name included in their design. Some would also have paper labels in addition to the embossed name, and later ones had painted-on names. We are generally only interested in embossed items, not painted or paper labeled. Below are examples of approximate prices for jars and trays that are complete with original lids and have no cracks or heavy chips. Jars with minor chipping along their rims will be only slightly less, but large rim chips or chips on other surfaces will greatly devalue items. Missing lids or trays with any chipping usually bring much less than perfect items. Also bought are spare lids.

Also buying very old, plain counter jars in ususual shapes and old penny candy jars or tops to any of these. Many of these, like those listed below with an* have been reproduced. Original Planters jars were only made in clear glass (none were colored) and are embossed 'Made in USA' on the bottom.

Abalone Cove Antiques
7 Fruit Tree Rd.
Portuguese Bend, CA 90275
310-377-4609 or fax 310-544-6792

We Pay

After Dinner Famous Peanuts Jar **80.00**
Barsam Bros Jar **90.00**
Beich's Jar...**70.00**
Dad's Cookies Jar...**90.00**
Elephant Peanuts Jar **120.00**
Hoffman's Chocolates, low tray, vaseline **45.00**
Nabisco Jar..**50.00**
Nut House Peanut Jars, various styles, ea.................................**45.00-70.00**
Pitcain Water Spar Jar **75.00**
Planters Peanuts Jar, corner peanut*...**200.00**
Planters Peanuts Jar, fishbowl* **60.00**
Planters Peanuts Jar, football **200.00**
Planters Peanuts Jar, 8-sided, lg* **85.00**
Planters Peanuts Jar, running Mr Peanut* **120.00**
Planters Peanuts Jar, sq..**60.00**
Squirrel Peanuts Jar **85.00**
Teaberry Gum Tray, clear w/pedestal...**40.00**
Teaberry Gum Tray, vaseline or white w/pedestal...............................**45.00**
Teaberry Gum Tray, amber, low...**45.00**
Water Spar Varnish Jar **85.00**

I am interested in buying all **unusual Planters Peanuts and Mr. Peanut memorabilia**, especially containers that held Planters products and point-of-sale display items. I am also interested in any material from the many Planters Peanuts stores that existed throughout the country, such as signs, neon clocks, etc. I will always reimburse your postage or UPS and insurance costs. A SASE will guarantee a reply to any written inquiry. Please write or call if unsure of any item or if not listed below. Unwanted items include magazine ads, plastic cups, metal dishes, pocket knives, plastic banks, and items made after 1970.

Sherwin Borsuk
80 Parker Ave.
Meriden, CT 06450
203-237-8042

We Pay

Boxes, cardboard, held Planters products ....**50.00+**
Store Display, cardboard or paper, featuring Mr. Peanut.......................**75.00+**
Coloring Books, unused, before 1950 ....**10.00+**
Glass Jars, clear glass (not reproduction), w/lids ....**25.00+**

Glass Jars, clear glass w/paper label(s)..**75.00+**
Letter Opener, from Planter's Chocolate & Nut Co **250.00**
Statue, metal, legs crossed..**250.00+**
Statue, rubber...**350.00+**
Store Display, metal...**250.00+**
Costume, Mr. Peanut...**200.00+**
Night Light, plastic Mr. Peanut ....**75.00+**
Figure, papier-mache Mr. Peanut..**125.00+**
Lamp, papier-mache or composition Mr. Peanut statue on base, electric...**1,500.00+**
Peanut Butter Pail ....**250.00+**
Toy, plastic vehicle driven by Mr. Peanut..**150.00+**
Postcards, showing Planter's stores or factories ....**2.00+**
Hand Puppet ....**350.00+**
Tin, held Planters Peanuts, pocket size ....**250.00+**
Tin, held Planters Nuts, under 1-lb size ....**15.00+**
Tin, held Planters Nuts, 5-lb size...**50.00+**
Tin, held Planters Nuts, 10-lb size...**200.00+**
Trolley Card Ad, cardboard..**75.00+**
Shipping Crates, Planters, wood ....**100.00+**

———

I buy **old advertising** of many kinds such as signs made of porcelain, tin, cardboard, and paper; lighted clocks and signs; containers used to hold coffee, tobacco, cosmetics, medications, food, or soda pop; thermometers; and small items such as pins, mirrors, jewelry, tops, crickets, lighters, and playing cards. I love to buy in quantity and will offer you a fair price. Other wants include **political memorabilia, radio premiums, and hunting memorabilia — especially anything relating to gunpowder**.

David Beck
P.O. Box 394
Mediapolis, IA 52637
319-394-3943

We Pay

Coffee Can, #1 key-wound style ....**up to 100.00**
Pocket Mirror...**up to 100.00**
Pins, farm machinery company ....**up to 75.00**
Sign, Coca-Cola, porcelain ....**up to 1,500.00**
Sign, Coca-Cola, tin ....**up to 750.00**
Sign, bottle form, die-cut bottle ....**up to 400.00**
Sign, oil company, porcelain, 24" dia...**up to 700.00**
Sign, corn or feed supplier...**up to 75.00**

Advertising

Sign, yard-long paper ....**up to 200.00**

Quality porcelain signs are wanted on a variety of subjects that were advertised from around 1890 to 1960. These can be found in many shapes and sizes. I'm mostly interested in those that have nice graphics. Age is not as much of a consideration as graphics. A sign book is available for sending $30.00 postpaid.

Mike Bruner
4103 Lotus Dr.
Waterford, MI 48329
810-623-4875

Signs	We Pay
Adams Express	200.00
Ace Flour	150.00
AT&T Long Distance	275.00
Bond Bread	60.00
Greyhound Bus	400.00
Hood Tires	370.00
Hood's Milk	550.00
Kool Motor	225.00
Pepsi-Cola	100.00
Postal Telegraph	250.00
Red Cross	30.00
Sapolin Paints	125.00
Sinclair Gasoline	160.00
Vitality Dog Food	200.00
Western Union	125.00

Tin cans that held a product such as aspirins, automotive items, condoms, cosmetic and shaving items, gums, medicines and veterinarian items, needles, polishes, typewriter ribbons, spices, and sample tins of coffee, cocoa, face powders, talcum, etc.

These products will photocopy beautifully, so send me a photocopy with your price, and I'll get back with you the very day I receive it. Please include your phone number.

I have a comprehensive list of over 1,500 tins I'm actively looking for with prices I'm willing to pay. If you send a SASE (three stamps) in at least a #10 envelope, I will send it to you. **No tins made after 1940s or any common tins** such as Tums, Sucrets, Bayer Aspirin, Kee-Lox, or Typewriter Ribbon are wanted.

I have published a book on the subject called *Encyclopedia of Advertising Tins (Smalls and Samples)* which is available for $29.95.

David Zimmerman
6834 Newtonsville Rd.
Pleasant Plain, OH 45162
513-625-5188

Private collector seeks **materials relating to British biscuit tins** such as trade cards, advertisements, calendars, pocket mirrors, giveaways, point-of-purchase items, etc. Brands may include Huntley & Palmer, Crawford's, McVitie & Price, Jacob's, MacKenzie, CWS, and others; but items must be British bisquit manufacturers only.

Bryon Fink
Hopkinson House, Apt. 605
Washington Square South
Philadelphia, PA 19106
215-923-9749

I am a collector of **General Electric refrigerator promotional items** from the 1920s through the 1930s pertaining to the monitor top refrigerator. I am in search of a refrigerator-shaped G.E. clock that is 8½" by 5" in size and has Telechron electric clockworks centered in the door. I'm also looking for a G.E. water bottle and a monitor top-shaped creamer and sugar bowl set. I'm also interested in Frigidaire, Sewel, Westinghouse, and Norge promotional items. Please send description along with your asking price.

Larry Wessling
2805 Kingsridge Dr.
Blue Springs, MO 64015

Wanted: **gasoline and advertising globes.** These may be one-piece etched or painted glass, have metal bands with glass faces, or have plastic bands with unusual glass faces. Long-time collector **will pay top prices for quality items.**

Wayne Priddy
P.O. Box 86
Melber, KY 42069
502-554-5619 or 502-444-5915

Advertising

I am a private collector of **early advertising signs from the turn of the century up to the 1920s depicting phonographs** such as Victor, Columbia, Edison, etc. Below is a small list of signs I am currently looking to buy. Quality is important. Please write, call or fax. Thank you.

Kirk Lahey
70 Collins Gr. Unit 22
Dartmouth, NS
Canada B2W 4E6
902-434-5699 or fax 902-435-7886

Phonograph Company Signs We Pay

	We Pay
Pathe, tin	400.00+
Pathe, porcelain	500.00+
Mandel, tin	300.00+
Columbia Records Thermometer, tin	600.00+
Victor Records Thermometer, tin	600.00+
Columbia Grafonola, tin, shows dancing couple	400.00+

Art

We are interested in purchasing quality **American and European paintings from the late 19th century to the mid-20th century.** Please send photos with descriptions, dates, condition, etc. All letters are answered within a few days. We are especially interested in garden scenes, mothers and children, beach scenes with people, western works, and still life paintings featuring money. We have listed below prices we are willing to pay for major examples of the following artists. We are interested in smaller examples as well as works by artists not listed. We will also purchase entire collections or estates of artists. Please feel free to call.

Cincinnati Art Galleries
635 Main St.
Cincinnati, OH 45202
513-381-2128 or fax 513-381-7527

Major Works by Artist We Pay

	We Pay
Adams, J.O.	10,000-25,000.00
Albert, E.	5,000.00-10,000.00

Amick, W.	5,000.00-10,000.00
Bacher, O.	25,000.00-50,000.00
Baker, G.	10,000.00-25,000.00
Bannister, E.	25,000.00-50,000.00
Beal, G.	10,000.00-25,000.00
Beal, R.	10,000.00-25,000.00
Beard, J.	5,000.00-10,000.00
Beard, W.	5,000.00-10,000.00
Beaux, C.	10,000.00-25,000.00
Beckwith, J.	25,000.00-50,000.00
Betts, L.	10,000.00-25,000.00
Birney, W.	5,000.00-10,000.00
Bischoff, F.	25,000.00-50,000.00
Black, L.	10,000.00-25,000.00
Blenner, C.	5,000.00-10,000.00
Bloch, A.	10,000.00-25,000.00
Bluemner, O.	25,000.00-50,000.00
Boggs, F.	5,000.00-10,000.00
Borein, E.	10,000.00-25,000.00
Botke, J.	10,000.00-25,000.00
Bradford, W.	25,000.00-50,000.00
Bricher, A.	25,000.00-50,000.00
Bridgman, R.	5,000.00-10,000.00
Brookes, S.	10,000.00-25,000.00
Brown, J.G.	10,000.00-25,000.00
Brown, W.	5,000.00-10,000.00
Brush, G.	25,000.00-50,000.00
Bundy, J.	5,000.00-10,000.00
Butler, T.	25,000.00-50,000.00
Butterworth, J.	25,000.00-50,000.00
Cadmus, P.	25,000.00-50,000.00
Cassidy, I.	10,000.00-25,000.00
Chalfant, J.	25,000.00-50,000.00
Christy, H.	5,000.00-10,000.00
Coleman, C.	25,000.00-50,000.00
Couse, E.	25,000.00-50,000.00
Cucuel, E.	10,000.00-25,000.00
Curran, C.	25,000.00-50,000.00
Davey, R.	10,000.00-25,000.00
David, S.S.	10,000.00-25,000.00
Davies, A.	10,000.00-25,000.00
Deas, C.	25,000.00-50,000.00
Delano, G.	5,000.00-10,000.00
Deming, E.	5,000.00-10,000.00
Dewing, M.	5,000.00-10,000.00
Dixon, M.	25,000.00-50,000.00
Dodge, W.	5,000.00-10,000.00
Dolph, J.	5,000.00-10,000.00

Art

Dougherty, P. 5,000.00-10,000.00
Dougherty, T. 25,000.00-50,000.00
Dow, A. 10,000.00-25,000.00
Dubois, G. 25,000.00-50,000.00
Dubreuil, V. 10,000.00-25,000.00
Dufner, E. 5,000.00-10,000.00
Duncanson, R. 10,000.00-25,000.00
Dunn, H. 10,000.00-25,000.00
Dunning, R. 10,000.00-25,000.00
Dunton, W. 10,000.00-25,000.00
Durand, A. 25,000.00-50,000.00
Durrie, H. 25,000.00-50,000.00
Duveneck, F. 25,000.00-50,000.00
Edmonds, F. 10,000.00-25,000.00
Ellis, F. 5,000.00-10,000.00
Enneking, J. 5,000.00-10,000.00
Fairman, J. 5,000.00-10,000.00
Forsyth, W. 5,000.00-10,000.00
Francis, J. 10,000.00-25,000.00
Frost, A. 5,000.00-10,000.00
Gamble, J. 10,000.00-25,000.00
Garber, D. 25,000.00-50,000.00
Gaspard, L. 25,000.00-50,000.00
Gaugengigl, I. 5,000.00-10,000.00
Gaul, W. 5,000.00-10,000.00
Gay, W. 5,000.00-10,000.00
Gignoux, R. 10,000.00-25,000.00
Gilchrist, W. 5,000.00-10,000.00
Gile, S. 5,000.00-10,000.00
Gollings, R. 10,000.00-25,000.00
Graves, A. 10,000.00-25,000.00
Gruelle, J. 5,000.00-10,000.00
Gruppe, E. 5,000.00-10,000.00
Guy, S. 25,000.00-50,000.00
Hahn, W. 25,000.00-50,000.00
Hale, E. 10,000.00-25,000.00
Hale, P. 25,000.00-50,000.00
Hall, G. 5,000.00-10,000.00
Hamilton, H. 5,000.00-10,000.00
Hart, J. 5,000.00-10,000.00
Hart, W. 10,000.00-25,000.00
Harvey, G. 10,000.00-25,000.00
Haseltine, W. 10,000.00-25,000.00
Hawthorne, C. 25,000.00-50,000.00
Hennings, E. 25,000.00-50,000.00
Henri, R. 25,000.00-50,000.00
Henry, E. 25,000.00-50,000.00
Henshaw, G. 5,000.00-10,000.00

Herter, A. 10,000.00-25,000.00
Herzog, H. 10,000.00-25,000.00
Hibbard, A. 5,000.00-10,000.00
Higgins, V. 10,000.00-25,000.00
Hill, T. 25,000.00-50,000.00
Hills, L. 5,000.00-10,000.00
Hirst, C. 5,000.00-10,000.00
Hitchcock, G. 25,000.00-50,000.00
Hoffbauer, C. 5,000.00-10,000.00
Hopkins, J. 5,000.00-10,000.00
Horton, W. 5,000.00-10,000.00
Hovenden, T. 10,000.00-25,000.00
Hudson, G. 10,000.00-25,000.00
Hunt, W. 10,000.00-25,000.00
Hurd, P. 10,000.00-25,000.00
Hurley, E. 5,000.00-10,000.00
Innes, G. 25,000.00-50,000.00
Johnson, D. 25,000.00-50,000.00
Johnson, E. 25,000.00-50,000.00
Johnson, F. 25,000.00-50,000.00
Jones, H. 5,000.00-10,000.00
Kaelin, C. 5,000.00-10,000.00
Kaye, O. 10,000.00-25,000.00
Keith, W. 10,000.00-25,000.00
Kensett, J. 25,000.00-50,000.00
Key, J. 5,000.00-10,000.00
Krieghoff, C. 10,000.00-25,000.00
Kosa, E. 5,000.00-10,000.00
Kroll, L. Jr. 5,000.00-10,000.00
Kuehne, M. 5,000.00-10,000.00
Kuhn, W. 25,000.00-50,000.00
Kuniyoshi, Y. 25,000.00-50,000.00
Lambdin, G. 10,000.00-25,000.00
Lane, F. 25,000.00-50,000.00
Laurence, S. 10,000.00-25,000.00
Lie, J. 5,000.00-10,000.00
Lorenz, R. 10,000.00-25,000.00
Marsh, R. 25,000.00-50,000.00
Maurer, A. 25,000.00-50,000.00
McCloskey, W. 25,000.00-50,000.00
McEntee, J. 10,000.00-25,000.00
Meakin, L. 5,000.00-10,000.00
Melchers, G. 25,000.00-50,000.00
Melrose, A. 10,000.00-25,000.00
Mignot, L. 10,000.00-25,000.00
Miller, A. 25,000.00-50,000.00
Moeller, L. 5,000.00-10,000.00
Mora, F. 5,000.00-10,000.00

Art

Moran, E.	5,000.00-10,000.00
Mosler, H.	10,000.00-25,000.00
Mowbray, H.	10,000.00-25,000.00
Mulhaupt, F.	5,000.00-10,000.00
Nourse, E.	25,000.00-50,000.00
Osthaus, E.	10,000.00-25,000.00
Palmer, W.	5,000.00-10,000.00
Parker, L.	10,000.00-25,000.00
Parrish, M.	25,000.00-50,000.00
Paxton, W.	25,000.00-50,000.00
Peterson, J.	10,000.00-25,000.00
Peto, J.	25,000.00-50,000.00
Phillips, B.	10,000.00-25,000.00
Picknell, W.	10,000.00-25,000.00
Pippin, H.	25,000.00-50,000.00
Raphael, J.	25,000.00-50,000.00
Redfield, E.	25,000.00-50,000.00
Reynolds, W.	5,000.00-10,000.00
Rungius, C.	10,000.00-25,00.00
Salmon, R.	25,000.00-50,000.00
Sawyler, P.	5,000.00-10,000.00
Schofield, W.	10,000.00-25,000.00
Selden, D.	5,000.00-10,000.00
Seltzer, O.	10,000.00-25,000.00
Shaw, J.	10,000.00-25,000.00
Shulz, A.	5,000.00-10,000.00
Shinn, E.	25,000.00-50,000.00
Simmons, E.	10,000.00-25,000.00
Silva, F.	25,000.00-50,000.00
Sontag, W.	10,000.00-25,000.00
Stark, O.	10,000.00-25,000.00
Steele, T.C.	10,000.00-25,000.00
Stewart, J.	10,000.00-25,000.00
Tanner, H.	25,000.00-50,000.00
Thayer, A.	25,000.00-50,000.00
Thieme, A.	5,000.00-10,000.00
Tooker, G.	25,000.00-50,000.00
Vogt, L.	5,000.00-10,000.00
Volkert, E.	5,000.00-10,000.00
Weis, J.	5,000.00-10,000.00
Wendel, T.	10,000.00-25,000.00
Wessell, B.	5,000.00-10,000.00
Wessell, H.	5,000.00-10,000.00
Whittredge, T.	25,000.00-50,000.00
Wiles, I.	25,000.00-50,000.00

I am buying **paintings, oils, and watercolors, etc. by early 20th-century California artists** including well-known impressionists to the not-so-familiar artists. Of special interest are plein-air landscapes. Large or small canvases wanted. The price I pay depends on the artist, composition, age, condition, and size of the painting.

Jacqueline D. Marie
P.O. Box 852
Morro Bay, CA 93443
phone or fax 805-772-9648

I collect the **works of Joseph Jacinto Mora (a.k.a, J.J. Mora or Jo Mora, 1876-1947)**. He was one of California's most versatile artists, a master sculptor, painter, photographer, author, muralist, book illustrator, draftsman, cartographer, cartoonist, linguist, and even a jewelry desiger — he did it all, and exceptionally well. By the time this book is published, I shall have published my own definitive book on Jo Mora. I am interested in anything in relation to this artist — the acceptable condition of which will depend on scarcity; but in most cases, fine condition or better is desired. I will pay cash or horse trade for items of interest.

Other wants include **a 1930s poster of the oceanliner, *Normandie*; Art Deco, cowboy and Indian bookends; a Bucking Horse statue and artwork by Till Goodan; and anything by Jo Mora**.

T.J. Ahlberg
1000 Irvine Blvd.
Tustin, CA 92780
714-730-1000 or fax 714-730-1752

Pictorial Posters   We Pay

Cowboy Rodeo Poster, Salinas ....100.00+
Cowboy Rodeo Poster, Levi ® ....100.00+
Indians of North America Poster ....50.00+
Oceanliner *Normandie* Poster, 1930s ....Call

Pictorial Maps (Cartes)   We Pay

California ....50.00+
Los Angeles ....100.00+
San Diego (the Marston Co.) ....100.00+
Carmel by the Sea ....30.00+
Monterey Peninsula ....100.00+

Seventeen Mile Drive..100.00+
Central America (The Grace Line)..100.00+
Grand Canyon ....25.00+
Yellowstone...100.00+
Yosemite...75.00+

Other Wants   We Pay

Original Artwork ....Call
Sculpture ....Call
Authored Books ....60.00+
Illustrated Books ....25.00+
Carmel Dairy Milk Bottles ....Call
Carmel Dairy Calendars ....Call
Christmas Cards ....Call
US Half Dollar, California Diamond Jubilee, 1925 ....300.00
Hotel Del Monte Menu, 12 different, ea.....................................50.00
Pop Ernest's Menu 50.00
Del Monte Bar Recipe Booklet..50.00
Animaldom Cartoon, c 1898-1910, *Boston Herald*, Sunday 25.00
Sterling Silver Buckles or Jewelry Work, any............................Call
Original Photographs of Mora 10.00
Animal Football Calendar, 1903..Call
Your Other Items ....Call

I am interested in buying **fine art**, particularly American and European artists from the 19th and 20th centuries. Quality, subject, matter, size, period of the painting, fame of the artist, trends, condition, and provenance are some of the factors that determine the current market value as well as the medium that was used (oil on panel, oil on canvas, watercolors, etc.). Important paintings are always valuable, but valuable paintings don't have to be important but maybe art of the day. Track records of an artist are to be considered as well as quality. Quality can bring in large dollars without a name signed. I am willing to pay top dollar for any piece of fine art. Items wanted include:

Master limited edition lithographs   Beach scenes
Early New England artists   Latin American art
Early Florida artists   Paintings with women and children
Artists of California   Sporting art
American Impressionists   Garden scenes
New York Ash Can School

Ann Marie Alexander Galleries
Fine Art and Antiques
P.O. Box 1002
Dania, FL 33004-1002
954-987-1485

Art Deco and Art Nouveau

Steven Whysel, L.L.C., an antiques and art buyer, seller, appraiser, and consultant specializes in: **Art Nouveau** (metal, porcelain, furniture, and art). Prices are based on artist/manufacturer, rarity of item, and condition.

In metal works, sterling and bronze are favored. In furniture, inlay (marquetry) is desirable. In porcelain and pottery, those pieces mounted with bronze or silver are sought after. In art, works by Mucha and Charpentier are favored.

19th- and 20th-century European and American art (including oil paintings, watercolors, and original drawings) are also wanted. Prices paid are based on artist, medium used, size, condition, and subject matter. Only signed pieces are sought. Send photo, size, and condition description with stamped, self-addressed envelope to:

Steven Whysel, L.L.C.
3403 Bella Vista Way (Rte. 71)
Bella Vista, AR 72714
501-855-9600 or 501-751-5115

Art Nouveau is a fluid artistic style which swept the world at the turn of the century. It is characterized by its use of flowing, graceful lines and also by its use of maidens and the female figure, most often with long, flowing hair. Often water and waves are integrated into the piece as well. I buy **fine examples of the Art Nouveau period**. I will buy damaged porcelain and pieces which need replating, but the better the condition, the more I will pay to you! I am a dealer in Art Nouveau, and I am always looking for that special piece. You will recognize Art Nouveau by its outstanding beauty and attention to detail. The more exquisite the item, the more it is worth to me and to you.

These are other items we buy: **Russel Wright, vintage costume jewelry, mesh handbags, vintage compacts and accessories, Roseville, Weller, Rookwood, Newcomb College, Grueby, McCoy, pre-1920 Van Briggle, and Art Deco accessories and lighting.**

Fred Stegmann, Jr.
P.O. Box 4894
Laguna Beach, CA 92652
714-249-3711

We Pay

Art Nouveau Silverplated Vases or Centerpieces....................................**400.00+**
Art Nouveau Silverplated Decorative Objects...**250.00+**
Art Nouveau Silver Decorative Objects ....**450.00+**
Art Nouveau Silver, w/applied insects of other metals ....**750.00+**
Art Nouveau Ceramics, w/figurals or animals...**350.00+**
Moorcroft Pottery, signed WM or WMoorcroft.......................................**350.00+**
Weller, signed Sicard or Sicardo...**250.00+**

Art Pottery

We are interested in purchasing **fine American art pottery**. We will buy single pieces or collections valued into the 7 figures. As one of America's premier pottery dealers, we are constantly searching for pieces to add to our inventory. We will travel for large collections and payment is immediate. Below are examples of potteries for which we are searching. We will need photos and descriptions sent to us for a more precise estimate. All letters are answered within a few days or give us a call if that is more convenient for you.

Buffalo Pottery	Norse
California Faence	Orverbeck
Chelsea Keramic	Owens
Clewell	Pewabic
Cowan	Pisgah Forest
Dedham	Roseville
Fulper	Shearwater
Greuby	Teco
Lonhuda	UND
Marblehead	Van Briggle
Matt Morgan	Vance Avon
Niloak	Weller
Newcomb	

We are buying Rookwood pottery. Prices shown are approximate ranges paid for undamaged artist-decorated Rookwood. For a more precise idea of price please send photos with complete descriptions.

Cincinnati Art Galleries
635 Main St.
Cincinnati, OH 45202
513-381-2128 or fax 513-381-5727

Rookwood   We Pay

Standard Glaze Floral	200.00-5,000.00
Iris Glaze Floral	500.00-20,000.00
Vellum Floral	300.00-5,000.00
Indian Portrait	1,000.00-20,000.00
Scenic	700.00-20,000.00

I collect **American art pottery**. I'm particularly interested in Roseville, McCoy, Hull, Rookwood, Shawnee, Watt, Weller, and just about any American pottery. All pieces must be in mint condition — no cracks, chips, crazing, etc. Items I collect include: cookie jars, salt and pepper shakers, planters, jardinieres, vases, wall pockets, and figurals of people, animals, etc. I also collect Goldscheider figurines. Austrian items are preferred but will consider USA Everlast. I'll pay fair prices. Call or write me and let's make a deal!

Gene Underwood
3962 Fruitvale Ave.
Oakland, CA 94602
510-482-2841

Roseville   We Pay

Freesia	30.00+
Iris	40.00+
Snowberry	40.00+
Zephyr Lily	40.00+

Wanted: **art pottery and art glass**. I'm paying up to $100.00 for fine, old art pottery and glass pieces. Items such as figures, vases, baskets, epergnes, perfume bottles, lamps, paperweights, etc., are wanted. Pieces must have no breaks, cracks, chips, or excessive wear. Because items are unusual, I can't give a price without seeing them. Please send a photo of front and back sides and bottom. Along with the photos please give description including: composition (how it appears to be made), height and width, markings (please spell out), color (including any use of gold), and provenance (age, origin, etc.).

When I receive your photo and description, I will judge the piece for quality, access the value, and then mail you an offer plus an amount for postage as a deposit along with packing and shipping instructions.

Please do not send the item until I have seen the photo, and we have agreed on a price, and I have instructed you regarding packing and shipping.

Dorothy Hodges
442 E 6th St.
Beaumont, CA 92223
909-795-3170 (evenings)

Arts and Crafts

I buy **mission-style furniture and decorative accessories manufactured from 1900 through 1920**. Gustav Stickley, Limbert, Roycroft, L. & J.G. Stickley, and Stickley Brothers all made dark-colored, oak furniture that is plain and heavy in appearance. The furniture often has exposed construction with doweled pegs or wedges that join different boards. I also buy hammered copper and sterling silver accessories made by Jarvie, Roycroft, Kalo, Stickley, Karl Kipp, Dirk van Erp, and others. The metal is frequently a dark brown color and shows hand-hammered workmanship. Leaded glass and reverse-painted hanging and table lamps by such makers as Jefferson, Pittsburgh, Handel, Pairpoint, Bradley & Hubbard, and others are sought for purchase as well as art pottery by such makers as Teco, S.E.G. Marblehead, Newcomb, Fulper, Grueby, and Walrath. Write for a free list of wants.

Bruce A. Austin
Rochester Institute of Technology
College of Liberal Arts
Rochester, NY 14623-5604
716-475-2879 or 716-387-9820 (evenings)

We Pay

Bookcase, Roycroft, single door, mahogany, copper hardware ....**3,000.00+**
Bookends, Roycroft, hammered copper, poppy design, 6" ....**400.00+**
Box, cigar; Roycroft, hammered copper, applied silver squares..........**1,000.00+**
Bowl, Fulper, ceramic, brown over yellow, 10" ....**125.00+**
Chair, rocking; Gustav Stickley, 5 vertical slats on back ....**800.00+**
Candlesticks, Jarvie, copper, disk base w/slender stem, 14", pr..........**1,200.00+**

Chest of Drawers, Gustav Stickley, 2 over 3 ....**1,500.00+**
Desk Set, Roycroft, hammered copper, 5-pc set ....**275.00+**
Footstool, J.M. Young, uneven stretchers, 15x20"..................................**450.00+**
Jardiniere, Dirk van Erp, hammered copper, 10x12"..............................**1,000.00+**
Lamp, table; Bradley & Hubbard, 14" sq hip shade, slag glass...............**600.00+**
Lamp, table; Duffner & Kimberly, 18" dia leaded glass shade ....**1,500.00+**
Lamp, table; Gustav Stickley, round top, 24" dia ....**2,750.00+**
Magazine Stand, L. & J.G. Stickley, wide slats on sides.........................**900.00+**
Morris Chair, Gustav Stickley, 5 slats under arms ....**6,000.00+**
Pen Tray, Gustav Stickley, hammered copper.......................................**100.00+**
Pitcher, Newcomb, ceramic, high-glaze floral design, 6"....................**1,500.00+**
Plate, S.E.G., ceramic, rabbit design on border, 3 colors, 4" dia............**125.00+**
Settle (sofa), L. & J.G. Stickley, even arms, slats under arms...............**2,500.00+**
Sideboard, L. & J.G. Stickley, 2 cabinet doors & 2 drawers, 48" ....**1,750.00+**
Tile, Grueby, ceramic, bunny eating grass, 4" sq...................................**200.00+**
Tray, Benedict Studio, hammered copper, 20" dia ....**1,000.00+**
Vase, Jugtown, bulbous form, blue over red, 5"....................................**150.00+**
Vase, Karl Kipp/Tookay, 4 buttresses & silver squares, 8"..................**1,500.00+**
Vase, Walrath Pottery, orange flower design on yellow, 8" ....**4,000.00+**

I am a private collector interested in **all types of arts and crafts items** —
commonly referred to as Mission. Below is just a partial listing of those items
I am looking to purchase. Please write or call with your information. I pay top
dollar, and guarantee a fast response to your correspondence.

John S. Zuk
106 Orchard St.
Belmont, MA 02178
617-484-4800 (home) or 617-349-0652 (office)

We Pay

Newcomb College Art Pottery ....**500.00+**
Fulper Art Pottery...**500.00+**
Roycroft Copper Accessories (desk sets, vases, candlesticks, etc.)...........**50.00+**
Oak Furniture (Stickley, Limbert, Roycroft, etc.) ....**100.00+**
Roseville Pottery...**50.00+**
Pairpoint Lamps...**500.00+**
Handel Lamps ....**500.00+**
Tiffany Lamps ....**500.00+**

I am a collector of **Roycroft**. I am interested in purchasing any Roycroft piece but especially desk sets consisting of stationary holders, ink wells, pen trays, bookends, letter holders, blotters, calendar corners, stamp boxes, letter openers, bookmarks, desk clocks, humidors, ashtrays, matchbook holders, smoking stands, poker chip caddies, hatpins, incense burners, door knockers, bowls, frames, trays, small boxes, vases, jardinieres, candle holders, bud vases, and other metal objects bearing the Roycroft mark. Highest prices paid for pieces I do not already have in my collection. Send photo and price, or call toll-free.

Francesca Gern
P.O. Box 2161
Hudson, OH 44236
888-786-7455

We buy, sell, and trade **Moorcroft pottery**. Please call or write and tell us what you have. My phone number is 612-872-0226. This is a voice mail since we seldom answer the phone. Call us and we will call you back. Please leave a time when we can reach you.

We also buy, sell, and trade **Royal Doulton character and Toby jugs as well as other character and Toby jugs, Battersea, and Billston boxes**.

John Harrigan
Great West Companies
1900 Hennepin Ave.
Minneapolis, MN 55403
612-872-0226 or fax 612-872-0224

Autographs

Hello, my name is Ralf G. Mulhern. We have a hobby that is quite interesting. We started this hobby a couple of years ago. It has grown to be a certain part of our lives. We are collectors, not dealers. We give what we collect a good home. It has become a part of us. When writing please send a Xerox copy and price you desire on each photocopied item. It is most helpful in determining an offer that will make both of us happy.

We want one item or a hundred items. Some categories to look for are: space, artists, actors, any presidential material, colonial, Civil War, military, inventors, explorers, etc. We have broken our price scale down to show you an idea as to our offers. Thank you for considering us in your needs as well as ours.

Ralf G. and Donna Mulhern
3722 Alabama St., #130
San Diego, CA 92104

We Pay

Cabinet Cards or Civil War Soldiers **15.00-100.00**
Documents, Hand-Written or Typed Letters.............................**50.00-300.00**
Signed Photographs **25.00-250.00**
Unsigned Photographs of Famous People **15.00-100.00**
Tintypes of Famous People **15.00-100.00**
Unusual Subjects (people being hanged, etc.).............................**15.00-100.00**
Other Items Wanted...**Write**

We have been paying top prices for signed letters, photos, books, contracts, sheet music, manuscripts, signed restaurant or store receipts, and cancelled bank checks. Passports and driver's licenses are okay. Other interests include **postcards, movie lobby cards, and posters.** Prices paid depend on content and condition.

The Movies, Sig Goode
P.O. Box 878
Capt. Cook H, Hawaii, 96707
808-328-8119

We Pay

Louis Armstrong...**up to 3,500.00**
The Beatles ....**up to 3,500.00**
Charlie Chaplin ....**up to 3,500.00**
Truman Capote ....**up to 3,500.00**
Albert Einstein..**up to 3,500.00**
William Faulkner ....**up to 3,500.00**
Ian Fleming...**up to 5,000.00**
Greta Garbo ....**up to 5,000.00**
Clark Gable ....**up to 5,000.00**
George Gershwin ....**up to 5,000.00**

Howard Hughes	up to 4,000.00
Alfred Hitchcock	up to 4,000.00
Al Jolson	up to 4,000.00
Ernest Hemingway	up to 4,000.00
F. Scott Fitzgerald	up to 2,000.00
Vivien Leigh, as Scarlett	up to 2,000.00
W.C. Fields	up to 2,000.00
Marx Bros.	up to 2,000.00
Margaret Mitchell	up to 2,000.00
Vladimir Nabokov	up to 2,000.00
Lou Gehrig, signed baseball	up to 2,000.00
Humphrey Bogart	up to 750.00
Cary Grant	up to 750.00
Cole Porter	up to 750.00
Ezra Pound	up to 1,500.00
Pablo Picasso	up to 1,500.00
Boris Pasternak	up to 1,500.00
Babe Ruth, signed baseball	1,500.00
J.D. Salinger	up to 750.00
John Steinbeck	up to 750.00
Duke Ellington	up to 750.00
Paul Robeson	up to 3,000.00
Jackie Robinson	up to 3,000.00
Thomas Wolfe	up to 3,000.00
Josephine Baker	3,000.00

Automobilia

Automobile **books and automobilia of all types** purchased. We will buy hard- and soft-bound books, in or out of print, new or used, remainders, surplus stock, large private collections or single copies. Our main interest is in books that deal with auto racing, history of cars and their manufacturers, motorcycles, famous automotive personalities, design, etc. We willingly purchase all automotive books. However, we specialize in European and exotic automobiles such as Ferrari, Maserati, Lamborghini, Mercedes, Porsche, Rolls Royce, etc. We also specialize in domestic manufacturers that are no longer in existence such as Packard, Studebaker, Auburn, Dusenberg, etc. We do not buy ex-library books, sales literature, owners or workshop manuals unless they are appropriate to those types of automobiles previously listed. We purchase automobilia such as race posters, art, period photographs, original design renderings, etc. We are aggressive buyers of top quality items regardless of age and quantity. Prices quoted are for books with dust jackets in top condition.

LMG Enterprises
9006 Foxland Dr.
San Antonio, TX 78230
phone or fax 210-979-6098

We Pay

Annual Automobile Review 1953/54 #1	**100.00**
Annual Automobile Review 1954/54 #2	**160.00**
At Speed (Alexander)	**80.00**
Autocourse 1964-65	**90.00**
Bentley 50 Years of the Marque (Green)	**60.00**
Boyhood Photographs of J.H. Lartique (Lartigue)	**100.00**
British Light Weight Sports Cars 78 (Japanese)	**140.00**
Cara Automobile (Pininfarina)	**80.00**
Comicar (Bertieri)	**50.00**
Delorean Stainless Steel Illusion (Lamm)	**40.00**
DMG 1890-1915 (German)	**180.00**
Errett Loban Cord (Borgeson)	**120.00**
Ferrari 80, 2nd edition (Italian)	**100.00**
Ferrari Yearbook, 1949-1970, ea	**70.00-400.00**
First Century of Portraits Celebrating Mercedes	**200.00**
Grand Prix Car, Vol. 1 & Vol. 2 (Pomeroy)	**160.00**
L'Art et L'Automobile (Poulain)	**60.00**
La Targa Florio (Garcia)	**80.00**
Les 24 Heures de Mans (Labric)	**160.00**
Piloti che Gente, 4th edition (Ferrari)	**140.00**
Spirit Celebrating 75 Years of Rolls Royce (Dallison)	**60.00**
Ten Ans de Courses (Montaut)	**600.00**

I will consider and buy **almost anything issued by the Ford Motor Company with the exception of cars, parts, and ads**. I am also willing to sell and trade. Especially wanted are employee factory badges issued from 1910 to about 1960, brochures and pamphlets promoting Ford products as cement, charcoal briquets, tires, gasoline, and Johansson Gage Blocks. Also wanted are **items printed or made for the following fairs**: Panama-Pacific Exposition 1915, Chicago World's Fair 1933-34, San Diego Exposition 1935, Dallas Exposition 1936, and the New York World's Fairs of 1939 an 1964. Also sought are pins, badges, and buttons that Ford issued over the years. Condition determines price. Other wants include **pre-1946 aviation memorabilia and items made from the US Frigate *Constitution*, Old Ironsides**, when she was rebuilt in the 1920s.

Tim O'Callaghan
46878 Betty Hill Rd.
Plymouth, MI 48170
313-459-4636

We Pay

Factory Badge, shaped as front of Model T **150.00**
Factory Badge, shaped as front of 1927 radiator **100.00-300.00**
Factory Badge, round w/employee photo, WWII **100.00-200.00**
Gear Shift Knob, from various Expos & Fairs **75.00-150.00**
Ford Times/News Magazine, 1908 to 1943, ea **10.00-25.00**
Dish, marked w/lg green Ford logo **20.00**
Coaster, Chicago World's Fair, rubber **20.00**
Salt & Pepper Shakers, rotunda shaped **100.00**

I pay cash for **most all automobilia items**. Send photocopy or picture of item along with a price. I will answer all letters received. No car parts wanted. Automobilia of Buick, Oldsmobile, Cadillac, Pontiac, Chevy, Fisher Body, A.C. Spark Plug, Dort, Durant, Reo, Packard, Hudson, etc., wanted. I'm looking for several types of badges, flags, rings, factory-award jewelry, buttons, senority tie tacs, photos, medals, and some promotional materials and advertising. Postage and insurance will be reimbursed.

Gary Abdella
1929 Windsor
Flint, MI 48507
810-235-9439

We Pay

1937 Sit-Down Medallion..**35.00**
Buick Triangle Badge...**25.00**
Fisher Body Tie Tac..**25.00+**
Chevy Hourly Badge **12.00**
Buick 1942 Ashtray...**40.00**
Buick 14K Pocket Watch **175.00**
Ford Ladies 50th-Anniversary Compact **50.00**
Ford Iron Mountain Badge **100.00**
Chevy Corvette Owner Pin **85.00**

Fisher Body Wooden Craftman Guild **250.00**
Factory Plant Protection Badge...**up to 50.00**

Wanted: car, truck, tractor (circa 1900 to 1972) sales brochures; catalogs; owners' and shop manuals; parts books; paint chip books and loose sets. Also wanted are auto magazines, good condition old license tags, hood and radiator ornaments. Auto parts may be new or old stock. Lenses, chrome trim, suspension, and brake parts are wanted. Good used hubcaps circa 1920s through the 1960s are sought. Please let me hear from you if you have any auto-related toys from the 1920s through the 1970s.

Wayne Hood
228 Revell Rd.
Grenada, MS 38901
601-226-9060

TMC Publications deals in automobile literature for **Mercedes, BMW, Jaguar, Lexus, Porsche, Audi, etc.** We are constantly on the look out for:

Original workshop manuals
Owner's manuals
Parts catalogs
Sales brochures

Posters
Old automobile toys
Miscellaneous old automobilia
collectibles

The prices that we pay depend on condition and originality of merchandise offered.

Jeffrey Foland
TMC Publications
5817 Park Hts. Ave.
Baltimore, MD 21215-3931
410-367-4490 or fax 410-466-3566

I buy any quantity of **original gasoline globes or signs** — one piece or collections. Globes or signs need not be perfect but in decent condition. On globes, single sides or inserts only are okay. Just call or write.

Oil Co. Collectibles
Scott Benjamin
411 Forest St.
La Grange, OH 44050
216-355-6608

We Pay

Glass Globe, glass inserts...250.00+
Metal Globe, glass inserts ....300.00+
Picture-Type Globe, w/airplane, etc ....400.00-2,000.00+
Sinclair Aircraft, 1-pc ....2,000.00+
Musgo, 1-pc...2,800.00+
Bezol, 1-pc..1,200.00+
Other 1-Pc Globes, ea ....500.00-2,000.00+

Aviation

Buying **pre-1946 airline timetables and factory airplane and sales brochures, as well as all pins, badges, and buttons.** As a Ford aviation historian and collector, I pay top dollar for any aviation item associated with the Ford Motor Company. Also I'm interested in most other Ford memorabilia and items made from the U.S. Frigate *Constitution*, Old Ironsides, when she was rebuilt in the 1920s.

Tim O'Callaghan
46878 Betty Hill Rd.
Plymouth, MI 48170
313-459-4636

We Pay

Ford Airplane Catalogs, from 1920s 100.00-150.00
Ford Airplane Factory Employee Badge 300.00
Airline Timetables 10.00-35.00
Airline Timetables Picturing Ford Airplanes................................30.00-60.00
Florida Airways 1926 Timetable Picturing Ford Airplanes.....................100.00
Medallion From Side of Ford Plane...400.00

I buy most items used by **commercial airlines** in their operations, advertising, and promotions. My main interest is in dining ware items such as china, glassware, and silverplate serving pieces such as coffeepots, creamers, and sugar bowls, etc. Of particular interest are butter pats and salt and pepper shakers made of china. Items may be from either domestic or foreign airlines and either old or new.

Also of interest are airline-issue playing cards, crew wings, junior wings, and metal travel agency-sized airline models. The only non-airline issue items purchased are the **Aero-Mini brand metal airplane toy models** which are about six inches in length.

Dick Wallin
P.O. Box 1784
Springfield, IL 62705
217-498-9279

We Pay

Air France, early Concorde china w/black design	**25.00-50.00**
American Airlines, china w/DC3 plane & flag logo	**500.00+**
American Airlines, silverware, Flagship, w/airplane nose handle	**15.00**
British Airways, butter pat, w/blue & yellow Concorde rim	**35.00**
Any Airline, butter pat, china w/top logo	**20.00+**
Cubana Airlines, any china or playing cards	**25.00-50.00**
Foreign Airlines, cup & saucer set, w/top or side logo	**15.00+**
Delta Airlines, bowl, w/Flying-D oval logo, Incaware	**25.00**
Eastern Airlines, DC8 glass, w/gold pinstripes	**20.00**
Panagra, any china or playing cards	**25.00-50.00**
Pan Am, china, w/dark blue winged globe logo	**400.00-600.00**
Pan Am, teapot, sugar bowl or creamer w/gold eagle & stars	**100.00+**
TAT-Arrow Logo Joint Air-Rail Service Items, any kind	**50.00+**
Ashtray, chrome plane on pedestal, any airline	**100.00+**

I am buying **commercial airline items from Pan Am and Panagra**. I am also interested in items from other airlines. I prefer items from 1930 to 1950 but I will look at all commerical airline items from 1927 to 1980. Of special interest are **items from the Pan Am flying boats** and anything unusual from other airlines.

Please provide written description with photocopy, photo, or accurate drawing. Please enclose a SASE. Note: I am **not** interested in any military items.

	We Pay
Pilot Wings	25.00+
Pilot Hat Emblems	25.00+
Flight Attendant Wings	25.00+
Flight Attendant Hat Emblems	25.00+
Ground Service Insignia	15.00+
Timetables	3.00+
Playing Cards	1.00+
Anniversary Pins	5.00+
Advertising Pins	.50+
Uniform Patches	.50+
Dining Service Items	1.00+
Junior Pilot Wings	1.00+
Junior Stewardess Wings	1.00+
Junior Flight Certificates	1.00+
In-Flight Safety Cards, Pan Am/Panagra only	.50+
Ticker Jackets	.10+
Seat Pocket Packets	1.00+
Commemorative/Inaugural Items	2.00+

William Gawchik
88 Clarendon Ave.
Yonkers, NY 10701
914-965-3010 or fax 914-966-1055
e-mail: panam314@aol.com

Back Bars

I am buying old saloon and soda fountain back and front bars. Preprohibition and post-prohibition styles wanted in any size, shape, or condition; also wanted are bar parts — i.e., columns, arches, cornices, fronts, etc. Condition always determines price.

Spiess Architectural Antiques
228-230 E Washington St.
Joliet, IL 60433
815-722-5639

We Pay

Back Bar Simple Straight Cornice, 2 columns.........................**1,000.00-5,000.00**
Back Bar Single Arch..**2,500.00-7,500.00**
Back Bar Triple Arch...**4,000.00-10,000.00+**
Back Bar, Victorian, 4 spindles, round mirrors.................................**2,500.00+**
Front Bar, Brunswick style w/4 columns, 20 ft. or larger.......**1,500.00-3,000.00**
Front Bar, Victorian, 4 spindles, lattice panels, 16 ft.............**1,500.00-3,000.00**

Backscratchers

All types of backscratchers are wanted — especially of unusual materials or from foreign countries. I will pay according to uniqueness or artistic appeal. Please write, thank you.

Manfred S. Rothstein
Fayetteville Dermatology Clinic
1308 Medical Dr.
Fayetteville, NC 28304

Banks

These tin (or tin with paper label) **miniature oil-can banks** are usually four ounces in size and represent a specialty within the collectible bank category. Beginning in the early 1940s, these banks were produced as a promotional tool for gasoline and motor oil dealers. In addition to motor oil, many other specialty oils and fluids were promoted with these banks including antifreeze, top oil, and lubricants. There are well over 100 to 150 versions known to date. Many oil companies offered five or six different banks representing most, if not all, of their oil products. The most common tin banks are Cities Service with Koolmotor for various grades of oil (HD, 5D, Premium, etc.). Another is Wolf's Head Motor Oil with a number of versions, the most desirable being Wolf's Head Light Duty or Heavy Duty Motor Oils. The Super Duty version is the most common.

Listed below are some of the brands I seek in order to expand my collection of oil-can banks. Please drop me a card with your find and desired price. **Price range is from $5.00 to $65.00** based on condition and rarity. I'll respond immediately.

Peter Capell
1838 W Grace St.
Chicago, IL 60613-2724
312-871-8735

Banks From These Companies	We Pay
Freeway Service Stations	75.00
Blue Flash Tiolene 'Can Take It'	75.00
Pacific Cooperative Heavy Duty Motor Oil	45.00
Pure Tiolene Motor Oil, celluloid & tin	60.00
RPM Delo Lubricants (Standard Oil California)	45.00
Sohio, The Standard Lubricant	45.00
Standard, glass block	60.00
Wakefield Castrollo Uppper Cylinder Lub	35.00

Plastic Figural Gas Pump Banks	We Pay
Pure	50.00
Shell	50.00
Sunoco	50.00

Barware

Wanted: **cocktail shakers, vintage cocktail recipe books, and barware**. Cocktail shakers of glass and chrome, all kinds including figural, lady's leg, Zeppelin, Penguin, Dumbell, Golf Bag, Roosters, Lighthouse, and those made by Revere, Chase, Manning Bowman are wanted. Enclose photo or sketch and description and write to:

Stephen Visakay
Cocktail Shakers
P.O. Box 1517
W Caldwell, NJ 07007

Baseball Cards

I buy mint-like condition commons baseball cards which I layout on grids and hot plastic laminate using industrial roll-feed laminators. When trimmed, I have desk mats and dinner placemats which are sold to better gift shops. Every year I buy several hundred-thousand clean, undamaged commons baseball cards only of any players, any brands, and any years. I even accept massive duplications of the same player.

Now paying one-half cent each for commons in mint-like condition manufactured after 1992. Now paying one-third cent each for all other commons issued in 1992 or before. Payment promptly sent day after cards are received and counted. Do not send bent, dirty, or damaged cards. Any bent, dirty, or damaged cards will be returned at the same time as payment is mailed out. First-time card shippers ship up to 10,000 mint-like commons only sorted by pay categories above. These are delivered prices to me. Pack well in sturdy box and tape well. Ship cheapest way, usually UPS. This is a great way to get rid of duplicates of all those commons you have in your collection that nobody else wants to buy just because they are commons. Send baseball cards only, no others, and I will advise about future shipments.

Beautiful Land Recycling
Blaine Moore, Recycler
2602 Hilltop Dr.
Marshalltown, IA 50158
515-752-5077 (day)

Baseball Memorabilia

We buy fine **baseball memorabilia from before the turn of the century to 1950**. We only buy items of Hall of Famers (including publicatations, programs, autographed items, and advertising pieces). We do not purchase damaged or lesser-quality items nor autographs that are not, or cannot, be properly authenticated. Prices paid depend on condition, year, and scarcity.

Frank J. Ceresi
3600 N Nelson St.
Arlington, VA 22207

Bauer

Bauer pottery, after its move to Los Angeles, was one of the first potteries to use bright colors and the first to introduce the distinctive ringware. I buy **Bauer ringware, vases, large jars, jardiniers, and garden urns and pots** in excellent to mint condition. In the ringware style, the mixing bowls come in various colors and have a number on the bottom such as a 9 or 12. Some colors are more desirable than others; pouring and serving pieces like ice pitchers with lips, carafes, covered casseroles, large platters, and coffee or teapots are also very collectible. As is often true in other collecting categories, vases are also in strong demand. I have been dealing in Bauer for over five years and have a good market and clientele. Condition and color are very important, so the more desirable the color and the better the condition, the more money I can pay out to you.

Fred Stegmann, Jr.
P.O. Box 4894
Laguna Beach, CA 92652
714-249-3711

We Pay

Ringware Mixing Bowls, sm..**10.00+**
Ringware Mixing Bowls, med ....**20.00+**
Ringware Mixing Bowls, #9..**45.00+**
Ringware Pouring Pieces ....**40.00+**
Ringware Serving Pieces..**40.00+**
Ringware Dishes...**10.00+**
Ringware Vases ....**45.00+**
Vases..**50.00+**
Jars, lg...**100.00+**
Garden Urns, Jardiniers & Pots..**45.00+**

Bells

We are interested in buying cast brass, bronze, or silverplated bells that have humans, animals, or other figures as well as bells that are figurines or have figural handles. Details of the metal casting should be distinct. Any identifying marks as to the subject, artist, country of origin, or year of origin are important to us. Also, the tone of the bell should be clear and resonate for some time after ringing. We prefer older bells (do not polish any patina) but more recent ones are okay if they are good quality. We do not buy cheap reproductions, rolled metal bells, souvenir bells, most India bells, or badly damaged or cracked bells. Two-piece bells and pewter bells are of little value to our collection. Photos or descriptions with sketches are essential.

Donald Mathews
3215 Garner Ave.
Ames, IA 50010-4225
515-232-0938

We Pay

Blackbeard, Ballantyne, 1992	**100.00**
Ponce de Leon, Ballantyne, 1990	**100.00**
James Bridger, Ballantyne, 1985	**140.00**
Roman Centurion, Huddy	**175.00**
Turtle Bell (Toledo), wind-up	**95.00+**
Hemony Bell (or Serke)	**50.00+**
Napoleon Bell	**20.00**
Welch Lady w/Spinning Wheel	**50.00**
Sally Bassett (two feet clappers)	**80.00**
George Sands (lady)	**75.00**
Martha Washington	**70.00**

Black Americana

I buy **all types of Black Americana**, especially salt and pepper shakers, spice sets, cookie jars, clocks, stringholders, wall pockets, egg timers, egg cups, head vases, sprinkler bottles, teapots, spoon rests, pie birds, tablecloths, kitchen towels, etc. A favored category is Black Americana advertising, including anything Aunt Jemima, Coon Chicken Inn, Cream of Wheat, Gold Dust Twins (please no magazine advertisements), any premiums, products, or advertising signs with a Black Americana theme or logo. I buy children's books and toys with a Black Americana theme (e.g., Little Black Sambo,

Nicodemus, pickaninnies, golliwogs, Beloved Belindy, Topsy-Turvy) as well as other folk art or manufactured dolls, toys, games, and puzzles. Other Black-related books bought are literature, poetry (e.g., Dunbar, Weeden), and humor (e.g., *Two Black Crows*). I want vintage entertainment-related minstrel material, Amos 'n' Andy, Josephine Baker, Hattie McDaniel, and various *Gone with the Wind* items. I *do not buy* African artifacts, slave, or Ku Klux Klan material.

Judy Posner
May through October
R.D. 1, Box 273 HW
Effort, PA 18330
717-629-6583 or fax 717-629-0521
e-mail: Judyandjef@aol.com
or
November through April
4195 S Tamiami Tr. #183HW
Venice, FL 34293
941-497-7149 or fax 941-493-8085
e-mail: Judyandjef@aol.com

We Pay

Book, any Little Black Sambo, various, ea	**35.00-65.00**
Book, *Ten Little Niggers*	**65.00-95.00**
Cheese Shaker, Mammy	**45.00-55.00**
Cookie Jar, Aunt Jemima, hard plastic	**200.00-250.00**
Condiment Set, Mammy & barrels, ceramic	**85.00-95.00**
Doll, Beloved Belindy, Knickerbocker, 1964	**150.00-175.00**
Doll, Topsy Turvy, folk art, various, ea	**45.00-65.00**
Egg Cup, Golliwog	**45.00-60.00**
Plate, child's; golliwog	**45.00-60.00**
Puzzle, Little Black Sambo	**25.00-35.00**
Record, Little Black Sambo	**35.00-40.00**
Salt & Pepper Shakers, Coon Chicken Inn, pr	**200.00-250.00**
Salt & Pepper Shakers, various, pr	**20.00-150.00**
Shipping Crate, Cream of Wheat	**55.00-60.00**
Spoon Rest, Mammy (or w/Chef), various, ea	**50.00-75.00**
Syrup Pitcher, Little Black Sambo	**50.00-65.00**

I'm always interested in adding different and unusual items to my collection. I'm interested in **sterling souvenir spoons, kitchen items, matchcovers, ink blotters, and advertising items** as product tins, bottles, containers, signs, etc. I am **not** interested in native-type items or dolls. A photo or photocopy is helpful along with a description including condition and your asking price.

Joyce Wolford
1050 Spriggs Dr.
Lander, WY 82520
307-332-5868

We Pay

Aunt Jemima Items	Write
Bottle, shows advertising	20.00+
Children's Storybook	18.00+
Coon Chicken Inn Items	Write
Cookie Jars	Write
Cookbooks or Recipe Booklets	18.00+
Ink Blotter	9.00+
Linens, printed, appliqued, or embroidered	20.00+
Matchcovers	8.00+
Souvenir Spoons, demitasse or teaspoon	55.00+
String Holders	60.00+
Salt & Pepper Shakers, unusual, pr	35.00+
Tiger, single shaker to Little Black Sambo set	Write
Advertising Items, tin	25.00+
Toothbrush Holder, figural	50.00+
Wall Pocket	45.00+

Honest, well-established dealer paying top prices for **quality Black Americana** including: humidors, china, toys, games, tins, advertising signs, egg timers, banks, puzzles, Mammy items, folk or outsider art, authentic slave items, Little Black Sambo, anything pertaining to Aunt Jemima, Coon Chicken Inn, or Cream of Wheat. Premium prices paid for any **golliwog** item, including Florence Upton books. No magazine ads, please. I respond to all inquiries and pay promptly by whatever method is desired; and I have many repeat sellers. References supplied with pleasure.

The Butler Did It!
Catherine Saunders-Watson
P.O. Box 302, 3 Ash St.
Greenville, NH 03048-0302
phone or fax 603-878-2171
mobile phone 603-566-0553
e-mail 76063.2114@compuserve.com

We Pay

Humidors	200.00-700.00

Black Americana

Early Aunt Jemima Pieces	up to 800.00
Coon Chicken China	100.00-300.00
Golliwog, Steiff, original	5,000.00-6,000.00
Golliwog Egg Timer	125.00-150.00
Tin Advertising Signs	up to 1,500.00
Tin Jigger Toys	275.00-450.00
Cream of Wheat Bowl	75.00-95.00
Photo, Black Civil War soldier	up to 300.00

I am interested in buying **all types of Black memorabilia**, especially Mammy, Aunt Jemima, Uncle Mose, Uncle Remus, and Little Black Sambo. Also anything from the F&F Mold & Die Work collection. Items must be old and in very good condition — no repros, African, or KKK materials or items are wanted. I will pay top dollar. Please send photo with description, condition, and your asking price along with your phone number. A few specific wants are listed here.

LaGail Daniel
334 Campbrooklyn Rd.
Fitzgerald, GA 31750

We Pay

Cookie Jar, Aunt Jemima, hard plastic	300.00+
Book, *Little Black Sambo*	up to 100.00
Book, *Ten Little Niggers*	75.00+
Book, children's; w/Blacks	25.00+
F&F Mold & Die Works Items	up to 300.00
F&F Mold & Die Works Spice Rack w/Spice Containers, red plastic	250.00+
Puzzle, Little Black Sambo	50.00+
Salt & Pepper Shakers, Coon Chicken Inn, pr	200.00+
String Holder	75.00+
Syrup Pitcher, Little Black Sambo	65.00+
Wall Pocket	50.00+

I am interested in **Black memorabilia from before 1950**. Items must be in good condition, anything unusual. Send photo for me to bid. Examples of items wanted follow.

Arthur Boutiette
410 W 3rd St., Ste 200
Little Rock, AR 72201

We Pay

Advertising Items, ea ....**25.00+**
Book, vintage Black Sambo, ea ....**35.00+**
Book, w/golliwog ....**30.00+**
Doll, Beloved Belindy ....**20.00+**
Game, for Black children ....**20.00+**
Lamp, Mammy ....**75.00+**
Photo, tintype ....**20.00+**
Photo, tintype of Black soldier ....**40.00+**
Salt & Pepper Shakers, Coon Chicken Inn, pr ....**100.00+**
Toy, Amos 'n' Andy, tin ....**150.00+**
Toy, Alabama Coon Jigger, tin ....**150.00+**

Books

We buy **good condition used and out-of-print reference books on antiques**. Particularly need books on art glass, cut glass, silver, R.S. Prussia, toys, furniture, folk art, shaving mugs, dolls, etc. Buy hardcover or paperback; one book or entire library. Send list with title, author, date, number of pages, condition, your phone number, and price wanted. We pay generous shipping allowance. Please list all titles you have available.

Antique and Collectors Reproduction News
Box 71174-WB
Des Moines, IA 50325
515-270-8994

I am interested in purchasing **new or modern signed editions for resale**. I am also interested in **Easton Press and Franklin Press all-leather volumes** both signed and unsigned. I collect the **signed volumes of Ted De Grazia**, a well-known Arizona artist. Some examples of the prices that I pay are listed below. The value of individual volumes is of course dependent on the condition (must be fine or better). I will appreciate any and all quotes. I ask that complete description of the book and its condition be sent with SASE. Thank you for your help.

Al-PAC, Lamar Kelley
2625 E Southern Ave., C 120
Tempe, AZ 85282-7633
602-831-3121 or fax 602-831-3193

We Pay

Easton Press Leather Volumes..**12.00**
Franklin Press Leather Volumes..**12.00**
Easton Press Signed Leather Volumes **15.00**
Franklin Press Signed Leather First Editions **15.00-25.00**
First Edition Signed Ted De Grazia...**20.00-25.00**
Modern Signed First Editions **10.00-40.00**
Other Volumes, older, full leather, by well-known authors **10.00-1,000.00**

We buy and sell new and out-of-print books on **antiques and collectibles**. Wanted are older references or price guides pertaining to specific subjects in antiques and collectibles. Send list of titles with condition, year, size, and price.

Collector's Companion
Perry Franks
P.O. Box 935
Mechanicsville, VA 23111

Advanced collector wishes to buy **Sherlock Holmes** items, i.e., pre-1960 books, sculpture, posters, photos, prints, dolls, toys, games, pins, etc. Anything associated with Sherlock Holmes or Dr. Watson, i.e., Victorian gasogene, dark lantern, tantalus, and 221B Baker Street furnishings as well as items associated with Sir Arthur Conan Doyle (Watson's literary agent) are wanted. Prices vary according to condition and rarity. Antiques should be circa 1880 to 1910.

Richard D. Lesh, B.S.I.
1205 Lory St.
Ft. Collins, CO 80524
970-221-1093

Sherlock Holmes Items   **We Pay**

Books, 1st editions by Doyle ....300.00+
Books by Other Authors, pre-1960..30.00+
Sculpture of Sherlock Holmes or Dr Watson..100.00+
Posters of Movies or Plays, pre-1960 ....100.00+
Cigarette Cards ....10.00+
Autographed Letters, Books or Photos...100.00+
Dr. Watson's Service Revolver, Adams .450, circa 1880........................150.00+
Gasogene (seltzer bottle)..100.00+
Tantalus (2, 3 crystal decanters)..100.00+
London Police Dark Lantern, tin..200.00+

———

I am searching for books written by **Ella Wheeler Wilcox**. Ella was born in
Wisconsin in 1850 and died in Connecticut in 1919. She wrote approximately
50 books — most of which were poetry. Her most famous poem was titled
Solitude and begins with the lines 'Laugh and the world laughs with you,
weep and you weep alone.'

Ella's writing was self taught and her work came from the heart. She
referred to her early poems as 'heart wails,' and she soon became the most
widely-read poet of her era. She was loved by the common man yet disdained
by the critics. I will pay $100.00 each for the titles I don't have.

John Hanson
1318 Camden Ln.
Ventura, CA 93001
805-643-2869

———

Wanted to buy: any early **Dick and Jane readers or related items** dating from
1935 on. Call for prices paid.

Sue Samuels
408-484-9272

———

We want to buy **children's series books from 1900 to 1970**. These books are popular literature for children. Each series, or set, has a continuing main character or group of characters, e.g., Nancy Drew, The Five Little Peppers, etc.

Until 1960, all of these books were published with a paper cover, called a dust jacket. If the series book has a copyright date prior to 1960, the book **must** have its dust jacket to be considered for purchase. After 1960, most series were published in a format called 'pictorial cover.' The binding is an embossed cardboard with a picture printed on the front cover. Ofen the book cover has a listing of other books in the same series. Also the spine of the book usually has a number somewhere mid-span (1, 25, 33, 47, etc.) showing where your particular title falls in the series.

We only buy very good, tight books. Dust jackets must be in good condition too. We do **not** buy Bobbsey Twins (except with paper doll dust jacket) or Happy Hollisters (except for numbers 30 through 33). SASE for immediate answer with reason(s) if we do not purchase. Please note the way we pay more for some wants if they are for first editions. Prices also depend on condition; feel free to inquiry about others not listed here.

We also are interested in the **Limited Editions Club** begun in 1929 by George Macy. Each book was limited to 1,500 copies and signed by the author, illustrator, publisher, or a combination of all three. The paper, binding, and illustrations were fine. Each book was in its own individual box. The LEC also issued thousands of pieces of individual letters, etc. This ephemera is also wanted. Some of the original artwork for LEC books is also available. We do purchase **original original oils or lithographs produced from the Limited Edtions Club.** We only purchase books in fine condition in fine boxes. Most books fall in the $15.00 to $50.00 range.

We also buy complete libraries, leather-bound books, modern first editions, art books, and other children's books.

Lee and Mike Temares
50 Heights Rd.
Plandome, NY 11030
516-627-8688 or fax 516-627-7822

Children's Series   We Pay

Nancy Drew, #1 through #41 nonpictorial covers	3.00-12.00
Cherry Ames, #5 through #23, w/dust jacket	3.00-8.00
Cherry Ames, #24 through #27, pictorial covers	5.00-25.00
Rich Brant, #4 through #20, w/dust jacket	3.00-10.00
Rich Brand, #21 through #24 pictorial covers	5.00-25.00
Tom Swift Jr., #5 through #18, w/dust jacket	3.00-5.00
Tom Swift Jr., #26 through #33, pictorial covers	5.00-30.00
Chip Hilton, #1 through #19, w/dust jacket	3.00-10.00
Chip Hilton, #20 through #20, pictorial covers	5.00-30.00
Judy Bolton, #3 through #34, w/dust jacket	5.00-30.00

Judy Bolton, pictorial covers **3.00-10.00**
Ken Holt, #3 trhough #17, w/dust jacket **3.00-10.00**
Ken Holt, #18, pictorial covers **40.00**
Five Little Peppers **3.00-5.00**
Ruth Fielding **1.00-5.00**
Rover Boys **3.00-5.00**
Tom Slade **1.00-5.00**
Dana Girls...**2.00-5.00**
Freddy the Pig, any..**3.00-15.00**
Betsy Tacy, any..**3.00-15.00**

Limited Edition Club   We Pay

Most Titles **15.00-50.00**
Lysistrate **1,500.00**
Ulysses **600.00-1,500.00**
Frost's Poems **100.00**
Miller, quarto, any **50.00**
Green Grow the Lilies **75.00**

Other Wants   We Pay

George Macy's Checkbook **100.00**
Lot of 50 Monthly Letters, issued by LEC...**50.00**
Original Artwork by Boardman Robinson, oil paintings for chapter
    headings..**200.00-400.00**
Picasso Prints, suite of 6 ....**2,000.00**

———————

I want to buy books on **blue and white Delft from Holland only**. I will pay reasonable prices.

Barbara Andrews
362 Hwy. 65 N
Conway, AR 72032
501-329-4032

———————

Automobile books and automobilia of all types purchased. We will buy hard and softbound books, in or out of print, new or used, remainders, surplus stock, large private collectons, or single copies. Our main interest is in books that deal with auto racing, history of racing cars and their manufacturers, motorcycles, famous automotive personalities, design, coach building, etc. We willingly purchase all automotive books. However, we specialize in European and exotic automobiles such as Ferrari, Maserati, Lamborghini, Mercedes, Porshe, Rolls Royce, etc. We also specialize in domestic manufacturers that are no longer in existance such as Packard, Studebaker, Auburn, Duesenberg, etc. We **do not** buy ex-library books, sales literature, owners' or workshop manuals unless they are appropriate to those types of automobiles perviously listed. We purchase automobilia such as rare posters, art, period photographs, original design renderings, etc. We are agressive buyers of top quality items regardless of age and quantity and prices quoted are for books with dust jackets in top condition.

LMG Enterprises
9006 Foxland Dr.
San Antonio, TX 78230
phone or fax 210-979-6098

We Pay

Annual Automobile Revue 1953/54 #1	**100.00**
Annual Automobile Revue 1954/55 #2	**160.00**
At Speed (Alexander)	**80.00**
Autocourse 1964-'65	**90.00**
Bentley, 50 Years of the Marque (Green)	**60.00**
Boyhood Photographs of J.H. Lartigue (Lartigue)	**100.00**
British Light-Weight Sports Cars 78 (Japanese)	**140.00**
Cara Automobile (Pininfarina)	**80.00**
Comicar (Bertieri)	**50.00**
Delorean Stainless Steel Illusion (Lamm)	**40.00**
DMG 1890-1915 (German)	**180.00**
Errett Loban Cord (Borgenson)	**120.00**
Ferrari 80, 2nd edition (Italian)	**100.00**
Ferrari Yearbook, 1949 through 1970, ea	**70.00-400.00**
First Century of Portraits Celebrating Mercedes	**200.00**
Grand Prix Car, Vol. 1 & Vol. 2 (Pomeroy)	**160.00**
L'Art et L'Automobile (Poulain)	**60.00**
La Targa Florio (Garcia)	**80.00**
Les 24 Heures du Mans (Labric)	**160.00**
Piloti che Gente, 4th edition (Ferrari)	**140.00**
Spirit Celebrating 75 Years of Rolls Royce (Dallison)	**60.00**
Ten Ans de Courses (Montaut)	**600.00**

Wanted: **beat generation and counter-culture books and ephemera**. Even though I am only 20, I have been seriously collecting this for one third of my life! Items from the late 1950s, '60s, and early '70s include poetry, sociology, song books, art, fiction, literature, newspapers, magazines, etc. Authors include Brautigan, Ginsberg, McClure, Corso, Rubin, Hoffman, Norse, Lamantia, Alpert (Ram Dass), Burroughs, Kerouac, Ferlinghetti, Leary, Warhol, Fante, Bukowski...just to name a few. I'm very interested in anything reflecting that time period. Price I pay is based on collectible value and condition. I will respond to all offers. Thank you.

Marcella Alice Cervon
10074 Ashland St.
San Buenaventura, CA 93004
805-659-4405 or fax 805-659-4776

I am a collector and buy **old books on most subjects: biographies, history, medicine, novels, etc.** Condition is very important. I need books in very good or better condition with dust jackets (where issued) in like condition. Please no book club, paperbacks, textbooks, or Reader's Digest editions. Any book should be first state, first printing, but there are always exceptions. My prices are top — better than you'll get at bookstores. I will buy one book or entire collections. Please send your list and prices. I answer all inquiries.

Ron Gibson
110 Windsor Cir.
Burlington, IA 52601
319-752-4588

I am interested in **books that are collections of the cartoons of a single artist.** No general collections of cartoons (Best of Punch), comic books, recent reprints, or storybooks based on cartoons are wanted please.

The marking of first editions varies with different publishers, though a majority of the books by the artists will state a first printing or edition, or have the number one still in the number series. Others will have a date on the title page matching the copyright date.

Prices are for books in fine to excellent condition — no tears, coloring, loose pages, bent covers, or broken spines. Prices vary greatly with condition. Listed here are some cartoon anthologies wanted. Publishers for these are Cupples & Leon Publishing Co., Star Co., Ball Pub. Co., and Cartoon Reprint Series (1900 through 1935). **I will pay from $15.00 to $75.00** for these books.

Bringing Up Father	Nebs
Dick Tracy	Percy & Ferdie
Dolly Dimples	Regular Fella's
Harold Teen	Smitty
Joe Palooka	Tillie the Toiler
Keeping Up With the Jones	The Gumps
Little Orphan Annie	Toonerville Trolly
Moon Mullins	Winnie Winkle
Mutt & Jeff	

Craig Ehlenberger
Abalone Cove Rare Books
7 Fruit Tree Rd.
Portuguese Bend, CA 90275
310-377-4609 or fax 310-544-6792 (6 am-9 pm PST)

Other Early Artists   We Pay

John McCutcheon..25.00+
Clare Briggs ....25.00+
Outcault (Buster Brown)..35.00+

Artist's Collections, First Editions Only   We Pay

Addams, Charles 12.00
Alain..10.00+
Arno, Peter ....10.00+
Corbean, Sam ....8.00+
Darrow, Whitney Jr. ....8.00+
Day, Chon (Brother Sebastion) ....6.00+
Dunn, Alan ....8.00+
Fisher, Ed ....8.00+
Giovannetti, Pericle L. ....8.00+
Hamilton, William ....12.00+
Hoff, Syd ....8.00+
Hokinson, Helen ....10.00+
Kelly, Walt (Pogo) (most are paperback without dust jackets) ....15.00+
Ketcham, Hank (Dennis the Menace), all say First, no dust jackets ....10.00+
Key, Ted (Hazel)..8.00+
Kovarsky, Anatol ....8.00+
Partch, Virgil (VIP)..5.00+
Petty, Mary ....10.00+
Price, George ....12.00+
Segar (Popeye)...30.00+
Shafer, Burr ....10.00+

Stevenson, James...10.00+
Syverson, Henry...5.00+
Taylor, Richard ....8.00+
Wilson, Gahan...8.00+

Bottle Openers

I buy **any figural bottle opener** that is a standing figure, three-dimensional figure, or wall-mount figure that I do not already have. And I'll buy a second one, if it is in better condition than mine, so that I can upgrade my collection.

Charlie Reynolds
2836 Monroe St.
Falls Church, VA 22042
703-533-1322

We Pay

Bear Head, wall mount, 2 holes under chin 1,500.00
Boots, brass 50.00-75.00
Boy w/Books, cast iron 2,000.00
Cardinal, cast iron...325.00
Dragons, cast iron...125.00
Drunk on Lamppost or Signpost, aluminum 200.00
Elephant, w/raised trunk, cast iron, 3*1/4*" 350.00
Eskimo Holding Bottle, pot metal 350.00
Knight, Syroco Wood...450.00
Lady w/Harp, cast iron 450.00
Monk, Syroco Wood 350.00
Nudes, brass or cast iron, ea...40.00-75.00
Rhino, cast iron, Japan...350.00
Roadrunner, opener in beak & tail 350.00
Turtle, brass, opener at bottom...200.00
Others ....**Top Dollar**

Bottles

Before 1900 all bottles were handmade. These can usually be distinguished from modern, machine-made bottles by looking at the seams on each side. On a machine-made bottle they go all the way to the top of the lip. If they end lower, if there are perpendicular seams, or if there are no seams at all, the bottle is handmade and probably collectible. Machine-made bottles have no value as collectibles.

I will consider purchasing **almost any type of handmade bottle, except fruit jars**. The most desirable have one or more of the following characteristics:

1. Embossed lettering, design, or picture
2. Pontil mark (round, rough gouge on underside of bottle where glass-blowing rod was broken off)
3. Unusual shape or color

Bottles without any of the above are probably of no value. Presence of a label or a crudely-made appearance adds to the value. I will not buy bottles with cracks, scratches, chips, bruises, iridescence, or with a condition known as 'sick glass' (a milky haze that will not clean off).

Please send me a full description with a drawing or photo if possible of whatever you have. I will respond to all communications (include a reply postcard or envelope). If I don't buy it, I will give you an informal appraisal. The huge variety of collectible bottles makes it hard to estimate prices without seeing a specific item. The prices below will give you a general idea of the minimums for the more collectible bottles in each category.

Michael Engel
29 Groveland St.
Easthampton, MA 01027
413-527-8733

Type	We Pay
Bitters	15.00-500.00+
Cosmetic (hair, perfume, cologne)	5.00+
Food or Household (unusual embossing, shape, or color)	3.00-10.00
Ink (unusual shape or color)	10.00-100.00+
Medicine (especially cures)	5.00-100.00+
Mineral Water (Saratoga-type)	10.00-100.00+
Peppersauce/Pickle (elaborate design)	20.00+
Poison	10.00+
Soda or Beer (attractive embossed designs)	5.00-10.00
Whiskey	5.00+

We purchase **perfume bottles of all types**: miniatures, Czechoslovakian crystal bottles, Baccarat, Lalique, DeVilbiss atomizers, and commerical perfume bottles. Commercial bottles are those that originally contained perfume when they were sold, such as Matchabelli Windsong in a small crown-shaped bottle. Commerical bottles should, if possible, have a label and the original box.

Monsen and Baer
Box 529
Vienna, VA 22183
703-938-2129 or 703-242-1357

Minatures   We Pay

Czechoslovakian, crystal, 2"...25.00+
Dior, Schiaparelli, Guerlain, or Coty..5.00+
Ceramic, metal crown top...40.00+

Atomizers   We Pay

DeVilbiss, 6"...100.00+
Volupte, 5"...75.00+
Lalique..300.00+

Lalique   We Pay

Apple for Ricci...100.00+
D'Orsay, black glass Ambre d'Orsay......................................500.00+
Molinard Calendal Nudes..500.00+
Roger & Gallet Le Jade, green glass.....................................1,500.00+

Commercial   We Pay

Vigny Le Golliwogg...100.00+
Hattie Carnegie, bust of woman..100.00+
Ciro Chevalier, knight, black glass, in box............................150.00+
Schiaparelli, Zut, woman's torso, in box................................600.00+
Schiaparelli, Success, Fou, green leaf, in box........................800.00+
Lucretia, Vanderbilt, bl glass, in box.......................................750.00+

Baccarat   We Pay

Elizabeth Arden, It's You, hand..800.00+
Houbigant, Buddha, in box...200.00+
Ybry, green square..200.00+
Ybry, purple or orange square...500.00+
Christian Dior, Diorissimo, in box..2,000.00+
Christian Dior, dog...5,000.00+

Bottoms-Up/Down

Bottoms-up cups were made by McKee in the 1940s. The nude is draped over the cup with her bottom 'up,' so that you must finish your drink before setting it down! These have a pattern number under the feet. The cups were sold with or without a coaster. Bottoms-down mugs are footed with her bottom hidden under the foot. Her legs form the handle and the pattern number is under the foot.

April and Larry Tvorak
HCR #34, Box 25B
Warren Center, PA 18851
or
P.O. Box 126
Canon City, CO 81215

We Pay

Bottoms-Up Cup, jade-ite	**40.00**
Bottoms-Up Cup, any other color	**35.00**
Coaster, jade-ite	**75.00+**
Coaster, any other color	**65.00+**
Coaster, crystal or crystal w/fired-on color	**10.00-15.00**
Bottoms-Down Mug, jade-ite	**150.00**
Bottoms-Down Mug, any other colored	**135.00**

Boxes

We collect **Victorian era boxes** which held collars and cuffs; gloves; brush, comb, and mirror sets; shaving sets; neckties; etc. Also wanted are photograph albums and autograph albums. The items we collect have lithographs affixed to the front or top of the piece. The lithographic prints usually show scenes or people. We prefer those which show close-up views of children or ladies, but will consider others. The print (or in some cases the entire album) is covered with a thin layer of clear celluloid. In other instances, part of the box or album will be covered with an abstract or floral print paper or colorful velvet material.

We are interested only in pieces in top condition: no cracked celluloid, split seams, or missing hardware. Condition of the interior of these boxes and albums is not as important as the condition of the outside. We are *not* interested in French Ivory celluloid boxes or solid celluloid dresser sets. If you see an exceptional celluloid box or album, but are uncertain about buying it for resale, please put us in touch with the owner. If we can buy it, we will pay you a finder's fee. Request our illustrated want list.

Mike and Sherry Miller
303 Holiday Dr.
Tuscola, IL 61953
217-253-4991

We Pay

Boxes, sm, ea	**40.00-75.00**
Boxes, med, ea	**50.00-100.00**
Boxes, lg, ea	**85.00-200.00**
Autograph Albums, ea	**25.00-75.00**
Photograph Albums, ea	**75.00-175.00**
Photograph Albums, musical, ea	**100.00-250.00**

Boyd Glass

We will pay the following prices for Boyd items. These must be mint and without factory flaws. We will consider buying your entire collection if you know the names of the pieces and can give descriptions and number of each type of design you have.

Chip and Dale Collectibles
3708 W Pioneer Pky.
Arlington, TX 76013

We Pay

J.B. Scottie, cobalt	**20.00**
J.B. Scottie, ruby	**22.50**
J.B. Scottie, complete collection	**400.00**
Joey the Horse, cobalt carnival	**30.00**
Airplane, vaseline	**18.00**
Hand-Painted Mini Vases	**10.00**
Debbie Duck, Firefly	**6.00**
Ducklings, vaseline	**2.50**
Hand-Painted Suee Pigs	**5.00-12.50**
Chick Salts	**3.50-45.00**
Patrick Bear, Enchantment	**14.00**

Bow Slippers...**3.50-20.00**
Cat Slippers..**4.00-22.00**
Hobo Shoes **3.00-8.50**
Elizabeth Dolls...**3.50-20.00**
Test Color Pieces...**10.00-50.00**

Breweriana

I am interested in purchasing ceramic items from **Anheuser Busch Brewery** such as beer steins, salt and peppers shakers, etc. Please send a complete description (with photo if possible), as well as the price you wish to receive to:

Scott Wheeler
213 Meadows Rd. South
Bourbonnais, IL 60914
815-933-5074 or fax 815-932-8792

Breyer Model Horses

I buy all makes of model horses including **Breyer, Hartland, Hagen-Renaker, and even customized and repainted models.** Fair prices given (see list below)! Send all lists. I also sell models from the 1970s to current editions of Breyer horses. Also available is a *Breyer Model Horse* value guide listing all models in all colors, the year(s) they were manufactured, and their resale values. This listing has been compiled from sale lists received from actual model horse hobbyists and show the price collectors are willing to pay. Most collectors are turned off by flea market prices from vendors who charge too much for beat-up models just because 'it's a Breyer!'

Carol Karbowiak Gilbert
Rolling River Farm
2193 Fourteen Mile Rd. #206
Sterling Hts., MI 48310

We Pay

Classic Black Stallion (flocked w/buggy)..**150.00**
Classic Ruffian (bay Lula)..**20.00**
Traditional Black Stallion (Ageless Bronze Hyksos)...............................**60.00**
Traditional Fighting Stallion (florentine or any decorator color)............**150.00**
Traditional Foundation Stallion (dapple gray Azteca)............................**40.00**
Traditional Lady Phase (sorrel)..**60.00-75.00**
Traditional Man O'War (chestnut)..**20.00**
Traditional Old Timer (dapple gray w/hat)..**45.00**
Traditional Sherman Morgan (alabaster Pride & Vanity)........................**100.00**
Traditional Sham (dark gray Rana)..**30.00**
Porcelain Arabian Mare..**175.00**

Buffalo Pottery

We wish to buy **Buffalo Pottery: Deldare, Blue Willow, jugs, and pitchers, as well as their advertising and identified commercial ware.**

Deldare is easily distinguished by the masterful use of hand-tinted scenes on the natural olive-green color of the body of the ware and generally portrays village and hunting scenes. Emerald Deldare, made with the same olive-green (and generally employed the same body shapes) depicts historical scenes and is highlighted with an Art Nouveau border or decoration.

Additionally, Buffalo Pottery produced Blue Willow ware, a series of jugs and pitchers, and served the needs of industry with its fine line of commerical ware for hotels, restaurants, railroads, steamship, and various government agencies.

Fred and Lila Shrader
2025 Hwy. 199 (Hiouchi)
Crescent City, CA 95531
707-458-3525

Deldare & Emerald Deldare   **We Pay**

Candlestick or Candle holder..**250.00+**
Chocolate or Demitasse Cup & Saucer.......................................**190.00+**
Deldare Advertising Plate...**600.00+**
Deldare Calendar Plate ....**600.00+**
Dresser Set (tray, powder jar & hair receiver)............................**200.00-500.00+**

Buffalo Pottery

Egg Cup ....150.00+
Humidor ....350.00+
Jardiniere & Pedestal ....Negotiable
Mugs, various sizes...100.00+
Tankard ....450.00+
Teapot or Chocolate Pot, various sizes ....200.00-400.00+
Toothpick Holder..200.00+
Tray, various sizes ....195.00+
Vase, various styles & sizes ....275.00+

Pitchers & Jugs
We Pay

Pitcher, 6" or larger ....250.00+
Pitcher, 6" or less ....75.00+
Jugs, 6" or larger ....250.00+
Jugs, 6" or less ....75.00+
Roosevelt Bears Creamer ....200.00+
Roosevelt Bears Pitcher ....500.00+

Other Items
We Pay

Advertising Mugs, Plates, Etc..20.00-100.00+
Blue Willow Place Setting Pieces (cups, saucers, plates, etc.)................20.00+
Blue Willow Serving Pieces (teapots, covered vegetable bowls, platters, cream-
    ers, sugars & pitchers) ....65.00-300.00+
Teapot w/Lid & Original Infuser ....50.00+

Buttonhooks

I am wanting to acquire additions to my large, internationally-known collection of buttonhooks, which includes all types of shoe hooks (large), glove
hooks (small), and collar/shirt buttoners (loop or closed hook). I am a collector, not a dealer, so I am not interested in duplicates of what I already have,
but I want 'new' additions to my collection. I am most interested in very large
(over 12"), folding/mechanical, in combination with other implements and
unusual designs or materials. I have no interest in common advertisers or
plain celluloid (faux ivory). **I pay from $10.00 to over $100.00 for individual
hooks depending on condition and need for my collection.** I have purchased
thousands of buttonhooks during the past ten years, most by mail from individuals around the world. I have also purchased several entire buttonhook
collections. Send photocopy of your buttonhooks to:

Richard Mathes
P.O. Box 1408
Springfield, OH 45501-1408

Buttons

We are manufacturers of a unique line of costume jewelry that is sold to shops throughout the U.S. Most of our jewelry items begin with 7 to 10 shirt-sized pearl buttons. For the most part, pearl buttons of this sort are not very collectible; but we find that many antique dealers and button collectors as well as sewing enthusiasts have quantities 'stashed away' — too good to throw away, but who wants them?

We do! And we are always buying. If you have pearl buttons in good condition (not rusty or extremely dirty, **not plastic**), we'd love to hear from you! Below is a guideline to what we pay, as well as a few other items we are always buying related to our business. If you have any of these items and seriously wish to sell, please contact us for further instructions. We pay your shipping costs as well.

B'see Boutiques
1441 N Market St. Ext.
E Palestine, OH 44413
330-426-2636

We Pay

Pearl, prefer white, shirt-size, per lb	**5.00-6.00**
Pearl, about size of quarter, ea	**5¢-10¢**
Pearl, w/carving, larger than quarter, ea	**15¢-25¢**
Mixed Lots of Better, Very Old Antique Buttons (we like metal), per lb	**10.00-15.00**
Old Watch Parts, Movements & Faces (no wrist bands or whole watches), per lb	**15.00**
Box Lots of Old/Antique Costume Jewelry (for parts)	**10.00-100.00**

California Perfume Company

In New York City, New York, in 1886, Mr. D.H. McConnell, Sr., founded the California Perfume Company (C.P.C.). These toiletries continued to be manufactured with the C.P.C. label until 1929 when 'Avon Products Inc.' was added. Both names appeared on the label until about 1939 when 'C.P.C.' was removed, and the labeling continued as 'Avon Products.' The name 'Perfection' was used on the household products issued by these companies.

Prior to the C.P. Company, another company called Goetting & Company (1871-1896) existed that was founded by Adolph Goetting. In 1896 it was bought out by the C.P. Company and Mr. Goetting became their chief chemist. Another French perfume company, Savoi Et Cie labeling, was marketed by the C.P.C. in retail outlets. Lastly the 1918 C.P.C. packaged Marvel Electric Silver cleaner (patent Jan. 11, 1910) and Easy Day or Simplex Automatic Clothes Washer (patent July 4, 1916).

I am a collector of these items and the additional items listed below. Items are wanted for my collection and research. I have listed a pay and up price; I am seeking the ones of interest to me that I do not have. A description, condition, price, and notes of importance are helpful. A large SASE is reguired for information seekers only. I **do not want any 'Avon' marked items**.

Mr. Richard G. Pardini
3107 N El Dorado St., Dept. W
Stockton, CA 95204-3412
209-466-5550 (early am hours or leave message)

Go-Withs . We Pay

Goetting & Company Products	**10.00+**
Savoi Et Cie Products	**10.00+**
Marvel Electric Silver Cleaner, patent Jan. 11, 1910, boxed	**25.00+**
Easy Day or Simplex Automatic Clothes Washer, patent July 4, 1916, boxed	**25.00+**

C.P.C. Items We Pay

Natoma Rose Fragrances Items, circa 1920	**20.00+**
Gift Sets, 1886 to 1929	**25.00+**
Catalogs, 1886 to 1914	**20.00+**
Outbooks, 1905 to 1929	**2.00+**
Items w/CP or Eureka Trade Marks	**10.00+**
Items w/126 Chambers St., New York USA address	**20.00**

Camark Pottery

We buy **Camark pottery of the 1920s and 1930s**, particularly hand-painted and Deco-styled pieces. These pieces, when marked, usually have the Camark die stamp or an impressed or ink-stamped state of Arksansas shape with the Camark name. Pieces are very often unmarked, and we are as willing to buy these as marked ones. Camark of the '30s is a light brown or cornmeal-type clay. Some damage is okay. Prices given are for drip or multicolor glazes, though solid glazes are desired at around half the price. The numbers given are found in catalog pages featured in books by Laetitia Landers and David Gifford. These pieces are the most desired, but we are just as interested in any earlier pieces, as well as any of the more rare later white clay pieces.

USArt Pottery
Tony Freyaldenhoven
P.O. Box 1295
Conway, AR 72033
501-329-0628 or fax 501-450-8046

Camark, 1920s-'30s	We Pay
Ashtray, #400, hexigonal, 4"	55.00
Bowl, #319, fluted w/handles, 11"	125.00
Bowl, #186, 15"	160.00
Candlestick, #180, 5" wide, pr	100.00
Ewer, #207, 9½"	140.00
Flower Frog, #413, fish design, 5¼"	125.00
Humidor, #173, hand-painted nude, Deco design, 7"	250.00
Humidor, #143, hand-painted nude, Modernistic design, 8"	300.00
Lamp, #L172, bulbous shape, 18"	275.00
Lamp, #L156, classic shape, 22"	275.00
Lamp, #L175, cylindrical shape, 23"	300.00
Lamp, #L195, 3-tiered Deco shape, 23"	400.00
Pitcher, #414, 9"	140.00
Vase, #206, embossed handles, 6"	125.00
Vase, #203, w/handles, 8"	175.00
Vase, #410, pillow form, 8"	200.00
Vase, #333, Deco design, 9"	200.00
Vase, #418, sea gulls in relief, 9½"	220.00
Vase, #403, globe form, 10"	250.00
Vase, #308, w/handles, 12½"	275.00
Vase, #137, Modernistic w/hand-painted bird, 13"	300.00
Vase, #174, Modernistic w/hand-painted nude, 13¼"	350.00
Vase, #193, urn w/loose handles, 16"	350.00

Vase, #194, w/handles, 18"	350.00
Vase, #188, embossed figure in ivory, 20"	400.00
Vase, #192, 24"	400.00
Wall Pocket, #166, 8"	200.00
Wall Pocket, #340, Deco design, 9½"	300.00

Camark, 1940s-'60s   We Pay

Basket, #805R, Iris ware, blue, 9¾"	100.00
Bookends, #125, female head, pr	75.00
Candlestick, #845R, Iris ware, blue, 6¼"	115.00
Centerpiece, #092, angel form, 7½"	35.00
Cigarette Box, #858, 3½" wide	25.00
Ewer, #358, ribbed, 12½"	45.00
Ewer, #800R, Iris ware, blue, 13½"	150.00
Flower Frog, #129D, hand-painted ducks, 9" wide	75.00
Pitcher, #200, duck form, 12"	80.00
Vase, #867, hand form, 5¾"	30.00
Vase/Rose Bowl, #792, 6½" dia	35.00
Vase, #866, ringed w/handles, 7"	30.00
Vase, #117, w/handles, 8"	40.00
Vase, #692, fluted w/3 handles, 8¼"	30.0
Vase, #650, urn form w/handles, 10½"	40.00
Vase, #651, ribbed-V shape, 11¾"	45.00
Wall Pocket, #795, 8¾"	50.00
Wall Pocket, #N7, sea horse form, 8"	50.00
Wall Pocket, #851R, Iris ware, blue, 9"	150.00
Wall Pocket, #265, goose form, 9" wide	50.00

Cameras

Classic, collectible, and usable cameras are wanted such as Canon, Minolta, Pentax, Nikon, Neica, Contax, Rolleiflex, Yashica, Zeiss-Ikon, and others. Prices paid range up to thousands of dollars for some rare editions.

Send list with description of cameras, or call for estimate or information (205-536-6893). We **do not buy** most Kodak (except Retina or Ektra) or Polaroid cameras, movie cameras, or the modern 'Point and Shoot' types of cameras. We buy lenses and accessories. Also, a long list of cameras for sale or trade is available. Call or write for list. Examples of prices paid are listed below. Prices are listed as a range reflecting good-operating condition to mint-condition cameras.

Gene's Cameras
2603 Artie St., SW, Ste 16
Huntsville, AL 35805
205-536-6893

We Pay

Canon A-Series 50.00-200.00
Canon F-Series 100.00-300.00
Canon FT, FX, TL, TX Series 25.00-100.00
Canon T-50, T-60, T-70, T-80, T-90 ....60.00-300.00
Canon Rangefinder Cameras 100.00-5,000.00
Minolta X, XK, XG Series 50.00-150.00
Nikon F, FG, FA, FE, FM, F3, & Others 75.00-400.00
Pentax M, LX, E, S, P Series, Spotmatics, Etc...........................50.00-200.00
Yashicamats 25.00-125.00
Leica Rangefinders..100.00-1,000.00
Contax SLR's & Rangefinders 75.00-300.00
Exaktas, all models 50.00-150.00
Other German & Japanese, many models ....**Call for Estimates**
Miniatures, Commemoratives, Stereos, Etc...........................**Call for Estimates**
Zeiss-Ikon, Lordomat, Minox, Mamiya, Praktica, Olympus, Fujica, Voight-
lander, & Many Others...**Call for Estimates**

I buy classic, collectible cameras, specializing in antique-view cameras of the cycle, field, and studio types. These are typically made of wood and are polished or leather covered and ideally have red or maroon leather bellows. Hardware should be brass or nickel. Condition, of course, determines price, along with rarity and with other factors of anything collectible. Do not hesitate to contact me, though, if you have broken, rough, or incomplete cameras as they are the only source of available parts. Sizes of cameras which I collect are 4x5", 5x7", and 'full-plate.' I cannot use 8x10" or larger.

These cameras were manufactured by Anthony, Blair, Buckeye, Century, Conley, Eastman, Rochester, Scovill, Seneca, and many others. My prices are fair and much higher than flea markets. Get that old relic out of the attic and make cash out of it. I'll consider any quantity. Write or call — I answer all inquires.

Ron Gibson
110 Windsor Cir.
Burlington, IA 52601
319-752-4588

Capo-Di-Monte

We are interested in purchasing all cherub-styled Capo-Di-Monte pieces including figurines. We prefer the older blue crown pieces. Some pieces may also be called Ginori, Docchia, or Royal Naples. Send picture and price requested. We are interested in single pieces as well as complete collections and will purchase from individuals as well as dealers. We reimbuse all shipping fees. We are the largest buyer of older Capo-Di-Monte in the country!

James R. Highfield
1601 Lincolnway E
South Bend, IN 46613
219-288-0300

We Pay

Box, 11"	500.00-1,200.00
Cup & Saucer	75.00-200.00
Figurine, lady, 6"	60.00-175.00
Plaque, 10x13"	200.00-450.00
Stein, 1 liter	500.00-1,200.00
Urn, 20", pr	2,000.00
Vase, 20", pr	2,500.00

Carnival Chalk Prizes

I buy **old carnival chalkware prizes that were produced to be given away at carnivals from about 1915 to 1950.** I am not interested in animals unless they were in the comics, such as Felix the Cat, Spark Plug the Horse, or Disney's Pluto. Some of the early prizes were Kewpie types while others have mohair wigs and dresses. I buy **old radio lamps made of plaster.** Examples of lamps would be Art Deco nudes or cowboys on bucking horses. The radio lamp was the ultimate carnival prize. I reimburse for UPS and insurance.

Tom Morris
P.O. Box 8307
Medford, OR 97504
541-779-3164

We Pay

Alice the Goon, from Popeye, 6" or 10", ea..**45.00+**
Amos & Andy, single or pr, 12" (varies)...**85.00+**
Betty Boop, 14½"...**125.00+**
Eugene the Jeep, from Popeye, 14"...**295.00+**
Felix the Cat, 12½"..**95.00+**
Hula Girls, 10" or larger...**30.00+**
Ma & Pa Yokum, 12½", pr..**120.00+**
Mae West, 13" to 14"...**45.00+**
Maggie & Jiggs, 8½" or larger, pr...**75.00+**
Miss America, 15¾"..**35.00+**
Moon Mullins, from Barney Google, 7"...**40.00+**
Nudes or Semi-Nudes, various sizes, ea..**35.00+**
Nude Art Deco Lamp, various sizes, ea...**85.00+**
Olive Oyl, from Popeye, 7"..**40.00+**
Pirate Lady, 13½"...**60.00+**
Popeye, 12" or larger, ea..**35.00+**
Sea Hag, from Popeye, 8"...**35.00+**
Shirley Temple, 9" or larger..**35.00+**
Spark Plug, from Barney Google, 7"...**155.00+**
Superman, 15"...**155.00+**
Uncle Sam, 15"..**50.00+**
Wimpy, from Popeye, 13½" or 16", ea...**40.00+**

Carnival Glass

I am wanting to buy old, Imperial glass or reproductions of Marigold carnival glass for my own personal collection. The items must be in the best of condition — no cracks, nicks, or chips. The items I am interested in buying are as follows.

Gladys Norton
2208 S College
Ft. Collins, CO 80525
970-484-0071

We Pay

Hobnail Spitton, lg...**50.00**
Bell...**45.00**

Miniature Punch Bowl & Cups ....**Call or Write**
Miniature Set (sugar bowl, cream pitcher, spoon holder & butter dish),
4-pc ....**Call or Write**

Cast Iron

I am buying cast iron as well as other collectibles listed below. I will purchase one item or an entire collection. Top, confidential prices paid for items I want. Please describe fully and include SASE with a phone number with your correspondence. Photos are appreciated and make dealing much easier. Original paint is very important on the figural cast iron. It affects the value greatly. No damaged or new pieces are wanted. I am a dealer collector with 27 years of statisfied customers and collector friends. Thanks.

Craig Dinner
Box 4399
Sunnyside, NY 11104
718-729-3850

Figural Cast Iron   We Pay

Advertising	10.00-3,000.00
Advertising Paperweights	10.00-250.00
Architectural	10.00-650.00
Bottle Openers	10.00-1,000.00
Curtain Tie Backs	10.00-65.00
Doorknockers	40.00-750.00
Doorstops	40.00-3,000.00
Governor Weights	25.00-1,500.00
Locks	5.00-400.00
Pencil Holders	10.00-75.00
Sad Irons	100.00-750.00
Shooting Gallery Targets	25.00-1,500.00
Windmill Weights	25.00-3,500.00
String Holders	75.00-500.00
Windmill Weights	25.00-3,500.00

Cast Iron   We Pay

Advertising	25.00-1,000.00
Architectural Items	10.00-300.00

Children's Cookware **15.00-1,500.00**
Coin Vending **75.00-750.00**
Cookware (includes Griswold, Filley, Wagner, etc.)...................**10.00-2,500.00**
Other Unusual Cookware **25.00-2,000.00**
Match Holders..**20.00-175.00**
Pencil Sharpeners, pre-1920 ....**25.00-1,000.00**
Sad Irons **10.00-450.00**
Signs..**25.00-500.00**
Toy Sad Irons **10.00-600.00**

Eclectic Pieces   **We Pay**

Advertising Match Holders, tin...**25.00-600.00**
Condom Tins..**2.00-500.00**
Lux Pendulette Clocks...**10.00-500.00**
Early Battery Clocks..**25.00-550.00**
Early Fans, ceiling & desk styles **25.00-1,000.00**
Laundry Sprinkler Bottles **10.00-300.00**
Stoneware Advertising **10.00-200.00**

I'm a buyer of a little of just about anything. I would like to buy **Wagner, Griswold Ware, Erie, and other cast-iron items**. Wanted are Griswold cake molds such as rabbits, lambs, and Santas. No repros wanted. Other wants include:

Miniatures and toys
Items marked No 2 and Erie
Large fry pans and lids marked Griswold, Erie, or Spider
Corn, wheat, muffin, bread, and cake pans
Kettles, oval roasters, and waffle irons
Ashtrays and mailboxes
Pup paperweight, aluminum, marked #30, 1⅝" tall

David W. Mayer
33 Mt. Vernon Pl.
Jamestown, NY 14701
716-487-1874

Cat Collectibles

I collect the cutest faced **B. Kliban cats**. They are black and white and may have sneakers or kisses, but always are adorable. A lot of people who liked cats had a Kliban in their home as sheets, pillows, candy dishes, figurines, banks, salt and pepper shakers, Christmas ornaments, coffee mugs, cookie jars, framed pictures, ceramic frames, bookends, stuffed animals, kitchen and bath towels, pot holders, books, magnets, cat feeders, candles and candle holders, glasses, ice buckets, airplane teapots, and so much more.

I prefer ceramic pieces but will consider all items offered. Photos are preferred and/or very good description with any damage cited in your note. I pay all postage and would prefer seller add their asking price in the note. Will also consider trades.

Sue Lucente
115 Marbeth Ave.
Carlisle, PA 17013-1626
717-249-9343

I collect cats in all areas of interest: ceramic, wood, metal, paper, glass, etc. — cookie jars, salt and pepper shakers, dolls, planters, statues, creamers, sugars, black cats — anything with a cat! What do you have to sell or trade? I belong to cat collectors, so if I'm not interested, I may know someone who will be looking for your item. Please send photo or proper description, the price (if you know value), and SASE.

Jean R. Ehrlich
120 E Liebl Ave.
Offerle, KS 67563
316-659-2374

Serious cat collector is looking for some serious cats. I am interested in any domestic cat items. Primarily I like the older items. **No reproductions please**. Books, prints, toys, stuffed (glass eyes only), games, tins, jewelry, cast iron, bronze, dishes, bottles, figurines, advertising, postcards, linens, quilts — you name it! I will pay good money to someone looking for a fair price. I still need several Copley and Goebel figurines for my collection. If you have any cat item that might fit these guidelines, please send description (a picture would be ideal) including size, color, specific markings, flaws if any, history if known, and an approximate price range you would expect for your piece(s). Please include your phone number as well as your address as I may need to call you with specific questions. Don't delay! I want your cat items today! Thank you.

Melissa Arbogast
25575 98th St.
Zimmerman, MN 55398
612-856-3370

I collect many cat figurines, but specialize in Goebel, Josef Originals, and Hagen-Renaker. Siamese cats are my favorite. Items that I'm most interested in are figurines and utilitarian pieces such as: salt and peppers, ashtrays, creamers, etc. Please send photos with markings and asking price. I have listed some of my wants below. There are many more I'm searching for, so call or write anytime.

Renae Giles
1033 Sunny Ridge Dr.
Carver, MN 55315-9355
612-448-7046

Goebel   We Pay

31-121-01, lying Persian w/slipper	**40.00**
31-122-01, standing Siamese w/ball	**40.00**
7581, gray cat rubber squeek toy, 5"	**35.00**
77-001-08, cat teapot w/flowers	**45.00**
77-001-04, cat teapot, tail is handle, front paws are spout, head is lid, 9"	**45.00**
CK 301, gray & white cat standing on base, 6"	**50.00**
CK 318, 2 small cats playing, 1-piece, 2½"	**35.00**
KZ 628, cat trump card indicator	**60.00**
KZ 707, cat ring holder	**45.00**
KZ 770, Art Deco cat planter	**55.00**
P 94 A&B, black cat & white cat hugging salt & pepper shakers	**50.00**
P 181 A&B, stylized cat & dog salt & pepper shakers	**50.00**
P 186 A&B, kitten & ball salt & pepper shakers	**55.00**
P 391 I&O, cat & dog salt & pepper shakers	**50.00**
P 394 I&O, kittens salt & pepper shakers	**50.00**

S182, match safe, black cat looking back at striker, mouth open, 3" long..**55.00**
S 194, white sitting cat creamer, loop at tail is handle, 5"........................**55.00**
S 636, match holder, black cat standing w/green box, 2"........................**55.00**
S 701, cat & dog creamer, 3" **60.00**
VP 107, yellow cat wall pocket, 6"..**50.00**
VT 28, cat vase, black or white, 6½" **45.00**
XP 47, yellow arch w/2 black cats as stoppers w/cork bottoms **50.00**

Josef Originals   **We Pay**

Cats, call or write for wants...**12.00-40.00**

Hagen-Renaker   **We Pay**

Cats, call or write for wants...**12.00-45.00**

———————

I collect **anything pertaining to cats**. I am particularly interested in prints and lithographs as well as any cats that are pre-1950. The price I will pay depends on the object and condition.

Eunice Gentry
1126 Prairie Ave.
Cleburne, TX 76031
817-556-3746 or fax 817-556-9929

———————

Catalina Island Pottery

I buy pieces marked **Catalina Pottery made by Gladding McBean**, shells, and some pieces marked with blue ink Made in USA. **G.M.B., Franciscan, Catalina Pottery advertising items, and price lists** as well as **some Franciscan dinnerware** pieces are wanted. All pieces must be in excellent condition. Send description or photo and price of your item or call and leave message.

Alan Phair
P.O. Box 30373
Long Beach, CA 90853
310-983-7020

Catalina Pottery/G.M.B	We Pay
Samoan Lady Holding Baby	up to 250.00
Fan Lady	up to 350.00
Hat Lady	up to 350.00
Reclining Lady	250.00
Mermaid	up to 400.00
Polynesian 'Painted Pieces'	up to 300.00
Encanto	up to 300.00
Ox Blood	up to 400.00
Signs for Franciscan, G.M.B., Etc.	up to 250.00
Shells	up to 150.00

Franciscan Dishes	We Pay
Wild Flower	up to 250.00
Twilight Rose	up to 250.00
Contours	up to 250.00
Ivy	up to 200.00
Small Fruit	up to 200.00

Ceramic Arts Studio

Ceramic Arts Studio was a pottery in Madison, Wisconsin, from 1940 to 1956. Beginning with hand-thrown pottery, the studio was particularly famous for highly-detailed figurines. The following is a list of Ceramic Arts Studio creations I hope to add to my collection. Please call with offers of mint-condition items only.

Tim Holthaus
P.O. Box 46
Madison, WI 53701-0046
608-241-9138
e-mail: ceramicart@aol.com

We Pay

Any Hand-Thrown Pottery, especially signed Rabbit	50.00+
Swirl & Swish Fish, swimming, 3½", pr	60.00+
Ram, stylized, 2"	40.00+
Spaniel, Honey, 6"	75.00+
Chick (nesting, 1½") & Nest (snuggle, 1"), pr	60.00+
Colonial Man, blue, 6½"	60.00
Colonial Woman, green, 6½"	60.00
Hans & Katrinka, chubby boy & girl, blue trim, pr	120.00+
Dutch Dance Boy & Girl, 7½", pr	175.00+
Egyptian Man & Woman, 9½", pr	250.00+
Harem Girl, lying w/feet behind, 6"	60.00+
Zulu Man & Zulu Woman, black, 5½" & 7", pr	180.00+
Zulu Man #2 & Zulu Woman #2, 5½" & 7¼", pr	180.00+
Zulu Man & Woman, white, pr	220.00+
Macabre Dance Man & Woman, pr	250.00+
Encore Woman, pink or black, ea	80.00+
Fire Man, burgundy & red, 11¼"	90.00+
Fire Woman, gray & brown, 11¼"	90.00+
Hamlet (plaque), 8"	90.00+
Water Woman, chartreuse, 11½"	80.00+
Swan Lake Man & Woman, pr	200.00+
Bird on Birdbath, for St. Francis, 4½"	40.00+
Water Well for Rebekah	40.00+
Madonna, w/Bible, 9½"	95.00+
Madonna, w/child, pink, 6½"	95.00+
Madonna, w/halo, 9½"	95.00+
Our Lady of Fatima, gold trim, 9"	95.00+
St. Francis, w/birds, brown or white, 7", ea	80.00+
Chubby St. Francis, w/birds, brown, 9"	80.00+
Sleeping Girl Angel, 3¼"	50.00+
Angel w/Candle, 5"	50.00+
Black Bobby, 3¼"	90.00+
White Willy/Ball Down (shelf sitter), 4½"	90.00+
White Winnie, 5½"	90.00+
White Woody, 3¼"	90.00+
White Rabbit, standing, 6"	90.00+
Goosey Gander (plaque), 4½"	75.00+
Jack Be Nimble (plaque), 5"	80.00+
Piper's Girl Praying, 3"	60.00+
Devil Imp w/Spear, 5"	75.00+
Devil Imp Sitting, 3½"	75.00+
Devil Imp Lying, 3½"	75.00+

Adult Band

We Pay

Accordion Lady, standing, 8½"	95.00+

Flute Lady, standing, 8½"..95.00+
Violin Lady, standing, 8½"..95.00+
Cellist Man, sitting, 6½"..95.00+
French Horn Man, sitting, 6½"..95.00+
Guitar Man, sitting, 6½"..95.00+

Balinese Dancers   We Pay

Lao, topless, 8½"...95.00+
Bali-Lao, standing, green, 8½"..70.00+
Bali-Gong, croutched, green, 5½"...70.00+
Balinese Girl, shelf sitter, 5½"...75.00+
Balinese Woman, brown or pair in blue..60.00+
Chinthe, 4"...50.00+
Burmese Temple..150.00+

Indian Group   We Pay

Seagull, fits on canoe, 2½"..50.00+
Birch Wood Canoe, blue trim...75.00+
Minnehaha, blue trim, 6½"..75.00+

My collection of Ceramic Arts Studio pottery (Madison, Wisconsin) has a few gaps I hope you can help me fill. The studio was particularly famous for highly-detailed figurines, but also made metal pieces to hang on the wall for displaying their ceramic work. The following is a list of Ceramic Arts Studio creations I hope to add to my collection. Please call with offers of mint-condition items only.

Jim Petzold
P.O. Box 46
Madison, WI 53701-0046
608-241-9138
e-mail: ceramics@execpc.com

                                                                                 We Pay

Salome, 14"..**25.00+**
Spring Leaf, green, 2" long..**40.00+**
Gremlin, standing, 4"...**75.00+**
Gremlin, sitting, 2"..**75.00+**
Mermaid, lying, 2½"...**75.00+**
Mermiad, sitting, 3"...**75.00+**

Ceramic Arts Studio

Sprite/Fish Down (plaque), 4½"..**95.00+**
Peek-A-Boo Pixie, 2½"...**50.00+**
Pixie Girl, kneeling, 2½"..**50.00+**
Pixie Riding Snail, 2¾"...**50.00+**
African Man (plaque), white trim ....**130.00+**
African Woman Head Vase, white trim ....**150.00+**
Skunky Bank, 4"..**95.00+**
Modern Jaguar, stylized, 5"..**80.00+**
Leopard Baby ....**75.00+**
Leopard, fighting, 6" or 8", ea..**125.00+**
Panther, fighting, 8"...**150.00+**
Panther, fighting, crouched ....**150.00+**
Dachshund, lying, 3½"...**40.00+**
Sassy & Waldo Dachshunds, 3¼", pr ....**80.00+**
Modern Dog, stylized, 5" ....**95.00+**
Donkey, 3¼" & 3", pr..**90.00+**
Elephant, bisque, w/trunk down, 5" ....**75.00+**
Horse Mother & Spring Colt, 4¼" & 3½", pr.................................**150.00+**
Zebra, amber & black, 5"...**150.00+**
Mouse, realistic, 3"...**40.00+**
Seal Mother, 6"..**75.00+**
Seal Pup, 3" ....**75.00+**
Seal on Rock, 5", pr...**160.00+**
Tortoise w/Hat, crawling, 2½"..**60.00+**
Kitten Washing, w/bow, 2"..**40.00+**
Kitten Sleeping, 1" ....**40.00+**
Bird of Paradise A & B, 3", pr..**80.00+**
Canary, left & right (shelf sitters), 5", pr.......................................**80.00+**
Cockatoo Male, wings spread (F), 5" ....**60.00+**
Cockatoo Female (shelf sitter), 5"...**60.00+**
Duck Mother & Duckling, 3¼" & 2¼", pr ....**70.00+**
Budgie & Pudgie Parakeets (shelf sitters), 5", pr..........................**70.00+**
Rooster & Hen, 3", pr...**60.00+**
Swans, neck up & neck down, 6" & 5", pr.......................................**90.00+**
Straight Tail Fish, lg & sm, pr...**60.00+**
Striped Fish Mother (plaque), 5"...**50.00+**
Striped Fish Baby (plaque), 3"...**50.00+**
Barber Shop Quartet Mug, 3½"...**75.00+**
Mountain Goat Caddy, oval, 5¼" ....**75.00+**
Paul Bunyan Plate, 6" dia ....**60.00+**
Buddah Pitcher, Wedgwood, bisque, 3½"...**60.00+**
Grapes Teapot, 2"..**50.00+**
Miss Forward WI, Wedgwood, 4"..**80.00+**
Toby Mug, 2¾"...**60.00+**

Metal Pieces   We Pay

Arched Window w/Cross, 14"...**50.00+**

Beanstalk for Jack, w/ladder, 13" ....**40.00+**
Bird Cage, w/perch for parakeets, 14"..**50.00+**
Corner Web, w/spider, 4" ....**40.00+**
Pyramid Shelf...**50.00+**
Sofa for Maurice & Michelle..**40.00+**
Staircase for Angel Trio...**50.00+**
Triple Ring, left & right, 15", ea..**50.00+**
Triple Ring w/Shelf, left & right, 15", ea...**60.00+**

Cereal Boxes

I buy **old cereal boxes from the turn-of-the-century to the late '70s**. Historical milestones like Post's Elijah's Manna; short-lived, trashy brands like Kream Krunch (freeze-dried ice cream and oats conncoction of the '60s); and packages featuring TV, sports, or cartoon characters as Roger Maris's All Pro, Quisp, and Cocoa Freakies are particularly sought after. Don't fret about condition; although I'll pay top dollar for a full box or a mint file copy (flat), I don't expect to see to many. I also buy **cereal premiums from the '50s through the '70s**. Please see my listing in this book under Premiums.

Scott Bruce
10 Notre Dame Ave.
Cambridge, MA 02140
617-492-5004
e-mail: scott@flake.com

Cereal Boxes   **We Pay**

Elijah's Manna, 1906 ....**200.00-300.00**
Corn Burst, 1960s...**100.00-200.00**
Kream Crunch, 1965 ....**100.00-200.00**
Sugaroos, 1960s **100.00-200.00**
Roger Maris' All Pro, 1968 ....**250.00-350.00**
Jelliphants, 1968 ....**100.00-200.00**
Yellow Sub Rub-Ons Rice Honeys, 1969.....................................**350.00-450.00**
Kaboom, 1969 ....**100.00-200.00**
Norman (sic), 1970s...**150.00-250.00**
Cocoa Freakies, 1970s..**100.00-200.00**
OOBopperoos, 1970s **150.00-250.00**

Character and Promotional Drinking Glasses

We are paying the following prices for mint examples of these glasses (no fading, cracks, or poor registration).

Collector Glass News
P.O. Box 308
Slippery Rock, PA 16057

We Pay

1930s & 1940s Character Glasses (Disney, Popeye, Warner Bros.), ea....**10.00-100.00**
Pepsi or Canadian Jungle Book, ea..**20.00-50.00**
Pepsi Mighty Mouse, ea...**200.00**
Pepsi Callahans Characters, ea **40.00**
Pepsi Walter Lantz Characters, ea...**10.00-100.00**
Pepsi Warner Bros. Interactions, ea **3.00-25.00**
1962 Hanna-Barbera Cindy Bear, Yogi Bear, or Huckleberry Hound, ea ...**30.00**
Canadian Pepsi Glasses, ea..**2.00-25.00**
Al Capp, ea..**5.00-25.00**
Coke Collegiate Crest, ea **5.00-25.00**
McDonald's Manager & Regional Glasses, ea....................................**3.00-100.00**
Dr. Pepper Star Trek, ea..**5.00-10.00**
Super Hero Glasses,ea **3.00-50.00**
Monster Glasses, ea...**10.00-35.00**
Sports Glasses, especially glasses that feature professional players ..**3.00-25.00**
Elby's Columbus CLippers, ea **10.00**
Kentucky Derby, Preakness & Other Horse Racing Glasses, ea.........**5.00-500.00**
Frosted Iced Tea Glasses Featuring Indians, State Themes, Etc., ea ..**2.00-10.00**

Character, TV, and Personality Collectibles

We buy all types of **Beatles memorabilia but specialize in toy or 3-D type**. We are basically interested in original '60s items. There are many reproductions out there, so give us a call if you have any questions on any item. We aren't really interested in records or paper items unless they are out of the ordinary. **Yellow Submarine items from 1968** are of special interest, so please give us a call or drop a line. All prices below are for excellent to near-mint items, and we are seldom interested in good or lower quality items unless rare. Remember these are just a *few* examples.

Bob Gottuso
BOJO
P.O. Box 1403
Cranberry Twp., PA 16066
412-776-0621

Beatles　　　　　　　　　　　　　　　　　　　　　　　　**We Pay**

Apron, white paper w/black & white pictures	**125.00**
Ball, black rubber w/white photo	**350.00**
Banjo, complete only	**500.00+**
Binder, vinyl, various colors	**80.00**
Bongos, by Mastro	**700.00+**
Bubble Bath, Paul or Ringo (condition is important)	**75.00**
Bubble Bath, Paul or Ringo, MIB	**150.00**
Clutch Purses, various styles, ea	**120.00+**
Colorforms, complete only	**300.00+**
Concert Tickets, complete w/photo & name (other than Suffolk Downs)	**80.00+**
Ticket Stubs	**40.00+**
Corkstopper, ea	**200.00**
Disk-Go-Case, plastic 45rpm record carrier, many colors, ea	**90.00+**
Doll, Remco, Ringo or Paul, w/instrument & life-like hair, 4", ea	**35.00+**
Doll, Remco, George or John, ea	**60.00+**
Dolls, Remco, set of 4	**225.00**
Doll, blow-up style, set of 4 (must hold air well)	**75.00**
Doll, bobbin' head, 8", set of 4, mint condition	**275.00**
Doll, bobbin' head, 8", set of 4, MIB	**475.00**
Drinking Glasses, many styles, ea	**60.00+**
Drum, by Mastro (hardest to find)	**600.00**
Drum, other manufacturers	**Wanted**
Guitars, many styles, ea	**250.00+**
Hair Bow, on sealed original card	**200.00+**
Hair Spray	**550.00+**
Halloween Costume, MIB	**350.00**
Halloween Costume, mint, missing box	**130.00**
Handbags, different styles & sizes available, ea	**180.00+**
Lamps, wall or table styles, ea	**300.00+**
Lunch Boxes, metal or vinyl, prices vary widely, mint condition	**240.00+**
Models, plastic, sealed contents, w/mint original box	**150.00+**

Character, TV, and Personality Collectibles

Paint by Number Kit, 4 portraits, unused ....450.00+
Pencil Case, various styles & colors ....80.00+
Pennants, felt, many styles & colors (many fakes)....................................25.00+
Pillows, any of 3 different styles, w/tag, ea ....90.00+
Puzzles, ea..75.00+
Record Player, mint condition 1,200.00
School Bag..400.00
Tennis Shoes, unused w/paper insert, MIB..400.00
Thermos, for lunch box 100.00
Wallets, various styles & colors, complete...65.00

I buy original 1960s **Beatles memorabilia**. I offer up to 75% of book value for these items. Any condition wanted. Here is a small list of items wanted: Beatle dolls, lunch boxes, buttons, notebooks, pencil cases, pins, bracelets, necklaces, record players, models, games, toys, clothes, overnight cases, posters, pillows, trays, glassware, trading cards, magazines, original packaging, fan club items, Yellow Submarine items, and much more. Please call or write if you have any items I may be interested in. Thank you very much.

Billy J. Burdette
1516 Bluebird Ln.
Anderson, SC 29621
864-375-0689

As a collector of Baby Boomer-era items and TV show collectibles (1948-1972), I am interested in endless numbers of items and toys produced as promotions for TV shows. I am looking for children's lunch boxes and thermoses, Beatles and Elvis items, rock 'n' roll memorabilia, Super Hero and other character dolls, cartoon character items, robots and space toys, cloth items (western motif and character related), cap guns and sets, original boxes (even if empty), and much more. Following is a listing of some of the items I am searching for and the prices I am willing to pay for items in excellent condition. Mint-in-box items would be higher. Please keep in mind that this is only a small sampling of items; any toys that are personality, advertising, or TV show-related will be considered for purchase or trade. Please send photos if possible and an SASE for a reply. I would like an opportunity to purchase your items. Thank you.

Terri's Toys & Nostalgia
Terri Ivers
419 S First St.
Ponca City, OK 74601
405-762-8697 or 405-762-5174
fax 405-765-2657
e-mail: ivers@pcok.com

Beatles   We Pay

Airflite Bag, vinyl...**200.00**
Alarm Clock **100.00**
Brunch Bag or Kaboodle Kit, ea **250.00**
Drinking Glass...**25.00**
Drums **200.00**
Guitar..**200.00**
Hat **25.00**
Lamp...**100.00**
Record Player **500.00**
Scrapbook..**100.00**
Shoes **50.00**
Thermos...**65.00**

Elvis Presley Enterprises Items   We Pay

Decanter ....**20.00+**
Dolls, ea...**20.00-300.00**
Guitar..**300.00**
Overnight Case **125.00**
Pillow **45.00**
Record Player **300.00**
Scarf...**35.00**
Scrapbook..**100.00**
Any Other Items...**20.00-50.00+**

Other Wants   We Pay

Cap Guns or Gun & Holster Sets (TV westerns or detective shows)....**up to 150.00**
Hopalong Cassidy Items, w/Hoppy name...................................**50.00+**
KISS or Monkees Items (no records)...**10.00+**
Playsets (Flintstones, Blue & Gray, etc) ....**40.00+**
Figures & Horses marked Hartland or Breyer ....**20.00+**
Advertising Items & Signs ....**20.00+**
Promotional Vehicles, plastic or plastic w/metal, 8" to 10"....................**30.00+**

I am buying all **Alvin and the Chipmunks, Chipettes, David Seville, and Clyde Crashcup** merchandise! These items are grouped in four different categories based on the eras in which they were released:

Pre-Alvin Show (1956-60)
Alvin Show (1961-70s)
Early '80s (1980-86)
Late '80s to 1990s (1987 to present)

Please note that the items in the pre-Alvin show era portray Alvin, Simon, and Theodore as small animals with traditional chipmunk markings and characteristics such as dark brown fur with black and white stripes and short tails; they were sometimes called 'The Three Chipmunks.' To be sure of their authenticity, look for the appropriate Bagdasarian and/or Monarch Music or Karman-Ross (Chipettes only) copyrights on these and all items. Beware of frauds which were common in the 1960s, namely record albums. The items listed are only a fraction of what was available. Please inform me about **any** unlisted items you might have. Note: all prices are for items in mint condition. Please write or call with information.

Kim Shriner
234 Lakeside Dr.
Tuckerton, NJ 08087
609-296-2322 (home) or (908) 901-5891 (business)

Alvin and Related Characters   We Pay

Alarm Clock, Chipmunks, wind-up style, 1990 ....**15.00**
Bandages, Chipmunk, 1990, MIB (sealed) **5.00**
Board Game, Three Chipmunks Acorn Hunt, 1960...................................**70.00**
Board Game, Three Chipmunks Big Record, 1960 ....**60.00**
Board Game, The Chipmunks Go Hollywood, 1983 ....**20.00**
Book, *The Chipmunk Adventure*, jigsaw & puzzles, 1987 ....**5.00**
Book, *The Ocean Blues*, 1966...**25.00**
Book, *Alvin's Lost Voice*, 1966 ....**25.00**
Card Games, Chipmunks, 1963-1983, ea **20.00**
Coloring Books, Chipmunks, about 1960 through 1966, ea **40.00**
Comic Books, Alvin (all issues except #2, Christmas Special, #8, #10, #16, #20
   & #28), 1962-1973, ea **15.00**
Comic Books, Clyde Crashcup, issued #1 through #4, 1963-1964, ea **15.00**
Cup Dispenser, Chipmunk, w/paper cups (5 designs: Jeanette not included),
   1984...**20.00**
Doll, Alvin, 1959, lg...**85.00**
Doll, Alvin w/Harmonica, wind-up musical, 1959 ....**85.00**
Doll, Alvin as Ragtime Cowboy Joe, wind-up musical, 1959....................**85.00**
Doll, Eleanor (of the Chipettes), soft, blond hair, brown eyes, 1984 ....**70.00**

Doll, Simon, talker, stuffed plush, 1983, 18", working **20.00**
Doll Outfit, for 10" plush dolls, Santa Claus, Alpine Skier, Undercover Agent
  or Swashbuckler, 1983-84, MIP, ea **20.00**
Doll Outfit, for 10" Chipette soft dolls, Slumber Party, Bareback Rider or Pink
  Fantasy, MIP, ea **20.00**
Halloween Costume, Alvin, vinyl w/mask, 1962 ....**150.00**
Hand Puppet, Alvin, plush, 1990..**10.00**
Fast Food Premium, Chipmunk figures, The Chipmunk Adventure, stuffed
  plush, Burger King, 1987, 7", ea...**8.00**
Kenner Give-a-Show Projector (originally included 16 shows, only 3 are want-
  ed: The Chipmunks, Clyde Crashcup, Lassie), 1964................................**35.00**
Lunch Box, Chipmunks, dark green vinyl (thermos not needed), 1963 ...**200.00**
Magic Drawing Slate (2 chipmunk designs, 1 Clyde Crashcup), 1962, ea..**35.00**
Mobile, Chipmunks' Treat, 1984..**25.00**
Mug, chipmunk-style Alvin walking down lane, heavy glass, 1959 ....**35.00**
Paint 'n Play Figures, Chipmunks (except Simon), Chipettes, or Uncle Henry,
  1984, unpainted, ea **20.00**
Pocket Book & Vinyl Wallet, chipmunk, 1959 ....**35.00-75.00**
Record Album, The Chipmunks Go Hollywood, 1983? **35.00**
Record Album, The Music of David Seville, 1957 ....**30.00**
Record Player, Chipmunks, 1965, working **75.00**
Slippers, Alvin, plush heads, 1990 ....**15.00**
Spoon & Fork Set, Chipmunk, 1990, MIB..**8.00**
Vehicle, Chipettes Picnic Buggy, 1984 ....**25.00**
Walkie-Talkie, Alvin, 1985...**30.00**

I am interested in purchasing memorabilia on the television series **Dallas**.
I am interested in buying any unusual items on the show or its stars. Please
send information and I will respond promptly, if it is one of the larger items
please include a photo. I am looking for good to excellent condition only, also
unique items not listed.

Cherie Kendall
P.O. Box 1618
Uniontown, PA 15401
412-439-3836

We Pay

J.R. Ewing Doll **100.00**
Any Other Dallas Doll..**75.00**
Ewing Oil Truck..**10.00-15.00**
Posters **10.00-15.00**

Character, TV, and Personality Collectibles

Puzzles 10.00-15.00
Greeting Cards..2.50-5.00
Postcards 2.50-5.00
Southfork Ranch Cookbook..15.00-20.00
Various Dallas Books 5.00-40.00
T-Shirt/Sweatshirts..10.00-25.00
Dallas Deodorant..5.00
Bumper Stickers, Pens or Pins 2.00-10.00
Calendars..10.00-15.00
Southfork Collection Clothes..**Call or Write**
Dallas Clothing Catalog 10.00-20.00

I am looking to buy any and all types of **Dick Tracy collectibles** including any strip-related characters such as Sparkle Plenty and Bonny Braids. Collectible interests include all toys, games, premiums, ephemera, posters, books, comics, guns, puzzles, dolls, figures, original art, store signs, and displays — anything. I also have hundreds of Dick Tracy items to offer in trade. Typical wanted items are listed here.

Larry Doucet
2351 Sultana Dr.
Yorktown Hgts., NY 10598
914-245-1320

Dick Tracy   **We Pay**

Game, Marble Maze, Hasbro, 1966..**100.00+**
Comic Book, Omar/Hancock Super Book Comic #1 ....**100.00+**
Doll, Little Wing, Ideal, in original box ....**250.00+**

I buy **vintage Disneyana of all kinds.** I'll buy any pre-1970 characters and items. My main focus is Disney porcelain and pottery. I want to buy figurines, children's china, tea sets, baby dishes, salt and pepper shakers, cookie jars, banks, planters, adult dinnerware, egg cups, egg timers, and toothbrush holders. I especially want items made by Brayton Laguna, Vernon Kilns, Evan K. Shaw, Hagen Renaker, Wadeheath, Goebel, Paragon, Salem, and Weetman. I'm especially interested in Fantasia pieces — both figurines and dinnerware. I collect the Disney female characters Alice in Wonderland, Snow White, Cinderella, Sleeping Beauty, and Tinker Bell. I seek Winnie the Pooh items. I do **not** buy recent Disney merchandise.

Judy Posner
May through October
R.D. 1, Box 273 HW
Effort, PA 18330
717-629-6583 or fax 717-629-0521
e-mail: Judyandjef@aol.com
or
November through April
4195 S Tamiami Tr. #183HW
Venice, FL 34293
941-497-7149 or fax 941-493-8085
e-mail: Judyandjef@aol.com

Vintage Disneyana   We Pay

Alice in Wonderland Figurines...50.00-300.00
Brayton Disney Figurines 50.00-500.00
Fantasia Figurines, Vernon Kilns..50.00-750.00
Fantasia Figurines, Evan K. Shaw..50.00-350.00
Fantasia Dinnerware, Vernon Kilns..25.00-1,000.00
Goebel Disney Figurines..50.00-750.00
Children's Dishes, marked Bavarian...50.00-500.00
Tea Set, Mickey Mouse, 1930s...100.00-500.00
Snow White & Seven Dwarf Figurine Sets..............................100.00-1,000.00
Wadeheath Snow White Series...75.00-750.00
Winnie the Pooh Ceramics...25.00-125.00
Salt & Pepper/Condiment Sets..25.00-600.00

Disneyland souvenirs and memorabilia wanted — anything from the California amusement park before 1980. My collection of Disneyland items is considered the world's best! I'm always looking for maps, guidebooks, tickets, food wrappers, brochures, ceramic items, special events programs, posters, passes, postcards and postcard folders, personal black and white or color photos, pin-back buttons, and any other type of souvenir. I love Disneyland and have been there more than once a month since the park opened in 1955! I would like to add your items to my collection and will give them a good home. No Walt Disney World in Florida, please. Prices depend on condition and age as per Tomart's *Disneyana Price Guide*.

Linda Cervon
10074 Ashland St.
San Buenaventura, CA 93004
805-659-4405 or fax 805-659-4776

Character, TV, and Personality Collectibles _____

Disneyland Souvenirs   **We Pay**

Guidebooks & Pictorial Souvenirs ....3.00-25.00+
Tickets & Ticket Books ....50¢-5.00+
Maps..5.00-20.00+
Postcards & Postcard Folders ....50¢-4.00+
Brochures & Folders ....1.00-10.00+

We buy **Ginger Rogers** memorabilia. Items in good to fine condition only are wanted. We're not interested in reproduction or poor quality posters, window or lobby cards. Please describe if applicable: title, size, and condition. We will pay for shipping and insurance.

If you have a large amount of sheet music or magazines, please send SASE for our want list. If you have questions, we'd like to hear from you.

Tom and Yvonne Morris
P.O. Box 8307
Medford, OR 97504
541-779-3164

                                                               We Pay

Autographs, pre-1950 ....50.00+
Book, *The Films of Ginger Rogers* ....20.00+
Buttons/Pins, advertising ....5.00+
Cigarette Cards ....8.00+
Commemorative Plates ....25.00+
Dixie Cup Lids ....5.00+
Greeting Cards, autographed ....10.00+
Standee Figure, full size ....95.00+
Lobby Cards ....15.00+
Magazines, complete w/Rogers on cover 15.00-30.00
Play Programs ....5.00+
Posters, Inserts, One-Sheets, Two-Sheets or Three-Sheets 50.00-500.00
Sheet Music, American or foreign 5.00-25.00
Song Books or Song Magazines 15.00
Window Cards..25.00+

We buy all toys depicting **the KISS rock group** in full-painted faces and costumes. We stay away from most paper and records but may be interested in tour programs or picture discs. Most of the items we are looking for were licensed by Aucoin and are from the 1977 to 1980 period. We are only interested in excellent or better condition items as they are not that old and are not that hard to find. All prices below are given for excellent to mint condition only. Please call if you have any questions. Thank you.

Bob Gottuso
BOJO
P.O. Box 1403
Cranberry Twp., PA 16066
412-776-0621

KISS   **We Pay**

Costume Jewelry	3.00-20.00
Backpack	50.00
Backpack, MIP (sealed)	100.00
Bedspread, MIP (sealed)	90.00
Colorforms, complete	45.00
Halloween Costume, MIB, ea	45.00
Cup, 7-11, by Majik Market, ea	12.00
Cup, Megaphone-Scream Machine	35.00
Curtains, MIP (sealed)	100.00
Doll, Paul or Gene, complete clothing, ea	55.00
Doll, Paul or Gene, MIB, ea	100.00
Doll, Ace or Peter, complete clothing, ea	60.00
Doll, Ace or Peter, MIB, ea	105.00
Game, On Tour, complete	35.00
Guitar, plastic	55.00
Guitar, MIP	100.00
Halloween Make-Up Kit, Kiss Your Face, MIP (sealed)	100.00
Jacket, paper w/flames	45.00
Lunch Box w/Thermos	80.00
Microphone, MIB	60.00
Model, Kiss Van, 100% complete in opened box	40.00
Model, Kiss Van, MIB (sealed)	60.00
Notebook, various photos on cover, ea	20.00
Pencils, set of 4, MIP (sealed)	25.00
Pencil, any group member, MOC (sealed), ea	25.00
Poster Art, MIP (sealed)	45.00
Puzzles, group photo, MIP (sealed), ea	25.00
Puzzles, group photo, 100% complete, opened package, ea	13.00
Puzzles, any group member photo, MIP (sealed), ea	35.00
Puzzles, any group member photo, 100% complete, opened package, ea	20.00
Radio, MIB	75.00
Radio, missing box	45.00

Record Player, MIB 250.00
Record Player, missing box 150.00
Remote-Control Van, MIB..125.00
Remote-Control Van, missing box..65.00
Rub 'n' Play Set, unused...40.00
Sleeping Bag, MIP 100.00
Sleeping Bag, missing package..50.00
View-Master Reel Set, w/booklet 20.00
View-Master Double-View on Card, ea 30.00
Wastebasket..65.00

I am always interested in purchasing good quality **Lone Ranger** items that I do not already have in my collection. I would like to have early items from the late 1930s through the early 1950s, but sometimes a brand-new item is needed for my collection. I do not care if the item is a newspaper article about some Lone Ranger/Tonto facts or a premium from some cereal company. I am after puzzles, pin-backs, toy guns, watches, etc., of our hero.

The Silver Bullet
Terry V. Klepey
P.O. Box 553
Forks, WA 98331
360-327-3726

The Lone Ranger   **We Pay**

Book, *The Lone Ranger Rides*, Putnam Publishing 100.00
Cereal Box, any company (Kix, Cheerios, Wheaties) 125.00
Cereal Box Back, Cheerios, Frontier Town #2 ....35.00
Doll, Lone Ranger or Tonto, early, 1938 ....**Call or Write**
Gum Cards, 1948, #28 through #48..20.00
Gum Cards, ca 1939, lg 100.00
Newspapers, early...25.00
Pulp Magazines, 1938-1938, ea 100.00
Premium, charm bracelet, 1938..200.00
Premiums, Lone Ranger Bread, paper, cards, letters, envelopes, ea..........25.00
Premium, ring, Lone Ranger Ice Cream Cone 150.00
Pocket Watch, 1940..150.00
Lone Ranger Ice Cream Cone Mold or Box ....**Call or Write**

I am looking for the following items on **Lucille Ball**. I collect magazines, comic books, plates, dolls, and other memorabilia on Lucille Ball and from her television shows. All items, magazines, and books must be in good to excellent shape.

Patrick Trubia
35 Beach Ave.
Copiague, NY 11726
516-842-0512

We Pay

Advertisements for Various Products **25.00-100.00**
Plate, Lucille Ball Tribute, artist Mike Hazel, 1982 ....**75.00**
Records **20.00-25.00**
TV Guide **50.00-250.00**
TV Magazine **30.00-100.00**
TV Weekly, Febuary 1980, *Los Angeles Herald Examiner* **50.00**
Comic Books, Dell or Gold Key **20.00-40.00**
Doll, I Love Lucy, Lucy Ricardo, rag type **500.00**
Doll, Effanbee, Legend Series, limited edition, 1985 ....**200.00**
Board Games **30.00-50.00**
Coloring Books **30.00-50.00**

I'm always interested in all types of **Lucille Ball memorabilia** — from her early motion picture days to becoming television's Lucy!

My search includes *I Love Lucy* coloring books and paper dolls, Ricky Jr. baby Dolls (American Character Co.), magazines, board games, signs, scripts, studio audience tickets, pencil tables, promotional items, collector plates, foreign memorabilia, etc. Somewhere out there is even a Pepsodent toothpaste carton with her picture. The search is on. If you can help, please write with description and asking price...and thanks.

Ric Wyman
408 S Highland Ave.
Elderon, WI 54429
715-341-6177

I am a serious buyer of any of the items sold by *MAD* magazine and any item picturing their mascot, Alfred E. Neuman. These items include T-shirts, jewelry, posters, busts, postcards, etc. Also I'm looking for earlier **(pre-1960) *MAD* magazines and paperbacks**. Please write or call.

Jim McClane
232 Butternut Dr.
Wayne, N.J. 07470
201-616-1538

Buyer is interested in **Neil Diamond memorabilia**, past and present. Buyer is interested in all items, but especially wanted are tour books, magazine articles, and photographs (standard stock photos and concert photos from fans). All offers considered. Send description of item(s) and asking price to the following address.

Joe Imhof
55 E Kings Hwy. #512
Maple Shade, NJ 08052
e-mail: cets33a@prodigy.com

Pogo was a daily newspaper comic strip character drawn and illustrated by Walt Kelly. Wanted are:

Comic strip paperback or hardback cartoon books
Pogo comic books published by Dell Comics
Small figures of Pogo Possum, Albert Alligator, Churchy Turtle, or Howland Owl
Pin-back buttons
Stamps
Records, 33 rpm or Canadian storybooks with small 78 rpm records
Other Pogo items

Because these items are usually subjected to hard use by children, prices will be according to condition. Also wanted are *Walt Disney Comics and Stories* by Dell Comics about Donald Duck and dated November 1947 through November 1951; *Walt Disney, the Wonderful Adventures of Pinocchio* by Dell Comics, January 1946; *Walt Disney's Snow White and the Seven Dwarfs*; *Walt Disney's Story of Pinocchio*; and children's books by Tony McClay: *Trouble on the Ark*, *The Downy Duck*, and *Raffy Uses His Head*. I will answer all letters.

David P. Norman
Normans Enterprises
542 Gettysburg Rd.
San Antonio, TX 78228-2058
210-732-7920

I am currently seeking **U.S. and foreign posters for 1930s Shirley Temple films**. Also wanted are lobby cards, window cards, half sheets, and inserts from the 1930s. I will pay current market price taking into consideration condition and rarity.

Gen Jones
294 Park St.
Medford, MA 02155
617-395-8598

I am a very serious buyer and collector of **The Three Stooges**, who will make payment within 24 hours on items from my want list. I send postal or bank money orders only! The Three Stooges are not just a hobby for me, but a way of life. Items of special interest are: 1930s-60s hand puppets, games, signed contracts, original candid photographs, canceled checks, all toys (late 1950s to mid-1960s), lobby cards, and one-sheet posters (from Columbia shorts and MGM short subjects). You have seen the other ads claiming to pay high prices — don't let them fool you. Forget the rest because I pay the best. I have spent over $250,000.00 collecting Three Stooges memorabilia. Remember I'll do moron deals! So call me first or last, you decide — just **please call**.

Robert Swerdlow
3503 Howard Blvd.
Baldwin Harbor, NY 11510
516-868-3017

1930s-1960s Items   **We Pay**

Bop Bag, without box	**1,000.00**
Bop Bag, in original box	**2,500.00**
Book Bags, 1950s-60s	**1,000.00**
Bowling Set, 1930s-60s, in original box	**2,500.00**
Canceled Check, signed by Curly Howard	**5,000.00**
Contract, signed by Moe, Larry & Curly	**1,500.00**
Contract, signed by Moe, Larry & Shemp	**1,000.00**
Colorforms Silly Riddle Games, 1950s-60s	**1,000.00**
Candy Sticks, by L.M. Becker	**500.00**
Candy Taffy Kisses, by Phoenix Candy Co.	**500.00**
Counter-Top Store Display, Pillsbury, 1937	**2,500.00**

Counter-Top Store Display, any for toys, 1950s-60s ....**1,500.00+**
Dolls, rag type by Juro, 1954, w/hang tag, ea..**500.00**
Fun Skates, 1950s-60s..**300.00**
Gum Cards Display Box, 1959..**500.00**
Halloween Costumes, by Spooktown & Ben Cooper, in original box.......**500.00**
Hand Puppets, composition, 1930s, ea..**1,000.00**
Hand Puppets, vinyl, 1959, in original package w/header card, ea..........**500.00**
Handwritten Letter, signed by Curley Howard...................................**5,000.00**
Finger Puppets, 1950s-60s, on original card..**1,000.00**
Flicker Rings, 1930s-60s, on original card..**500.00**
Hat, made by Clinton Co., plastic, 1950s-60s **1,000.00**
Kenner's Sparkle Paint Sets, 1950s-60s **1,000.00**
Lobby Cards, 1934 through 1939, 11x14", depending on title..............**1,500.00**
Looney Slim Jims Box, 1950s-60s **500.00**
Milk Carton, w/Stooges shown **500.00**
Musical Kazoo, 1950s-60s **500.00**
Nutty Putty, made by Nadel & Sons, on original card...............................**500.00**
Pencil Coloring Sets..**500.00**
Poster, Pillsbury 1937, for moving picture machine, 27x41" actual size ...**2,500.00**
Poster, Pillsbury 1937, for moving picture machine, 14x22" acutal size ...**2,000.00**
Posters, 1934 through 1939, folded one sheet, 27x41" actual size, depending
    on title...**10,000.00+**
Punching Balloons, on original card...**500.00**
Rubber Stamp Sets, Colorforms, 1960s **500.00**
Spin Toy, 1950s-60s, on original display card **1,000.00**
Anything Else Not Listed from 1930s-60s..**Call**

Chewing Gum Memorabilia

I am buying old **(pre-1940) chewing gum wrappers**. I am interested in 'usual' brands like Adams, Beech-Nut, Clark's, Wrigley's, Beeman's, Dentyne, Chiclets, Zeno's, Orbit, Sen-Sen, Black Jack, Yucatan, etc. Also, I am interested in old gum packs and whole or empty gum boxes. I can be interested in old gum store displays, signs, tins, and vendors. I am **not** interested in any large bubble gum items, gum cards, or gum magazine ads. I can use many duplicates of old gum wrappers. The price I pay very much depends on the rarity, age, and condition of these.

Miroslav Nikl
P.O. Box 7
16200 Praha 616
Czech Republic
phone or fax: 011422/3163036

Chewing Gum Wrappers   We Pay

Adams ....7.00+
Beech-Nut...5.00+
Clark's..5.00+
Wrigley's ....2.00+
Beeman's ....6.00+
Dentyne ....3.00+
Chiclets...6.00+
Zeno's ....6.00+
Orbit ....4.00+
Sen-Sen ....8.00+
Black Jack ....6.00+
Yacatan..8.00+

Chewing Gum Packs   We Pay

Adams ....25.00+
Beech-Nut...25.00+
Clark's..25.00+
Wrigley's ....12.00+
Beeman's ....25.00+
Dentyne ....10.00+
Chiclets...10.00+
Zeno's ....25.00+
Orbit ....15.00+
Sen-Sen ....35.00+
Black Jack ....25.00+
Yacatan..25.00+

———

This collector is looking for **anything and everything connected with gum**. Wrigley wartime gums such as Orbit, K Ration, and PK (Packed tight — Keep right!). Gums are wanted as well as Wrigley premium gift items and advertisements. Collector would love to find Fleer Funnies starring PUD and Bazooka Comics, packages of Topps celebrity and movie cards, Topps Goofy Groceries, Wacky Packages, and Crazy Spray Can series, gumball tubes with novelty toppers (filled or empty), and all flavors, makers, and styles of bubble gum dispensers.

Old or new, if it's GUM, I'm the One! Reach in your 'pack' and share or sell a 'piece' of gum with me. I'd love to 'chew' on fun facts and history too! Any Wrigley, Topps, or Fleer workers out there? Don't let the puns fool you — this collector is very serious! Please write or surf the net and e-mail me.

Chewing Gum Chronicles
10115 Greenwood Ave N, #M157
Seattle, WA 98133
e-mail: tmgum@worldnet.att.net

Children's Dishes

I buy children's dishes. I collect **Akro Agate, Jeannette Glass Co. children's dishes such as Cherry Blossom and Doric & Pansy.** I am also buying old transparent colored or clear pieces such as candlesticks, butter dishes, and any children's kitchen-related items. The Akro Agate colors I collect are transparent blue, green, and amber. I buy all marbleized colors: blue and white, maroon (red) and white, lemonade and oxblood, and green and white. Prices vary according to pattern, size, and individual piece.

Terry Semon
5414 Fleming St. #B
Everett, WA 98203
206-290-6805

	We Pay
Cereal Bowl	4.00-40.00
Creamer	10.00-40.00
Cup	10.00-40.00
Pitcher	12.00-20.00
Plate	4.00-15.00
Saucer	3.00-12.00
Sugar	15.00-60.00
Teapot	18.00-75.00
Tumbler	7.00-15.00

I want to buy children's **Blue Willow** tea sets or individual pieces in porcelain, tin, or plastic — no new please. The following prices are for porcelain.

Janet Luedtke
5110-103rd Ave.
Grand Junction, MI 49056
616-434-6884

Porcelain	We Pay
Complete Set in Box	110.00
Teapot w/Lid	15.00
Covered Vegetable	15.00
Platter	8.00
Creamer	5.00-8.00
Sugar Bowl w/Lid	5.00-8.00
Cup & Saucer	5.00-8.00
Plate	3.00-5.00
Lids for Teapots or Sugar Bowls	2.00

I am interested in buying **children's tea sets made of china or glass.** I prefer older sets made before 1950 and decorated with floral patterns, small children, Blue Willow, etc. I'm also looking for **children's spice and canister sets.** Photos and descriptions would be helpful when you reply.

Diane Genicola
25 E Adams Ave.
Pleasantville, NJ 08232
609-646-6140

China and Porcelain

We buy **all patterns of Blue Ridge china and dinnerware made by Southern Potteries.** We don't buy any crazed, chipped, or cracked pieces. If pattern name is not known a color photo is helpful. Send listing of number and kinds of pieces for sale with prices wanted.

Oscar Hubbert
P.O. Box 1415
Fletcher, NC 28732
704-687-0350

'Chintz' is the generic name for English china with an all-over floral transfer design. This eye-catching china is reminiscent of chintz dress fabric. It is colorful, bright, and cheery with its many floral designs and reminds one of an English garden in full bloom. It was produced in England during the first half of this century and stands out among other styles of china. I am interested in **'Chintz' pieces made by Royal Winton, Grimwades, James Kent, Lord Nelson Ware, and Crown Ducal**, among others. Pattern names often found with the manufacturer's name on the bottom of pieces include Anemone, Chelsea, Chintz, Delphinium Chintz, June Roses, Mayfair, Hazel, Eversham, Royalty, Sweet Pea, Summertime, Springtime, and Welbeck, among others.

I am interested in buying individual pieces or complete breakfast, luncheon, or tea sets. Prices vary depending on pattern and manufacturer. All pieces must be in perfect condition, no chips, cracks, crazing, or other damage. I buy all English 'Chintz' pieces and am especially interested in teapots, toast racks, pitchers, wash sets, and other large or unusual pieces. Items of interest are listed here. I hope you tell me about any 'Chintz' china you have for sale.

Biscuit Jars	Jam Jars
Breakfast Sets	Jardineres
Butter Pats	Loving Cups
Candlesticks	Musical Boxes
Candy Dishes	Salt and Pepper Shakers
Cheese Dishes	Sugar and Creamer Sets
Comports	Teapots (all sizes)
Condiment Sets	Toast Racks
Cruets (on stands)	Toilet Sets
Cups and Saucers	Trays
Egg Cups	Vanity Items
Fruit Bowls	Vases
Humidors	Wall Pockets

Marjorie Geddes
P.O. Box 5875
Aloha, OR 97007
503-649-1041

I buy **English Chintz china in all patterns**. These are all-over floral patterns made by Royal Winton, James Kent, Shelly, Royal Tudor, Lord Nelson, Grimwades, and others. Prices paid will depend on condition, pattern, and rarity of pieces. Especially looking for bowls, teapots, vases, pitchers, trays, lamps, or other unusual pieces. Cups and saucers and plates will be considered but price will reflect their more general availablity. If you do not know the name of your pattern, send a picture with correspondence.

Pam Rappaport
P.O. Box 823911
South Florida, FL 33082-3911

We Pay

Tea Set	**300.00+**
Covered Cheese Dish	**80.00+**
Breakfast Set	**300.00+**
Serving Bowl	**45.00+**
Lamp	**250.00+**

I am interested in purchasing **Crooksville China in Apple Blossom pattern** and especially want the creamer and sugar bowl. I have my mother's set of dishes that she purchased back in the 1940s and am trying to find missing pieces. There isn't much information available about any of the patterns which is really too bad. So if anyone out there knows what was made in this pattern or has any pieces to sell (good condition only), please let me know.

Linda Morrissey
24 Cliff Street
East Haven, CT 06512
203-466-6970

We purchase **Hall china and dinnerware** in any amount from single pieces to entire collections. Preferred patterns include **Autumn Leaf (Jewel Tea), Rose Parade, Silhouette (Taverne), Crocus, Red Poppy, Orange Poppy, and Morning-Glory**. All pieces should be free of chips, stains, or crazing. Any china or dinnerware sent to us will be evaluated promptly and an offer made within two weeks of receipt. We pay shipping both ways. Send SASE for shipping information.

Carousel Antiques
1006 Meyer at Fourth
Seabrook, TX 77586

Hall's Red Poppy pattern consists of a red floral decal with black leaves. Each glass piece has a narrow silver band on the edges. It was manufactured from the mid-'30s until the '50s. The Grand Union Tea Company used this pattern as a premium. We are interested in buying any unusual pieces — especially the metal accessories. We prefer only pieces in mint condition.

Mac and Jo Ann McKuegtch
4206 Abbeydale Dr.
Charlotteville, NC 28265
704-536-0507

We wish to buy **Shelley china** to better accommodate our Shelley china replacement service. We particularly wish to buy the 6-flute Dainty shape in full dinner sets as well as individual pieces. Additionally, we seek Shelley figurines (Mabel Lucie Attwell's children, animals, and particularly characters), chintz wares, advertising, and other items, Early Shelley wares marked with an intertwined 'CW' (Charles Wileman) are also of interest.

Fred and Lila Shrader
2025 Hwy. 199 (Hiouchi)
Crescent City, CA 95531
707-458-3525

We Pay

Advertising Pieces, as signs, brochures, figures, pre-1967	**Please Inquire**
Bell	**45.00+**
Butter Pat, various shapes	**25.00+**
Coffeepot, various sizes	**95.00+**
Cup & Saucer, various sizes & shapes	**35.00+**
Cup & Saucer, Chintz, various sizes & shapes	**40.00+**
Cup & Saucer, miniature, various shapes	**85.00+**
Festival of Empire Series	**95.00+**
Intarsio Ware	**100.00+**
Mabel Lucie Attwell Wares, Figures, Etc.	**85.00+**
Napkin Ring	**50.00+**
Pitcher & Bowl Set	**155.00+**
Place Settings, 5-pc or more, various shapes	**55.00-80.00+**
Plate, Dainty shape, various sizes	**15.00-65.00+**
Platter, Dainty shape, various sizes	**75.00+**
Salt & Pepper Set	**50.00+**
Teapot, various sizes and shapes	**95.00+**

Wanted: **all fine china from England, France, Germany, America, Japan, etc.** Pieces must be in mint condition. For offers send name of manufacturer, pattern, and pieces for sale — or photocopy both sides of dinner plate for possible identification. Mail order only. Write or call. The best time to call is from 7 pm to 11 pm EST.

Jay Adams
245 Lakeview Ave., Ste. 208
Clifton, NJ 07011
201-365-5907

Wanted: **Phoenix Bird dinnerware**, a blue and white china of the early 1900s. Made by many Japanese manufacutures, its pieces encompass nearly 500 forms — many coming in various sizes as well as shapes. Wanted are those **pieces in unique shapes other than the usual place settings seen today** (i.e., soap dish with cover, washbowl, castor set, cracker jar or cracker trough).

Joan Oates
685 S Washington
Constantine, MI 49042
616-435-8353

Wanted to buy: **restaurant-grade commercial china**. Especially wanted are cups and saucers, mugs, platters, plates, bowls, etc., with logos of drive-ins, luncheon diners, transportation, oil companies, steamship lines, airlines, and buslines. Hamburger and sandwich lines such as White Tower, White Castle, Royal Castle, Silver Castle, Krystal, Little Tavern, Whimpys, Baltimore Dairy Lunch, Waldorf Lunch, Globe Lunch, etc. — any pieces with interesting graphics. Please, no chips or cracks; items must be in very good to mint condition.

Dave Lathom
P.O. Box 5053
Bellingham, WA 98225
360-676-0715

We Pay

Transportation China	**25.00-500.00+**
Restaurant China	**25.00-250.00+**

Wanted: **porcelain pieces with missing lids** such as Nippon, Limoges, R.S. Prussia, German-marked items, and others.

Ronald D. Cowan
918 N Oleander Ave.
Daytona Beach, FL 32118
904-252-2756

I am buying **fine china that is signed by W. Wilson**. Walter Wilson was a painter in Meriden, Connecticut, during the late 1800s and early 1900s. He painted full lines of table china and vanity pieces as well as some decorative pieces. His motif was generally floral, including delicately painted pansies, violets, tulips, roses, forget-me-nots, iris, etc. Generally, his china was ivory in color with gold trim. An assortment of china blanks were used and included Limoges and Japan.

The signature, W. Wilson, is most often found on the face of the plate, but occasionally may be signed (printed) on the back in black lettering. Salt and pepper shakers and procelain pins are not signed. The price I pay depends upon the pattern. Pieces must be in excellent condition with no chips. A photo would be helpful but not always necessary. If you find an extra pretty piece of china, take a second look for the W. Wilson signature.

Sandra D. Hunt
380 N Main St.
Wallingford, CT 06492
203-269-1952

Christmas and Other Holidays

I am looking for **early German papier-mache candy containers**. From the turn of the century to the early 1930s, the Germans made a fabulous variety of different candy containers to represent all of our holidays. They were constructed of composition or a cardboard and papier-mache material. The price I pay depends on age, condition, size, and rarity. Please send a clear photo with a full description of size, markings, any flaws, hairline cracks, repairs, repaints, paint chips, or paint crazing.

Jenny Tarrant
Holly Daze Antiques
4 Gardenview
St. Peters, MO 63376
314-397-1763

German Santa Candy Containers   We Pay

Santa on Sleigh, 4"...**85.00-95.00**
Santa on Log Pile, Houses, Stumps, or Other Objects.................**150.00-185.00**
Santa, pulls apart at waist, 4".......................................**150.00-185.00**
Santa, pulls apart at waist, 5".......................................**175.00-195.00**
Santa, pulls apart at waist, 6".......................................**200.00-250.00**
Santa, pulls apart at waist, 7".......................................**225.00-275.00**
Santa, pulls apart at waist, 8".......................................**250.00-300.00**
Santa, pulls apart at waist, 9".......................................**300.00-350.00**
Santa in Long Robe, pulls apart at knees, 5"..................**225.00-275.00**
Santa in Long Robe, pulls apart at knees, 6"..................**250.00-300.00**
Santa in Long Robe, pulls apart at knees, 7"..................**300.00-350.00**
Santa in Long Robe, pulls apart at knees, 8"..................**350.00-400.00**

Other Santa Candy Containers   We Pay

Net Bag, Japan...**50.00-85.00**
Celluloid, standing **25.00-35.00**
Celluloid, in cars, houses, etc. **35.00-45.00**
Bisque, standing, sm...**35.00-55.00**
Bisque, on houses, in cars or planes **55.00-95.00**

Turkey Candy Containers   We Pay

Papier-Mache or Composition, lead feet, head removes, 3"............**45.00-55.00**
Papier-Mache or Composition, lead feet, plug on bottom, 3" **35.00-40.00**
Papier-Mache or Composition, lead feet, head removes, 4"............**55.00-65.00**
Papier-Mache or Composition, lead feet, plug on bottom, 4" **45.00-50.00**
Papier-Mache or Composition, lead feet, head removes, 5"............**65.00-75.00**
Papier-Mache or Composition, lead feet, plug on bottom, 5" **55.00-60.00**
Papier-Mache or Composition, lead feet, head removes, 6"............**75.00-85.00**
Papier-Mache or Composition, lead feet, plug on bottom, 6" **65.00-75.00**
Papier-Mache or Composition, lead feet, head removes, 7"............**85.00-95.00**
Papier-Mache or Composition, lead feet, plug on bottom, 7" **75.00-80.00**

Patriotic Candy Containers   We Pay

George Washington Bust, papier-mache, 3"....................**65.00-75.00**
George Washington Bust, papier-mache, 4"....................**75.00-95.00**

Christmas and Other Holidays

George Washington Sitting on Stump, papier-mache, 4".................85.00-100.00
George Washington on Horse, Boat, Box or Other Object...............95.00-125.00
Tree, papier-mache, 4"..35.00-45.00
Tree, papier-mache, 5"..45.00-65.00
Tree, papier-mache, 6"..55.00-75.00

German Rabbit Candy Containers   We Pay

Begging Brown Rabbit, papier-mache, head removes, 4"..................75.00-85.00
Begging Brown Rabbit, papier-mache, head removes, 5"..................80.00-95.00
Begging Brown Rabbit, papier-mache, head removes, 6"...............85.00-100.00
Walking Brown Rabbit, papier-mache, head removes, 4".................85.00-95.00
Walking Brown Rabbit, papier-mache, head removes, 5"..............95.00-110.00
Walking Brown Rabbit, papier-mache, head removes, 6"...........100.00-120.00
Brown Rabbit on Candy Box, papier-mache, 4"..............................85.00-100.00
Clothed Rabbit on Candy Box, papier-mache, 3"...........................95.00-110.00
Clothed Rabbit on Candy Box, papier-mache, 4".........................110.00-125.00
Clothed Rabbit on Candy Box, papier-mache, 5".........................125.00-165.00
Clothed Rabbit, papier-mache, head removes, 3"..........................100.00-125.00
Clothed Rabbit, papier-mache, head removes, 4"..........................125.00-150.00
Clothed Rabbit, papier-mache, head removes, 5"..........................150.00-175.00
Clothed Rabbit, papier-mache, head removes, 6"..........................195.00-225.00
Clothed Rabbit Nodder, papier-mache, 5"......................................120.00-145.00
Clothed Rabbit Nodder, papier-mache, 6"......................................150.00-165.00
Rabbit Pulling Wood or Moss Cart, papier-mache, 5"..................100.00-125.00
Rabbit Pulling Wood or Moss Cart, papier-mache, 6"..................120.00-140.00
Rabbit Pulling Wood or Moss Cart, papier-mache, 7"..................135.00-155.00
Rabbit Pulling Wood or Moss Cart, papier-mache, 8"..................145.00-175.00

St. Patrick's Day Candy Containers   We Pay

Man's Bust, composition, 3"..45.00-55.00
Man's Bust, composition, 4"..55.00-65.00
Child on Candy Box, 3"..75.00-85.00
Child on Candy Box, 4"..85.00-95.00
Child or Man, head removes, 4"..100.00-110.00
Child or Man, head removes, 5"..120.00-135.00
Pig, head removes, 3"...35.00-45.00
Pig, head removes, 4"...55.00-65.00
Pig, head removes, 5"...75.00-85.00

We are collectors that buy **older Christmas items from the 1880s through the 1950s.** If you have one item or a collection of older items to sell, please contact us. We love it all! We are interested in old figural glass ornaments, feather trees with round or square wooden bases, old Santa figures, cotton batting ornaments, Dresden ornaments, revolving musical tree stands that are key wound, old paper Christmas-themed items, clockwork Father Christmas nodders and reindeer, bubble and matchless star lights and many more items. Samples of prices paid can vary greatly due to condition, age, rarity, and country of origin. Items marked Germany are worth more than items marked Japan if they are in the same condition. An item in poor condition may be worth $20.00 while the same item in excellent condition could be worth $200.00. The following prices listed can't accurately cover all of the variables that exist. We are willing to pay more for many items listed in Christmas price guides that we need. Due to the vast amount of Christmas items produced over the years, it can help us most if you can include a photo of items you wish to sell. We will pay you the very best price for items we are seeking so we encourage you to call or send a note for all old Christmas you have to sell.

The Murphy's
216 Blackhawk Rd.
Riverside, IL 60546
708-442-6846

We Pay

Ornament, figural glass	**25.00-250.00**
Ornament, spun cotton, scrap face	**125.00-200.00**
Ornament, Italian w/annealed arms & legs	**35.00-65.00**
Feather Tree	**75.00-300.00**
Revolving Musical Key-Wound Antique Tree Stand	**250.00-400.00**
Santa, German w/fur beard	**125.00-400.00**
Santa or Reindeer Nodder, w/clockwork	**1,350.00+**
Bubble Lights	**3.00-20.00**
Matchless Star Wonder Lights	**22.00-75.00**
Papier-Mache Items	**20.00+**

We want to buy all types of **old Christmas items from the 1880s through the 1950s!** We buy figural Christmas tree light bulbs, old German figural glass ornaments, German feather trees, old Santas, Belsnickles, cotton batting ornaments, early Santa Claus storybooks, old light sets in original boxes, bubble light trees, bubble lights, German nativity sets, German stick-leg animals, celluloid figures and toys, lithographed scrap ornaments, papier-mache items and candy containers, hard plastic Santas and toys from the 1940s and 1950s, all types of lighted decorations, and any other unusual old Christmas items. Sample prices are below. We answer *all* letters. Please see our listing under Halloween in this book.

Bob and Diane Kubicki
R.R. #2
West Milton, OH 45383
513-698-3650

We Pay

Light Bulb, standing Indian...250.00+
Light Bulb, green Father Christmas..100.00+
Light Bulb, milk glass army tank...175.00+
Light Bulb, Uncle Sam...300.00+
Ornament, glass Indian's head, German, old..125.00+
Ornament, figural cotton girl w/scrap face..75.00+
Ornament, spun cotton fruit, 3" ....15.00+
Feather Tree, green, German, 6-ft..400.00+
Father Christmas Clockworks Nodder ....1,500.00+
Belsnickle, German, 8"..250.00-450.00
Santa Claus Storybook, 1905..20.00+
Boxed Light Set, early 1920s ....10.00+
Wooden Box, for early Christmas light set ....100.00+
Porcelain Socket Light String 30.00
German Nativity Set 35.00-75.00
Bubble Light Tree, green, 18-socket..100.00+
Plastic Bubble Light Santa...15.00
German Santa, w/rabbit fur beard, 8"...200.00+
Glass Santa-on-Chimney Lamp, black glass base ....500.00+

We buy select old Christmas lights, ornaments, and decorations to use and add to our collection. We especially like the **pre-1920 ornaments and Christmas decorations made in Germany**. Quality, condition, and rarity are important to us. We want lights to work but remember that many of the old ones are 15-volt, so it is not wise to plug them into 110. Use a 15-volt battery to test them. Please describe fully, and photographs are very helpful. What do you have?

J.W. 'Bill' and Treva Courter
3935 Kelley Rd.
Kevil, KY 42053
phone or fax 502-488-2116

We Pay

Belsnickle...100.00+

Bubble Lights, Royal, Paramount, Noma, Glolite, Etc................................**3.00-5.00**
Bubble Lights, these 'pour' slowly, usually w/clip..........................**10.00-25.00**
Bulb, Santa, Japan, lg...**50.00+**
Doll, Father Christmas..**25.00-500.00**
Lamp, Santa Claus, sm, complete...**500.00+**
Light Cover, Dresden (condition very important!)....................**35.00-100.00**
Lights, Matchless Wonder-Star, sm, single row.....................**12.00-30.00**
Lights, Matchless Wonder-Star, lg, double row.....................**35.00-85.00**
Ornaments, pre-1940 glass such as Noah's Ark, Indian, doll head, baby in cradle, ea..**75.00+**
Postcard, hold-to-light, die-cut Santa....................................**100.00+**
Postcard, hold-to-light, die-cut angels.............................**15.00-25.00**
Postcard, transparency w/color or black & white Santas, ea...................**20.00+**

Wanted: **Christmas items from the 1940s and prior years.** Anything used for the season, i.e., but not limited to these items is wanted: Santa Claus, all ornaments, nativity sets, animals, celluloid toys, candy containers, etc. Please send list and asking price. I will answer all SASE letters.

Sue Murphy
29668 Orinda Rd.
San Juan Capistrano, CA 92675
714-364-4333

Wanted: **holiday items from the 1950s to the present.** I collect almost anything Christmas and am interested in Halloween and Easter as well. Don't throw away your old boxes of holiday decorations, let me give them a home! Rarity, age, and condition of your item will determine what I will pay. If you will send a photo or detailed description, SASE, and the value you want for your item, I will respond.

Beth Summers
233 Darnell Rd.
Benton, KY 42025

Cigarette Lighters

I am an avid collector of **Zippo cigarette lighters and Case knives**. Below is a list of items I need and the prices I will pay. I also will pay a finder's fee for locating these items. Please call or write with your information or questions.

Clayton V. Vecellio
Box 298
Lewis Run, PA 16738
814-368-5294

Zippo Lighter	We Pay
1932, plain	500.00+
1933, w/diagonal lines	700.00+
1944, black crackle	20.00+
1979, w/elephant	75.00+
1979, w/donkey	75.00+
1969, moon landing	75.00+
1970, Bush-Gorbachav	80.00+
1970, Regan-Gorbachav	80.00+
1971, w/Donald Duck	75.00+
1972, w/Mickey Mouse	100.00+

Clocks

I buy **American-made clocks manufactured from 1800 to 1920**. Seth Thomas, Waterbury, Ansonia, E.N. Welch, Gilbert, New Haven, Ithaca Calendar Clock Co., Willard, Chelsea, and E. Howard are among the manufacturers whose clocks I am looking to purchase. Of special interest are large, wall-hung clocks that are weight-driven; two-dial calendar clocks that both tell the time as well as day, date, and month; weight-driven banjo-style clocks; ornate Victorian-style wood-case shelf or wall clocks; clocks with advertising on them; and tall case or shelf clocks made by Stickley. Replaced dials (i.e., faces) and movements (i.e., works) hurt the value of a clock. Top dollar paid for clocks that are in mint, original condition.

Bruce A. Austin
Rochester Institute of Technology
College of Liberal Arts
Rochester, NY 14623-5604
716-475-2879 or 716-387-9820 (evenings)

We Pay

Advertising Wall Clock, Baird Clock Co., Molescorium ....**850.00+**
Ansonia, figure-8 style wall clock, rosewood ....**300.00+**
Ansonia, steeple clock, mahogany, 8-day time & strike..........................**175.00+**
Atkins, schoolhouse-style wall clock, ripple molding, rosewood..........**300.00+**
Atkins, miniature Empire-style shelf clock, rosewood ....**275.00+**
Birge & Fuller, triple decker, reverse-painted glasses, mahogany.........**500.00+**
J.C. Brown, beehive clock, ripple molding, etched glass ....**800.00+**
Gilbert, fancy schoolhouse-style wall clock w/owl on glass ....**450.00+**
Gilbert, Amphion, heavily carved walnut Victorian shelf clock...........**500.00+**
Gustav Stickley, shelf clock, Seth Thomas movement, oak................**5,000.00+**
E. Ingraham, Treasure Island banjo, mahogany.....................................**350.00+**
Ithaca Calendar Clock, Parlor model, walnut, glass pendulum...........**2,000.00+**
Ithaca Calendar Clock, Shelf Library, walnut.......................................**500.00+**
Asa Munger, Auburn (NY), Empire-style carved column self model..**1,000.00+**
New Haven, Victorian shelf clock, reverse-painted glass, walnut..........**150.00+**
New Haven, ornately carved shelf clock, walnut, gilt trim....................**550.00+**
Sessions, store regulator, pressed oak case, simple calendar ....**475.00+**
Eli Terry, pillar & scroll, reverse-painted glass, mahogany ....**1,200.00+**
Seth Thomas, #2 Regulator, oak, single brass weight............................**600.00+**
Waltham, banjo, reverse-painted glasses, mahogany, 42"....................**1,500.00+**
Waterbury, ornate oak wall clock, open pendulum & 2 weights.........**1,500.00+**
E.N. Welch, weight-driven wall clock, walnut, 60"..............................**4,500.00**

I buy **antique clocks, especially clocks made before 1890**. Single pieces or entire collections are wanted. Travel distance is not a problem. Send photos or call 1-800-277-5275. Listed below are prices for mint, original clocks.

Mark of Time
24 South Lemon Ave.
Sarasota, FL 34236
800-277-5275

Maker's Name or Type of Clock	We Pay
Welch Spring & Co.	**up to 3,000.00**

Clocks

S.B. Terry ....**up to 1,500.00**
Eli Terry ....**up to 4,000.00**
English Weight-Driven Wall Clocks ....**up to 4,000.00**
American Weight-Driven Wall Clocks.........................**up to 10,000.00**
German Weight-Driven Wall Clocks............................**up to 4,000.00**
English Grandfather Clocks ....**up to 7,500.00**
American Grandfather Clocks......................................**up to 30,000.00**
China Clocks..**up to 1,200.00**
Fancy Repeating Carriage Clocks................................**up to 3,000.00**
F. Kroeber ....**up to 1,000.00**
Ansonia..**up to 5,000.00**
Seth Thomas ....**up to 9,000.00**
Waterbury ....**up to 4,500.00**
French Statue Clocks...**up to 7,500.00**
American Fusee Clocks..**up to 2,500.00**
English Fusee Clocks..**up to 7,500.00**

I collect **novelty clocks and am especially interested in Lux, Keebler, Mi-Ken pendulette clocks, and Oswald moving-eye clocks.** We buy only clocks in excellent condition. Only original clocks are wanted, *no reproductions or clocks that have been repainted.*

I'm also purchasing pressed wood items by Syrocowood, Ornawood, Durawood, etc. Price depends on item and condition.

Carole Kaifer
P.O. Box 232
Bethania, NC 27010
910-924-9672

We Pay

Lux, Liberty Bell 300.00-350.00
Lux, Scottie Dog...325.00-375.00
Lux, Capitol...300.00-350.00
Lux, figural 150.00-200.00
Mi-Ken (Japan), plastic 20.00-25.00
Mi-Ken (Japan), wood...25.00-35.00
Oswald (moving eye), Dog..250.00-350.00
Oswald (moving eye), Owl 300.00-350.00
Oswald (moving eye), others.......................................350.00+

I am interested in buying **out-of-print and antiquarian books as well as antique clocks**. We pay a percentage of the current market value for books and depending on condition this could be $1.00 to $1,000.00.

The Whale's Tale
Norma Wadler
P.O. Box 1520A
620 S Pacific
Long Beach, WA 98631
360-642-3455 or fax 360-642-2626

Clocks   **We Pay**

Chiming, up to 8" tall..70.00+
American, key-wound, chimes, before 1900, working.............................65.00+
American, key-wound, chimes, 1900-1929, working...............................45.00+
European or English, working...45.00+

Clothing and Accessories

You might even have some valuable items in your own closet! We buy so many different items, at great prices, we can't even list them all. Some of the items we are buying include **vintage (older) Levi's, Lee, and Wrangler jeans, Nike shoes, and military jackets**. Of special interest to us are denim jeans made by the above listed companies from the 1930s until about the 1980s. We buy a wide range of these jeans depending on size, condition, year made, and rarity of the particular item. The older the item and the better the condition, the more money we can pay you. If you're a collector, dealer, garage sale person, or just someone looking for a way to make some extra cash, we can help you. We have published a magazine detailing the kinds of items we would like to purchase from you. If you want to know more, give us a call.

Farley Enterprises
112 North 1200 West
Orem, UT 84057
801-224-3130
hhtp://www2.farley.com/farley/buy4us.html

Levi's Jeans   We Pay

Red Lines, double stitch, depending on waist size & grade............**33.00-120.00**
Red Lines, double stitch, depending on waist size & grade............**40.00-300.00**
BIG E 501...**400.00-600.00**
BIG E 505 (w/red line) **300.00-500.00**
FF1 ZXX, w/paper tag **400.00-800.00**
FFI ZXX, w/leather tag **700.00-1,500.00**
501XX, w/paper tag **700.00-1,200.00**
501XX, w/leather tag (Every Garment Guaranteed) **1,000.00-2,500.00**
501XX, WWIIXX (pocket paint) **1,500.00-5,000.00**
501XX, buckle backs..**3,000.00-10,000.00**
Regular 501, 28" to 36" waist, 1st or 2nd grade **12.00-20.00**

Other Jeans   We Pay

Lee 101, M.R. circa 1970s, 32" to 42" waist **67.00-140.00**
Lee 101, only, circa 1960s, 32" to 42" waist....................................**160.00-400.00**
Lee Cowboy, no buckle back **1,500.00-5,000.00**
Lee Cowboy, buckle back **3,000.00-10,000.00**
Wrangler IIMW, blue bell, 1960s, 32" to 42" waist.......................**120.00-240.00**
Wrangler IIMW, blue bell, 1950s, 32" to 42" waist.......................**200.00-800.00**
Wrangler Buttonfly, blue bell, 1960s **200.00-800.00**
Wrangler Buttonfly, blue bell, 1950s **400.00-1,200.00**

Coca-Cola

We buy **pre-1965 Coca-Cola advertising memorabilia** in excellent to mint condition. Areas of interest include calendars; tin, porcelain, cardboard, and paper signs; diecuts and window displays; festoons; light-up signs; playing cards; clocks; thermometers; trays; salesman's samples and miniatures; trucks and toys; etc. Our experience includes over 10 years of collecting soda-pop memorabilia, editors for several antique and advertising price guides, and writers of a monthly column dedicated to Coca-Cola and soft drink collectibles. As collectors we can offer top dollar for quality pieces and collections. Condition and rarity are important factors that must be taken into consideration when determining the value of an item. We are willing to travel to purchase items or pay for shipping and handling. Besides purchasing for our collection, we assist in determining the authenticity, age, and value of items at no charge. Please feel free to call us or write with your inquiries. A clear photograph is always helpful for a quick response.

Craig and Donna Stifter
P.O. Box 6514
Naperville, IL 60540
630-717-7949

Coca-Cola   We Pay

1924 Calendar, complete pad	**700.00+**
1936 Calendar, complete pad	**400.00+**
1937 Sign, cardboard w/running girl	**250.00**
1938 Sign, cardboard, signed Sundblom, 29x50"	**400.00+**
1922 Window Display, cardboard w/aquaplane girl	**1,000.00+**
1950s Porcelain Button Sign, shows bottle, 24" dia	**200.00+**
1930s Tin Sign, Take Home a Carton, shows 6-pack, 19x54"	**200.00+**
1950s Tin Sign, Drink Ice-Cold Coca-Cola, bottle on right, 20x28"	**100.00+**
1960s Tin Tire Rack Sign, Enjoy Coca-Cola While We Check Your Tires	**300.00+**
1950s Porcelain Fountain Service Sign, shows ribbon, 12x28"	**200.00+**
1920s Paper Hanger Sign, shows boy eating hot dog, 12x20"	**350.00+**
1944 Cardboard Cutout, service girl, 17"	**100.00+**
1953 Cardboard Santa Cutout, The Gift For Thirst	**100.00+**
1958 Festoon, sports cars, 5 pieces	**275.00+**
1928 Playing Cards, Bobbed Hair Girl, complete deck w/jokers & box	**250.00+**
1951 Playing Cards, Girl at Party, complete deck w/jokers & box	**250.00+**
1950s Light-Up Sign, 2-sided plastic, Shop Refreshed	**175.00+**
1960s Light-Up Sign, plastic & tin, rotating lantern style	**85.00+**
1942 Serving Tray, Roadster Girls	**150.00+**
1930 Serving Tray, Telephone Girl	**250.00+**
1941 Thermometer, shows 2 Coke bottles	**175.00+**
1950s Clock, lights up, shows bottle	**150.00+**
1939 Salesman Sample Floor Cooler, closed front style, w/case	**2,000.00+**
1960s Buddy L Truck, yellow w/cases & dollies	**90.00+**

I have particular interest in **Coca-Cola calendars from 1931 through 1949** in near-mint to mint condition. This includes Norman Rockwell Boy Scouts as well. I'm a collector looking to add to my current small collection. They must have full pads and cover sheets with no tears or noticeable stains. I can accept minor problems. The better the condition, the more I pay! If trading is your preference rather than selling, I have several nice Coca-Cola cardboards comparable in price. I will also pay a finder's fee of 10% for information leading to purchase of these calendars. I will consider other calendars up to 1959 based on their condition. The prices below reflect well above book price but certainly can be higher if condition dictates.

Chris Young
318 Old Timey Trails
Moultrie, GA 31768
912-985-0751

Coca-Cola Calendars	We Pay
1931	1,350.00+
1932	850.00+
1933	850.00+
1934	950.00+
1935	950.00+
1936	1,000.00+
1937	900.00+
1938	800.00+
1939	800.00+
1940	800.00+
1941	550.00+
1942	500.00+
1943	600.00+
1944	400.00+
1945	not available
1946	750.00+
1948	450.00+
1949	400.00+

Coffin Plates

Produced in the 1800s through the early part of the 20th century, metal coffin plates helped relatives memorialize the deceased and are sometimes found in shadow boxes along with other mementos. Most are rectangular, but some are shaped as the objects they depict, such as clocks, flowers, lambs, etc. Usually they are made of a silver-colored base metal, but sometimes are silver-plated or painted. Most coffin plates have two small holes. The most desirable plates have personalized engravings, such as with a name and date of birth and/or death. Foreign language plates are also desirable. More common are coffin plates engraved 'Our Darling,' 'At Rest,' 'Mother,' or 'Father.' Please send a self-addressed stamped envelope or a fax or e-mail address.

Adrienne Esco
4448 Ironwood Ave.
Seal Beach, CA 90740
310-430-6479 or fax 310-598-1585
e-mail: escoebliss@earthlink.net

We Pay

Engraved 'Our Darling,' 'At Rest,' 'Mother,' or 'Father' **5.00-10.00**
Engraved, name & date or foreign language.....................................**7.50-12.00+**
Unusual Shape or Design **10.00-18.00**
Personalized, w/plain border **7.50-10.00**

Coin-Operated Machines

I am a private collector interested in purchasing all types of arcade and coin-operated machines in any condition. Below is a partial listing of items I am looking to purchase. I am also paying finder's fees for assistance in purchasing these items. Please write or call with your information.

John S. Zuk
106 Orchard St.
Belmont, MA 02178
617-484-4800 (home) or 617-349-0652 (office)

We Pay

Wurlitzer 1015 Jukeboxes..**4,000.00+**
Other Jukeboxes (78 rpm & 45 rpm)..**500.00+**
Pre-1940 Slot Machines..**900.00+**
Trade Stimulators ....**100.00+**
Gumball Machines..**20.00+**
Games of Skill ....**75.00+**
Player Pianos..**500.00+**
Mills Violano Virtuoso (coin-op violin/piano)....................................**5,000.00+**

Slot machines, introduced in San Francisco about 1890, and any soda machines (especially Pepsi, Dr. Pepper, 7-Up, and off brands), slot and arcade machines, as well as any advertising signs or related memorabilia relating to these items are wanted. Other soda advertising and collectibles of any sort relating to anything previously mentioned or anything pertaining to Coca-Cola, Pepsi-Cola, Dr. Pepper, Tiny Grape, Nehi, or still others such as Gunther Beer are wanted. I also collect **Catalin radios**.

Richard O. Gates
P.O. Box 187
Chesterfield, VA 23832
804-748-0382 or 804-794-5146

Wanted: **old cast iron or cast aluminum gumball or peanut machines** in any condition, including broken machines, parts, or globes. Also interested in small breath pellet or candy machines, match or other small vending machines. Machines should be circa 1900 through 1940. **I will pay $100.00 to $500.00** and up for the right machines. Finder's fee paid on machines purchased from your leads.

Donald Pom
414-238-9045 (weekdays after 6 pm CST or weekends)

Slot machines, introduced in San Francisco about 1890, are any machine with a coin slot that involves gambling or speculation. They pay out in either money or tokens. The 1930s and 1940s were the golden years when most bars, gas stations, grocery stores, clubs, and private organizations had them in plain sight for all to play. Throughout most of history, they were illegal except for casinos. Today, ownership is legal in about half of the states — provided they are not used for gambling or illegal purposes.

The early machines nearly all had wooden cases. They came in floor models as well as counter-top styles. The next type were made of cast metal. Then came the metal fronts and wooden sides. The electronic machines are illegal in nearly all states.

There are many others wanted besides the ones listed here, so send photo for information.

Arcade machines used to be in all the penny arcades. They were found by the boardwalks along the shores and were made for amusement only. We all remember the fortuneteller that could move and give you your fortune on a card and the diggers that for a nickel you could maneuver and try to grab a prize. There were all types of machines to try your strength and some that by turning the crank would flip cards around so fast that they seemed to make movies. Arcade machines were found in amusement parks and carnivals, too. I collect these remembrances of my happy youth.

Thomas J. McDonald
2 Ski Dr.
Neshanic Station, NJ 08853

Arcade Machines   We Pay

Diggers	1,000.00+
Floor Model Fortunetellers (w/figure)	2,000.00+
Mutoscope, cast iron	1,500.00+
Mutoscope, counter-top type, tin or light metal	500.00+
Self-Playing Banjo (coin-operated)	5,000.00+
Violin Virtuoso	7,500.00+
Electric Energizer (Spear the Dragon)	1,500.00+
Lion Lung Tester	1,000.00+
Quartoscope (Mills Novelty Co.)	1,500.00+
Owl Lifter (Mills Novelty Co.)	750.00+
The Illusion (how you will become skeleton)	1,000.00+
Harvard Stamper (dispenses tokens)	750.00+
1937 World Series (Rock-Ola Mfg. Co.)	1,500.00+
Play Golf (Chester Pollard Amusement Co.)	1,000.00+
Play the Derby (Pollard)	1,500.00+

Slot Machines   We Pay

Floor models, wood, 1890-1910	3,000.00+
Counter-Top Models, wood	2,000.00+
Cast Iron Machines, 1910-1920	1,500.00+
Average Mills or Jennings, 1920-1960	750.00+
Bonus Machines	1,000.00
Baseball Vendor Bell	1,000.00+
Jennings & Mills Golf Ball Vendors	2,000.00
Fey Liberty Bell	50,000.00+
Buckley Bones (dice slot machine)	3,000.00
Bally Spark Plug (horse race slot)	2,500.00+
Mills Futurity, w/counter	2,000.00+
Rol-A-Top (Watling Mfg. Co.)	2,500.00+

Coins

We are major buyers of **all types, designs, and denominations of copper, silver, and gold coins of the United States minted prior to 1920**. A few of these issues were minted in very small quantities and command very high prices today. Others are quite common in low grades but command substantial premiums in new or near-new condition. All U.S. gold coins are collectible and quite popular. As always, condition is everything. Prices listed are for circulated coins with all designs and lettering that is complete and clearly readable. Cleaned or damaged coins are worth substantially less. A few examples are listed below. Please call or write about any examples not listed.

Glenn G. Wright
P.O. Box 311
Campellsport, WI 53010
800-303-8248

U.S. Coins	We Pay
Half Cent 1793	750.00+
Half Cent 1794 to 1797	100.00+
Half Cent 1800 to 1857	10.00+
Large Cent 1793	500.00+
Large Cent 1794 to 1795	80.00+
Large Cent 1796 to 1814	12.00+
Large Cent 1816 to 1857	4.50+
Flying Eagle Cent 1857 to 1858	7.00+
Indian Cent 1859 to 1909	50¢+
Two-Cent Piece 1864 to 1873	4.00+
Three-Cent Piece (nickel) 1865 to 1889	4.00+
Three-Cent Piece (silver) 1851-1873	6.00+
Shield Nickel 1866 to 1883	3.50+
Liberty Nickel 1883 to 1912	40¢+
Half Dime 1829 to 1836	9.00+
Half Dime 1837 to 1873	3.00+
Dime 1809 to 1836	8.00+
Dime 1837 to 1891	3.00+
Dime 1892 to 1916	55¢+
Twenty Cent Piece 1875 to 1878	25.00+
Quarter 1838 to 1891	4.50+
Quarter 1892 to 1916	1.50+
Half Dollar 1796 to 1797	7,000.00+
Half Dollar 1807 to 1838	18.00+
Half Dollar 1839 to 1891	8.00+
Half Dollar 1892 to 1915	3.50+
Silver Dollar 1794 to 1797	250.00+

Silver Dollar 1798 to 1803 ....**150.00+**
Silver Dollar 1836 to 1873 ....**50.00+**
Silver Dollar 1878 to 1904 ....**5.00+**
All U.S. Gold Coins ....**Call or Write**

I am a collector/dealer with 40 years of experience at the same location. I pay top prices for coins and can purchase any amount you may have. Ship insured by mail, my offer by check same day. We also need anything in **gold scrap or silver, jewelry, pocket watches, sterling flatware, gold wristwatches, and old fountain pens.** We pay market prices for all items shipped to to us. Also wanted are all U.S. silver coins, circa 1900-1964 at three times face value.

Dobmeiers Coins/Collectibles
505 Hallock St.
Jamestown, NY 14701
716-487-9731

U.S. Coins   **We Pay**

U.S. Large Cents, ea **2.00-500.00**
U.S. Half Cents, ea **2.00-500.00**
U.S. Gold Coins, ea **100.00-1,000.00**
U.S. & Foreign Gold Goins w/Holes, ea **50.00-500.00**
U.S. Silver Dollars, 1793-1935, ea.....................................**5.00-700.00**
Indian Head Cents, ea...**30¢-100.00**

Scrap Gold, Per Penny Weight   **We Pay**

10K..**6.25**
14K..**9.25**
16K...**10.25**
18K...**11.25**
22K...**12.25**

I am a coin buyer with 51 years of experience. All offers entertained.

Clarence Francis Chun
dba Eastern Spring
P.O. Box 22512
Honolulu, HI 96823
808-597-2270

I am interested in purchasing **foreign coins as well as United States coins, tokens, and medals**. I am not interested in parking tokens, sales tax tokens, or transportation tokens. I am especially interested in Western states 'Good For' tokens. My fondness for foreign coins is for Germany, Japan, and China as well as all other countries. I will pay the following prices.

Fred E. Hopkins
P.O. Box 2263
Peoria, AZ 85380
602-848-9229

We Pay

German 5 Marks, 1951 to present	**2.75-1,000.00+**
German Silver Coins, (1,2,3,5 Marks), before 1912	**5.00-5,000.00+**
German Minor Coins	**1¢-1,000.00+**
German Gold Coins	**75.00-1,000.00+**
Japanese 1 Yen (silver dollar size), 1870-1914	**5.00-3,000.00+**
Japanese Gold Coins, 1870-1932	**300.00-40,000.00+**
Other Foreign Coins	**up to 5,000.00+**
Good For Tokens	**25¢-300.00**
Canadian or Mexican Common Coins, per lb.	**3.50+**

Comic Books

I am interested in buying mostly older comics but will also buy new ones. I'm just starting to collect them and would like to have a big collection fast; so, if possible, I would like large quantities. I'm not too old, so I don't have very much money, but I will pay a good price. I prefer to buy first prints. If you think you have what I'm looking for, write and send a list of your comic books. Or call me at 941-421-4296.

Eric Greenhow
153 Oak Hollow Dr.
Haines City, FL 33844
941-421-4296

Compacts

We collect figural compacts (powder compacts with cases in the shape of various objects such as a guitar, binoculars, or a globe). Generally we do not purchase conventional round, square, or rectangular compacts even if they have an embossed, engraved, or a three-dimensional figure on the lid.

One of those exceptions we would like to find is a round, square, or rectangular compact enameled mint green or orange with the 1933-34 Chicago World's Fair 'A Century of Progress' theme and comet logo on top. We also collect **mesh vanity bags**. See our listing under purses in this book for descriptions and prices.

Only mint or near-mint compacts will be considered. Scratches, dents, or excessively-worn finishes will cause us to elimintate even the most sought-after pieces from consideration. The condition of the mirror is important, but in some cases we may still be interested in the piece even if the mirror is discolored or broken. Highest prices paid for compacts in mint condition complete with puff and original box. Below are just a few examples of figural compacts we're trying to find. Request our more complete, illustrated want list.

Other wants include: **advertising and ephemera about mesh purses (circa 1920 through 1935), beaded glass purses (18-20 beads per inch), Victorian autograph and photo albums (with lithographed print on cover), photographs of women carrying purses (circa 1925), Art Deco picture frames with reverse-painting, jewelry catalogs (circa 1920 through 1935), Bakelite jewelry, *Moulin Rouge* lobby card dated 1934, Moxie 'Doll House' bottle carton, and sheet music titled *Maid of Mesh* by Irving Berlin and dated 1923.**

Sherry and Mike Miller
303 Holiday Dr.
Tuscola, IL 61953
217-253-4991

Figural Compacts   **We Pay**

Bird, by Elgin (signed Dali)	700.00+
Jockey's Cap	100.00-150.00
Christmas Ornament Ball	75.00-100.00
Padlock	60.00-80.00
Fox (face), marked Italy	100.00-150.00
Cat (face), marked Italy	100.00-150.00
Book, by Raquel, red or green	50.00-75.00
Beach Umbrella	125.00-175.00
Binoculars, by Wadsworth	100.00-150.00
Guitar, by Samaral	150.00-200.00

Compacts

Drum, by Charbert	**125.00-150.00**
Hand w/Painted Nails, by Volupte	**125.00-150.00**
Hand w/Black Glove, by Volupte	**175.00-200.00**
Navy Officer's Cap, blue & white	**40.00-50.00**
Roulette Wheel, by Majestic	**75.00-90.00**
Hand Fan, by Wadsworth, engraved blades	**40.00-50.00**
Globe, by Kigu, musical	**275.00-350.00**
Hot Air Balloon	**175.00-225.00**

I collect **old powder compacts and anything with a compact in it or as part of it**. Such as purses, lighters, etc. The amount I am willing to pay depends on condition. I will answer all replies with SASE enclosed. Please send photocopy and asking price.

Sue Murphy
29668 Orinda Rd.
San Juan Capistrano, CA 92675
714-364-4333

We are buying **old compacts and carryalls** in mint or near-mint condition. Of special interest are sets in original boxes. We purchase all types including Bakelite, Lucite, porcelain topped, silverplate, and all metals. The age of the piece and whether it is signed will increase the value. We also purchase related feminine items such as **dresser sets, old perfume bottles, vanity purses, and old mesh and beaded handbags**. We are a dealers so we must purchase at a price that can be marked up for resale. We do purchase in volume.

Grandma's Memories
1827 Shoal Run
San Antonio, TX 78232
phone or fax 210-490-5988

Compacts, Carryalls, Vanity Bags	We Pay
1950s, compact, w/puff, common type	**10.00+**
1940s, compact, gold-tone, w/puff	**20.00+**
1930s, carryall, gold-tone, w/all puffs, lipstick case, etc.	**50.00**
1920s, carryall, silver, w/puffs, box, etc.	**80.00+**
1920s, vanity bag, silver	**100.00+**

I am buying **vanity bags** in silver mesh, enamel mesh, beaded, or Bakelite — especially with round top or unusual shape; also wanted are compacts on a chain, gold-tone bags with rhinestones on a chain, and purses with a unique frame or opening. Items must be pre-1950s but may be in any condition. I am paying prices according to rarity and condition. I also collect **baby-related items (mainly rattles)**, but will consider other items. Please, no dolls.

Jennifer Sykes
9018 Balboa Blvd. #595
Northridge, CA 91325
818-993-1916 or fax 818-993-7612
e-mail: Veedal10@aol.com or Veeda@ix.netcom.com

I am interested in compacts of all kinds from events such as the oval one from the 1939 Golden Gate International Exposition. Also wanted are unusual shapes with florals, fruit, or royal decorations. Please state your price.

Kayla Conway
4500 Napal Ct.
Bakersfield, CA 93307
805-833-0291

We Pay

Royalty Commemoratives	20.00+
Dated Expositions	20.00+
Sterling, fancy	30.00+
Attractive, sm	5.00+

Cookie Jars

The following are cookie jars that I would like to add to my collection and the prices that I am willing to pay for those jars in excellent condition. Marks on each jar are noted inside parenthesis.

Debbie Yates
P.O. Box 440
Norcross, GA 30091-0440
770-232-9799

Halloween   We Pay

Jack O'Lantern, w/green lid (McCoy USA) **450.00**
Black Cat (USA) **275.00**
Haunted House (Huia Clay, Hawaii) **45.00**
Skeleton Rising From Pumpkin (Hand Painted, USA)............................**55.00**

Animals   We Pay

Squirrel w/Holly & Red Berries (McCoy)...**300.00**
Kittens Playing in Basket Bed (McCoy)..**300.00**
Basset Hound (Metlox) **100.00**
Brown Cat on Black Coal Bucket (219, McCoy)......................................**175.00**
Winnie Pig w/Green Shamrocks (Winnie or USA)..................................**225.00**
Smiley Pig w/Clover Blooms (Smiley or USA)..**170.00**
Cow Jumped Over Moon w/Flasher Sun (806 USA) **175.00**

People   We Pay

Davy Crockett (Sierra Vista) **225.00**
Little Red Riding Hood w/Sunflowers on Skirt (967 Hull).....................**250.00**
Little Red Riding Hood (Poppytrail) **175.00**
Dutch Boy or Girl w/Gold & Decals (Happy or Cooky) **225.00**
Dutch Boy or Girl in Amish Outfits (USA) **150.00**
Dutch Boy in Blue, paint under glaze (USA)..**75.00**
Dutch Girl (54-200) **150.00**
Little Girl w/Birds Decorating Her Skirt (USA Brush) **200.00**
Tony Veller (Tony Veller on front) **160.00**
Astronauts (USA)..**300.00**
C3PO, gold robot (Star Wars)..**250.00**

Christmas   We Pay

Rudolph the Red-Nosed Reindeer (RLM)..**160.00**
Christmas Tree (McCoy, USA, 1959) **350.00**
Christmas Gentleman (Uncle Mistletoe) **250.00**

Miscellaneous...We Pay

Patriotic Hat, upside down, red, white & blue (no mark).........................**200.00**
Brown English Stagecoach w/Prancing Horses (no mark) **350.00**
Ear of Corn, 1 standing (McCoy) **90.00**

Walt Disney   **We Pay**

Snow White w/Dwarfs on Skirt (Walt Disney Prod.) **300.00**
Mickey Mouse w/Drum (805 or 964) **150.00**

Cracker Jack Items

I am an advanced Cracker Jack collector looking for **all early marked Cracker Jack items**. I look for pre-1940s prizes, boxes and display signs, and salesman's promotional items. I also look for the same items in **Checkers**. I am *not* interested in plastic items or items marked Borden.

Other wants include:
Angelus Marshmallow Items
Radio Premiums: Rings, decoders, manuals, maps, etc. — from Buck Rodgers, Capt. Midnight, Green Hornet, Orphan Annie, Lone Ranger, Tom Mix, Shadow, Sgt. Preston, Sky King, Superman, and Space Patrol
Miniature Irons: Swans, Wood Grip, Potts, Sensible, two-piece styles, and advertising
Tin Windup Toys and Tin Toys: Featuring comic strip characters or marked Occupied Japan, Marx, Structo, Chein, Girard, Kingsbury, Lehmann, Lindstrom, Strauss, Unique, Bing
Iron Toys: Marked Arcade, Hubley or Kenton
Still and Mechanical Banks
Old Dells Souvenir Items: Marked Kilbourn (plates, cups, postcards, photos, etc.

Phil Helley
629 Indiana Ave.
Wisconsin Dells, WI 53965
608-254-8659

Cracker Jack	We Pay
Advertising Mirror	50.00
Bank, tin book	35.00
Baseball Card	20.00-75.00
Baseball Score Keeper	55.00
Calendar, paper, 1928, round	55.00
Cracker Jack Box, 1930s	65.00
Jack at Chalkboard, arm moves, paper	35.00
Jigsaw Puzzle, paper w/zepplin, 1930s	75.00
Train Engine, No 512	65.00
Train Car, any of 3 circus animals, ea	85.00
Horse-Drawn Wagon, pot metal	125.00
License, Model T Ford, 1916	250.00
Orphan Annie Stand-Up, tin, oval	45.00
Pencil Clip	130.00
Pin-Back Button, w/Cracker Jack Boy, tin	100.00
Pin-Back Button, celluloid	35.00
Sign, Cracker Jack, cardboard, 1920s	300.00

Crackle Glass

I collect all colors, sizes and shapes of **crackle glass in any brand** — not just Pilgrim. Items must be in perfect condition — no chips. I might make an exception in the case of a very unusual item, but when offering an item a photo must be sent if at all possible. I will pay for shipping costs. Sample prices are listed here. I pay more for tumbler sets or crackle animals or unusual figures.

I also collect **milk cans**. No new ones or reproductions are wanted. They do not have to be in perfect condition, but better condition will command a higher price. Must send photograph and SASE. Shipping costs will be paid. **I will pay up to $50.00** or possibly more.

Melissa M. Khan
12 Sholefront Park.
South Norwalk, CT 06854
203-853-6110

Crackle Glass

We Pay

Small Item **5.00**
Medium Item **10.00**
Large Item **15.00**

Credit Cards

I want your **old, expired credit cards before 1970**. They can be plastic, plastic coated, paper, metal charge coins, celluloid, fiber — anything that extended credit to the user. Some go back to before the turn of the century. They can also be oil companies, Western Union, stagecoach passes, freight company passes, bank credit cards, travel cards, airline company cards, etc.

Walt Thompson
P.O. Box 2541
Yakima, WA 98907-2541
phone or fax 509-452-4016

We Pay

American Express, paper credit cards **50.00**
Diners' Club, paper credit booklets..**20.00**
Celluloid Cards (Kresge, Hahne, L.S.P. & Co., L. Bamberger, etc.) **15.00**
Oil Company, paperboard, before 1920, nice condition **75.00**
Oil Company, paperboard, before 1930, nice condition **20.00**
Oil Company, paperboard, before 1940, nice condition **10.00**
Oil Company, paperboard, before 1960, nice condition **5.00**
Airline Company, paperboard, before 1960, nice condition........................**5.00**
Bank Card, paperboard, before 1960, nice condition **5.00**
Specialty Shop, credit card, before 1960, nice condition **5.00**
American Express, platinum cards, before 1990 ....**25.00+**
American Express, gold cards, before 1973 ....**30.00**
Pre-Paid U.S. Telephone Cards, before 1990 ....**8.00**

Cuff Links

I am always buying **cuff links**; no quantity is too large or too small. Several factors determine my offers: condition, age, and whether in original box. Naturally, I also pay more for precious metal than for costume jewelry. Size and unusual designs are also factors in my evaluations. The mass-produced SWANK, Anson, and Hickok Cuff Links of the '40s, '50s, and '60s are generally worth much less than the older and hand-crafted pairs. Typically, my offers range from 50¢ to $10.00 per pair. But unusual designs or superior workmanship can be worth more.

In addition to cuff links, I also buy **tie tacks, collar buttons, shirt studs, money clips, stick pins, and lapel buttons**. Many people are surprised to learn that I also buy single cuff links; they need not be in pairs!

I have earned an excellent country-wide reputation for fair and prompt offers. That is why people send me their merchandise and I mail them a check or an offer (whichever the seller prefers). And, unless you are sending precious or rare items, there is probably no need to incur the high cost of insurance. Examples of recent prices paid are listed here.

Eugene R. Klompus
P.O. Box 346
Prospect Hts., IL 60070

We Pay

Cuff Links & Tie Bar Set, abalone & sterling, ca 1898	**145.00**
Cuff Links, SWANK brand, plastic Art Deco/base metal, ca 1965	**6.00**
Cuff Links, SWANK brand, fishing lure theme, ca 1965, in original box	**6.00**
Cuff Links, Anson brand, metal, fleur-de-lis design, ca 1970	**3.00**
Tie Bar, mother-of-pearl, ca 1920, 1", EX	**4.00**
Shirt Studs, Fox brand, 10K-gold filled, set of 5	**75.00**

I am a collector of **vintage cuff links**. I am primarily searching for the double-sided and snap-type pairs that were prevalent in the period of 1900 to 1930. Of special interest to me are pairs with enamel, pairs in their original boxes, and pairs with reverse-painted glass. I am also interested in silver and gold-filled pairs as well as celluloid pairs. I also purchase mother-of-pearl pairs.

Thomas W. Hudson
502 Jackson Ave.
Wilmington, DE 19804
302-892-2859

Double-Sided Cuff Links   **We Pay**

Enamel, 1 color on sterling...**50.00+**
Enamel, 2 or more colors on sterling ....**60.00+**
Enamel, 1 color on brass or other base metal ....**30.00+**
Enamel, 2 or more colors on brass or other base metal...........................**40.00+**
Celluloid..**15.00+**
Gold Filled ....**10.00+**
Silver Base..**10.00+**
Reverse-Painted Glass...**25.00+**

Snap-Type Cuff Links   **We Pay**

Kum-A-Part, enamel w/sterling tops, MIB..**75.00+**
Kum-A-Part, enamel ....**40.00+**
Other Brands, enamel ....**30.00+**
Push-Button Closures, all brands...**20.00+**
Pull-Button Closures, all brands ....**20.00+**
Reverse-Painted Glass...**25.00+**
Celluloid..**15.00**
Gold Filled ....**10.00+**
Silver Base..**10.00+**
Mother of Pearl..**10.00+**

Czechoslovakian Collectibles

At the close of World War I, Czechoslovakia was declared an independent republic and developed a large export industry. The factories produced glassware, pottery, and porcelain until 1939 when the country was occupied by Germany. I am especially interested in **Peasant Art pottery**. Pieces must be marked 'Made in Czechoslavakia.'

Delores Saar
45 Fifth Ave. NW
Hutchinson, MN 55350
320-587-2002

Peasant Art Pottery	We Pay
Bowl, 4½"	45.00
Creamer	25.00
Chocolate Pot, 8¼"	75.00
Egg Cup, 3½"	25.00
Mayonnaise Jar	35.00
Pitcher, w/lid, 7"	75.00
Pitcher, milk; 5½"	50.00
Vase, 7½"	50.00

_____

Decoys

I am interested in Mason and Wisconsin decoys, Ducks Unlimited pins circa 1937 through 1972, state Ducks Unlimited pins, live decoy items, duck calls, old hunting photos, Wisconsin game warden badges, old sporting magazines and books, as well as Winchester and other gun advertising pins. Other wants include **Hubley iron doorstops, paperweights, etc.; Barbie dolls, and Madame Alexander international dolls.**

Dean Dashner
349 S Green Bay Rd.
Neenah, WI 54956
414-735-4350

_____

Wooden decoys of all types are wanted including duck, swan, goose, crow, owl, shorebirds, and fish. Only old wooden items are wanted but will consider items in any condition, including separate heads and bodies. For an accurate offer include a side-view photo.

Art Pietraszewski, Jr.
60 Grant St.
Depew, NY 14043
716-681-2339 (5 pm to 10 pm)

Delaware Items

I buy Delaware collectibles for my personal collection. I am particularly interested in paper money, medals, and tokens. Delaware-related books and sheet music wanted. Delaware pattern pressed glass, antique advertising material, lottery tickets from the 1800s, bank checks, metal savings banks, paper ephemera, and limited edition prints of Delaware subjects are sought. Describe items fully in the first letter; include SASE.

Terry A. Bryan
189 South Fairfield Dr.
Dover, DE 19901-5756

We Pay

Badge, lodge	15.00+
Badge, pin-back	5.00+
Bank, Youth Savings Bank, metal	15.00+
Book, Delaware history from the 1800s	250.00+
Book, poetry collection, 1st edition	50.00+
Lottery Ticket, 19th century	15.00+
Medal, silver	15.00+
Medal, other than silver	5.00+
Medal, military	20.00+
Paper Money, colonial notes	45.00+
Paper Money, state bank notes	80.00+
Paper Money, merchant scrip	75.00+
Paper Money, national currency, lg	200.00+
Paper Money, national currency, sm	100.00+
Bank Checks, 19th century	5.00+
Pattern Glass, Delaware, common piece	45.00+
Pattern Glass, Delaware, toothpick holder	75.00
Sheet Music	20.00+
Sheet Music, *Sounds From Fort Delaware*	100.00
Tokens, marked 'Good For'	15.00+
Tokens, agricultural	4.00+

Depression Era Glassware

I am interested in several items:

Cambridge Co.: Nudes and Keyhole asparagus platter, sauceboat, faceted pointed-handled glass fork and spoon salad set
Lancaster Co.: open work pieces, apple green or pink, plain, not etched
Lancaster Co.: Jubilee Blanks, Apple green or pink
Paden City Co.: speakeasy cocktail shakers, any covered cigarette boxes, wall pocket vases, cabinet knobs and drawer pulls, cologne and perfume bottles, puff boxes, bobeche and prisms and/or holders that fit onto candlesticks, sugar shaker jars, and covered batter jugs
Depression glass: apple green rolling pin, double-spouted mixing bowls, canning funnels; pink strawholder
Hocking Co.: beer or coffee mugs
Sneath Co.: spice and cannister jars
Usglan Co., pink Swirl pieces
Washboard with crystal insert
Other wants include:
Compacts: for rouge, cake mascara, etc.; in solid brass with bows or cherubs
Cara Nome flower basket; also especially any with heart form
Victorian photo albums: with or without stands, having heart-shaped beveled mirror on cover, brass-trimmed albums with bows, hearts, or cherubs
China (I buy and sell), **Minton 'Marlow' pattern** only
Flatware (I buy and sell), **Oneida stainless 'Alexis' pattern** only
Diecast metal cars: Mercedes 380SL
Playing cards: with pinups by Vargas, Elvgrin, Petty, etc.

Mary Faria
P.O. Box 32321
San Jose, CA 95152-2321
408-258-0413

I am looking for several items. Please see the below listing. Also would like other **1920s through 1940s kitchen glassware items.**

Clara Louthan
HC64 Box 58
Coldwater, KS 67029
316-582-2850

We Pay

Sylvan Green Parrot Pieces ....**up to 50.00**
McKee Butter Dish & Lid, green **10.00**
Canister Set, clear w/Flour, Sugar, Coffee, Tea, w/tin lid, set of 4 ....**45.00**
Salt & pepper shakers, green, square......................................**10.00**
Salt & pepper shakers, white w/red flowers **10.00**
Salt & pepper shakers, clear **4.00**
Dazey Butter Churn, qt **50.00**
Dazey Butter Churn, gal..**40.00**
Hazel Atlas Butter Churn..**30.00**
Butter Molds...**6.00**
Dewdrop by Jeanette, any piece.......................................**up to 10.00**

Tea House Rose, by Danisco Dinner Ware   **We Pay**

Soup Bowl...**2.00**
Platter **6.00**
Coffeepot **15.00**
Chop Plate **6.00**

We are buying **Depression glass for resale.** We buy most patterns and colors. All glass must be in perfect condition — free of chips, nicks, cracks, and scratches. We also buy elegant glass of the Depression such as Heisey, Fostoria, Cambridge, Fenton, Duncan Miller, Paden City, Westmoreland, Indiana, and Imperial. Also wanted are **glass kitchen items** from this time such as juice reamers, canisters, mixing bowls, measuring dishes, etc. We also buy **glassware of the '40s, '50s, and '60s.** Please send a list of what you have for sale and your asking price. Pictures are also helpful. Mint condition glass only, please! Other wants include, but are not limited to the following:

Willow Ware (red and blue other than dinnerware items)
Children's glassware and china dishes
Coors
Fiesta
Franciscan
Goebel Friar Tuck Monks
Hall
Hull
Marx Toy Trains, 027 gauge
Roseville
Royal China (Currier and Ives, Memory Lane)
Liberty Blue Pattern 1976 by Staffordshire

The Glass Packrat
Pat and Bill Ogden
3050 Colorado Ave.
Grand Junction, CO 81504

Depression-era glass bought and sold, mail order only — Cambridge, Heisey, Fostoria, Tiffin, etc. Write or call (the best time to call is from 7 pm to 11 pm EST).

Jay Adams
245 Lakeview Ave., Ste. 208
Clifton, NJ 07011
201-365-5907

I am buying **pink** Depression glass in the following patterns: **Adam, American Sweetheart, Florentine #1 and #2, Mayfair (by Hocking), Princess, Royal Lace, and Sharon.** In **cobalt blue, Royal Lace** is wanted. I'm also buying elegant glassware in **pink** made by **Cambridge and Fostoria.** In **pink kitchenware**, I am looking for juice reamers, canister sets, mixing bowls, refrigerator boxes, measuring cups, and spice sets. All items should be in perfect condition. Photos and descriptions would be helpful when you reply.

Diane Genicola
25 E Adams Ave.
Pleasantville, NJ 08232
609-646-6140

Dolls and Dollhouses

Wanted to buy: **boudoir dolls of the 1920s through early 1930s** for my collection. Flapper type, movie stars, smokers, French, silk mask faced, musical, glass or sleep-eyed, male, Blossom Co., and unusual-sized dolls are wanted. I'm interested in very pretty or unusual dolls and prefer allover excellent condition but I also do repair so I will consider dolls that need work for a reasonable price. Also wanted are high heeled shoes and outfits for boudoir dolls that are in excellent condition. Please send price, description — and a clear photo of the doll helps too!

Bonnie Groves
402 N Ave. A
Elgin, TX 78621
512-281-9551

We Pay

Dolls	**35.00+**
Outfits	**5.00+**
Shoes	**5.00+**

I am a Kiddleholic and am always in search of **Mattel's Liddle Kiddles and all items that are related to the Kiddles**. I buy Kiddles mint in box, loose, whole collections, or just one doll. "These Liddle Kiddles" — I've got to have them all! I'm especially interested in gift sets, vinyl wallets, story displays, as well as exclusives and foreign Kiddles. Prices paid are according to the condition. All letters answered with SASE or call 504-733-0667.

Also wanted are all **small vinyl dolls from the 1960s and 1970s such as Upsy Downsys, Petal People, Flower Darlings, Tiny Teens Flatsy, Dolly Darlings**, plus many more.

Paris Langford
415 Dodge Ave.
Jefferson, LA 70121
504-733-0667

Liddle Kiddles   **We Pay**

The First 24 Kiddles, 4"	**25.00-100.00**
Storybook Kiddles	**50.00-150.00**
Skediddle Kiddles	**10.00-50.00**
Playhouse Kiddles	**20.00-50.00**
Kiddle in Kars	**15.00-30.00**
Kolognes and Locket Kiddles	**up to 20.00**
Kola Kiddles and Sweet Treats	**20.00+**

Dolls and Dollhouses

Jewelry and Pop-ups	**10.00+**
Zoolerys and Kozmics	**up to 100.00**
Chitty Chitty Bang Bang Kiddles	**20.00+**
Playhouses and Cases	**10.00-50.00**
Storybook Sweethearts and Baby Kiddles	**20.00-60.00**
Paper Goods	**15.00+**
Games and Miscellaneous Items	**50.00+**
Expo 70 Postcard	**50.00**
Wallet, vinyl	**100.00+**
Baby Items	**100.00+**
Gift Sets and Story Displays	**150.00+**
Kiddle Kopies and Competitors	**10.00-25.00**
One-of-a-Kind Items, unusual and rare	**200.00+**

I buy **all dolls from the 1950s, 1960s, and early 1970s**. I am particularly interested in Barbie dolls, Liddle Kiddles, Tammy and family, and Tressy. Mint in box, old store stock, and childhood collections are especially desired. What I pay for items generally depends on condition and rarity. I will pay double or triple the amount for a mint-in-the-box item than I will for the same item in played-with condition. The following is a sample of what I pay but I will pay more if an item is especially unusual.

Cindy Sabulis
P.O. Box 642
Shelton, CT 06484
203-926-0176

Barbie   We Pay

#5 or #6 Ponytails	**50.00-200.00**
Bubblecuts	**25.00-100.00**
1965-1966 Bendable Leg Barbies, marked ©1958	**200.00+**
Skipper	**25.00+**

Liddle Kiddles   We Pay

1st Series of Kiddles, complete w/accessories	**25.00-50.00**
Storybook Kiddles, complete w/accessories	**50.00-100.00**
Skediddle Kiddles, MIB	**25.00+**
Kozmic Kiddles, complete	**75.00+**
Liddle Kiddle Wallet	**50.00+**
Liddle Kiddle Puzzles	**25.00-100.00**

Tammy   We Pay

Tammy, MIB 25.00-35.00
Black Tammy 50.00-100.00
Bud, Tammy's boy friend ....100.00+
Misty, MIB..35.00-100.00
Tammy LP Records 10.00-25.00

Tressy   We Pay

Tressy, MIB 25.00-35.00
Tressy's Apartment...50.00+
Pre-Teen Tressy ....35.00+
Sister Cricket..15.00-25.00

Other Dolls   We Pay

Flatsy Dolls, in original frames..20.00
Dawn Dolls, MIB 15.00
Dolly Darlings, MIB 15.00-25.00
Remco's Littlechap Family...10.00-30.00
Celebrity Dolls ....10.00-100.00+

Barbie doll collector seeks vintage dolls and accessories circa pre-1970. Will pay top dollar for quality items. Sell your items to a collector instead of a dealer. Send a good photo along with price wanted to:

Lois Burger
2323 Lincoln St.
Beatrice, NE 68310
402-228-2797

Barbie Dolls   We Pay

#1 ....500.00-5,000.00
#2 ....500.00-5,000.00
#3 ....100.00-1,000.00
American Girls..100.00-1,000.00
Color Magic 100.00-1,000.00
Bubble Cut...50.00-250.00

Accessories   We Pay

Car **35.00-150.00**
Plane...**100.00-1,000.00**
Vinyl Items..**20.00-500.00**

I buy **dolls from the 1960s and older**. Price paid depends on condition. I belong to a local doll collector's club, so even if I don't want to buy your particular doll, I will know someone who will be interested. I also buy **old baby Christening dresses**. Price paid depends on detail and quality of the dress.

Annette Nichols
5732 Edward Ware Cir.
Garden Grove, CA 92845-2624
714-898-7407

Composition   We Pay

Shirley Temple, 1930s...**100.00+**
Buddy Lee ....**100.00+**
Baby Dolls, 24" & taller...**50.00+**
Miscellaneous Girl or Mama Dolls...**50.00+**

Hard Plastic   We Pay

Buddy Lee ....**75.00+**
Chatty Cathy Brunette...**25.00+**
Chatty Cathy Blond...**20.00+**
Chatty Baby ....**15.00+**
Terri Lee, 16"...**100.00+**
Nancy Ann Storybook ....**20.00+**

Vinyl   We Pay

Shirley Temple, 1957, 12" ....**35.00+**
Shirley Temple, 1957, 17"...**50.00+**
Shirley Temple, 1957, 19"...**75.00+**
Shirley Temple, 1957, 36" ....**500.00+**

I am buying **old dolls, doll parts — wigs, heads, eyes, and bodies**. My special wants are mint-in-box hard plastic dolls and 30-inch tall or larger antique bisque dolls. Please look in your attics, basements, and sheds to find the lost dolls of yesteryear. I don't mind dolls that need TLC. I will pay accordingly.

Sue Fishwick
523 West Osage
Pacific, MO 63069
314-271-4416

We Pay

Doll, bisque, 30"	**400.00+**
Doll, hard plastic, M	**75.00+**
Doll, hard plastic, MIB	**100.00+**
Doll, TLC, bisque, depending on kind, size & condition	**50.00+**
Doll, TLC, hard plastic, depending on kind, size & condition	**15.00+**
Doll, TLC, composition, depending on kind, size & condition	**15.00+**
Doll Head, old, depending on size & condition	**40.00+**
Bodies, BJ	**75.00+**
Bodies, kid	**50.00+**
Eyes, old	**20.00+**
Wigs, mohair	**15.00+**
Wigs, human	**10.00+**
Wigs, synthetic	**3.00+**

We are looking for **Holiday Barbie and Bob Mackie Barbie dolls**, both in or out of the box. We do prefer that their condition be excellent to mint. Please include your asking price and condition when contacting us.

Deana Jones
745 State Rte. 2151
Melber, KY 42069
and
Elli Konrad
Box 882
Calvert City, KY 42029

Wanted: **6½" Topper Dawn dolls (1970-1972)**. The female dolls have rooted eyelashes and hair; male dolls have molded hair. Topper Corp. is on the back side and there are holes in the soles of the feet. I am interested in dolls, fashions, accessories, ads, Japanese or Canadian releases, information, printed material, umbrellas, lunch kits, advertisements — anything. I am also looking for any boxed or carded copy-cat dolls, fashions, or accessories (Barbara's Fashions, Diana, Dizzy Girl, City Joy). Especially wanted are those that refer to Dawn ('also for Dawn..,' etc.).

Also I'm searching for these dolls: **Kenner's Blythe and Darcy; Hasbro's Love, Leggy, Jem, and Disco Girls; Mattel's Liddle Kiddles, Talk-Ups, Major Matt Mason, and Upsy Downsys; Galoob's Baby Face; American Character's Emerald the Witch; and Ideal's Flatsys (boxed or carded only please)**.

I am also interested in any of the following from the **1960s through 1970s: any catalogs (Sears, Service Merchandise, Aldens, etc.) that include toys or dolls, Thingmakers, cereal prizes, Oily Rubber Creatures marked R.D.F., and TV stuff.**

Joedi Johnson
P.O. Box 565
Billings, MT 59101-0565
phone or fax 406-248-4875

I am paying up to thousands of dollars for **vintage (circa 1959 through the early 1970s) Barbie collections**. This includes Barbie, Francie, all her other family and friends, their clothing, accessories, structures, etc. Condition, scarcity, and desirability affect the price of any given item, but in general I pay higher prices for mint and complete or mint-in-original box items.

Susan Anderson
410 N Hayford Ave.
Lansing, MI 48912
517-484-7069

Doll	We Pay
#1 Barbie	2,000.00+
#2 Barbie	1,500.00+
Other Ponytail Barbies	125.00+
Francie	60.00+
Black Francie	400.00+
Bubblecut Barbie	50.00+
American Girl Barbie	200.00+

TNT Barbie, Stacey or Casey, ea ....60.00+
Other Barbie & Family Dolls ....**Call**

I enjoy collecting **dolls, furniture, dishes, and accessories dating from the mid-1950s to the mid-1960s.** I am especially interested in Mattel's Barbie but also look for Betsy McCall, Ideal 18" and 21" teen fashion dolls, multi-jointed Dollikin dolls, and most any doll-related merchandise from this time period. The price I will pay very much depends on the rarity, age, and condition of your item. If you will send a photo or detailed description, SASE, and value you want for your item, I will respond.

Beth Summers
233 Darnell Rd.
Benton, KY 42025

Private collector will pay top dollar for **any loose or mint-in-box Barbie or Barbie family dolls and related items**, especially before 1980. Always buying: Barbie, Ken, Midge, Allan, Skipper, Skooter, Ricky, Francie, Stacey, Casey, Twiggy, Julia, Christie, Tutti, and friends. Also wanted are houses and other cardboard structures, transportation vehicles, vinyl items (lunch boxes, change purses, notebooks, record players, cases, etc.), paper items, and any condition of clothing — absolutely anything Barbie! Box lots of parts, accessories in any condition are also welcome. I'm also buying loose or never-removed-from-box newer Barbie dolls and family from 1980 to present day. Reference available upon request.

Denise Davidson
7321 Seymour Rd.
Owosso, MI 48867
517-723-4611

Wanted to buy: **right arm** for 12" boy doll with molded hair, jointed at arms and legs and has a c in circle with '1968 Mattel, Inc. U.S. & For. Pat. Other Pats Pending Mexico' printed on his buttocks. The doll has a tight smile with his teeth showing.

Flora Belle Allen
26 S Prospect Ave.
Liberal, KS 67901-3634

————————

Clean out your attic and check your basement. I want to buy any **old Barbie dolls or Barbie clothes**.

Sharon Thompson
401 Marty Dr.
Bowling Green, KY 42101
502-782-0033

————————

Please help me locate a doll I saw in Bea Skydell's catalog in 1985-1986. She is a 21" vinyl dancer named **Rehearsal #0013 by Abigail Brahms (Associated Dollmakers)**. Her hair is red. I will pay up to $200.00 for a mint-in-box doll. I have her sisters and we would appreciate a happy reunion.

Susan Schoenemann
1607 Main
Humboldt, TN 38343-2903
901-784-5848

————————

I am searching for **Chatty Cathy clothes, shoes, and accessories to fit the early-style doll that was available between 1961 and 1964.** Clothes should be marked as Chatty Cathy with a cloth label inside. Also I'm interested in Charmin' Chatty items such as clothes and working records.

Robbie Spees
120 Oakview Cir
Paducah, KY 42001

————————

We buy **Raggedy Ann dolls and miscellaneous Raggedy Ann items made prior to the 1970s.** We buy one piece or an entire collection. (Sorry — no handmade dolls.) Of special interest are Raggedy Ann dolls made by the P.F. Volland Co. in the 1920s, The Mollye Goldman Doll Outfitter's in the 1930s, the Georgene Novelties Co. from the 1930s through 1960, and the Knickerbocker Toy Co. in the 1960s. Prices paid will depend on age, condition, and rarity of the item. Remember: we buy one piece or an entire collection. What do you have?

On the internet? We can be reached at the following e-mail address: Raggedyman@aol.com. Also see our home page for further offerings at: http//home.aol.com/RAGGEDYMAN.

Larry Vaughan
Raggedy's & Teddy's
6337 Nightwind Cir.
Orlando, FL 32818-8834
407-884-5483

Raggedy Ann Items   **We Pay**

15" to 18" P.F. Volland Raggedy Ann or Andy Doll, original clothing, G...**500.00+**
15" Mollye Goldman Raggedy Ann or Andy Doll, original clothing, G...**300.00+**
15" Georgene Novelties Co. Raggedy Ann or Andy Doll, 1938 to 1943, black outlined nose..**300.00+**
12" Georgene Novelties Co. Raggedy Ann or Andy Awake/Asleep Doll, 1938 to 1940 ....**200.00+**
15" Georgene Novelties Co. Raggedy Ann or Andy Doll, 1944 to 1962, original, clean..**75.00+**
15" Knickerbocker Toy Co. Ann or Andy Doll, 1963 to 1970s, M in original M box ....**50.00+**
15" Knickerbocker Toy Co. Ann or Andy Doll, 1963 to 1970s, original, clean ...**15.00+**
Doll House, Fisher-Price, 1970s, MIB ....**50.00+**
Kitchen Furniture (stove, refrigerator, sink), original, clean, ea...............**25.00+**
Book, various titles, circa 1920 through 1940, VG ....**20.00+**

I am buying **old Raggedy Anns and Andys, Belindys, Uncle Clem, Pirate, Blue Camel, and related characters**. These can be manufactured by the following companies: Volland, Georgene, Mollye, or selected Knickerboker dolls. Prices given are for good-condition dolls. Condition determines prices. Other raggedy dolls or related items priced on individual basis.

Other wants include **Halloween, dogs (definite breeds), buttons and sewing (antiques or interesting), 1904 St. Louis World's Fair items (no clear glasses or plates), Pepsi, Bakelite, Barbie dolls and clothes made before 1969, teddy bears (early jointed mohair in good condition), Santa (old only), and papier-mache character nodders of the 1950s.**

Gwen Daniel
#1 Charlestown Plaza
St. Charles, MO 63303
314-978-3190
e-mail: gdaniel@mail.win.org

We Pay

Volland Ann or Andy ....750.00+
Voland Belindy ....750.00+
Mollye Ann or Andy...400.00+
Mollye Baby ....750.00+
Georgene Ann or Andy...50.00+
Georgene Black-Outline Nose Ann or Andy..100.00+
Georgene Belindy, sm..300.00+
Georgene Belindy, lg..400.00+
Georgene Camel w/Wrinkled Knees..**Premium Price**
Knickerbocker Ann or Andy, talker..40.00+
Knickerbocker Belindy ....200.00+
Blue Camel w/Wrinkled Knees ....50.00+

Wanted to buy: **old, small bisque or china dolls from Germany or France** circa 1860 to 1930 and measuring from 2" to 14" tall. Also wanted are old jointed mohair teddy bears of any origin and circa 1904 through 1930s, old small Santas (especially German), old glass Christmas ornaments, old feather trees, wind-up toys from the 1930s through 1940s, and old small doll-sized furniture.

Linda Katzopoulos
P.O. Box 713
Mountain City, TN 37683-0713
423-6237

The Little Falls Railroad and Doll Museum Ltd. is constantly looking for **dolls and railroad memorabilia** to enhance and expand the museum. We are primarily looking for porcelain dolls or heads to place on display. We appreciate histories with the dolls and especially desire dolls from the 1880s to early 1900s. We are able to give recognition for donations on a tax exept basis. We can be reached by phone, fax, or mail. All contacts will be answered.

The Little Falls Railroad and Doll Museum Ltd.
P.O. Box 177
Cataract, WI 54620-0177
608-272-3266

———————

I'm looking for **Barbie and her friends**. Any dolls including new ones (if they are mint in box) are wanted. Prices depend on doll, age, condition, etc. I'm also interested in **Marilyn Monroe, Gone with the Wind, Elvis, Star Trek, Star Wars, GI Joe, and the Dionne Quintuplets,** or any dolls similar to these. Please send SASE along with your asking price for a reply. Photographs are always helpful.

T.L. Rodrick
R.R. #2, Box 163
Sumner, IL 62466

———————

I am looking to purchase **anything Betsy McCall related**. I prefer excellent to mint condition but will consider any item. Will buy one piece or entire collection. I will reimburse actual UPS and insurance charges. Please contact me with your Betsy items first! I *love* this doll!

Marci Van Ausdall
P.O. Box 946
Quincy, CA 95971
916-283-2770 or fax 916-283-4449

We Pay

Doll, nude, 8", EX	**75.00+**
Doll, all original clothes, 8", EX	**125.00+**
Doll, all original clothes, 14"	**125.00+**
McCalls Patterns for Betsy	**5.00+**
Individual Outfits	**25.00+**
Packaged Outfits	**30.00+**
Designer Studio Boxed Set	**200.00+**
At the Ranch Boxed Set	**250.00+**
A Day With Betsy McCall Boxed Set	**200.00+**
Original Pamphlets	**15.00+**
Standard Plastics Carrying Case	**50.00+**

Dolls and Dollhouses

Puzzle ....**10.00+**
Record Albums ....**15.00+**
China Bowls (Betsy or Jimmy)...**25.00+**
Cookie Cutter ....**10.00+**
Trunk, 14"...**45.00+**
Betsy's Dachshund, Nosey..**25.00+**
Lamb, Knickerbocker..**25.00+**
Original Wrist Tag...**15.00+**
Golden Book...**10.00+**
Empty Doll or Clothing Boxes...**15.00+**
Any Unusual Betsy Item..**Your Price**

———————

I collect **Ginny Dolls** made by the Vogue Doll Company, Dakin Co., etc. A complete description of the doll you wish to sell and an SASE would be helpful along with your asking price. I would like the opportunity to trade some of my 200 Ginny Dolls also. Wanted are international brides, Ginny dolls from foreign lands, porcelain dolls, and Ginny Furniture.

I also collect **Wizard of Oz and Return to Oz books and dolls**. And I would like the opportunity to purchase your **first edition Little Golden Books copyrighted before 1970**. Covers must be intact with limited pencil marks and no tears on pages. I am willing to trade Little Golden Books as well. Thank you.

Donna Patacchiola
132 Hemlock Dr.
Lunenburg, MA 01462

———————

I collect and buy **Oriental dolls — Japanese and Chinese made from the 1900s to the 1950s**. Dolls have bisque or composition heads covered with gofun (crushed oyster shell) and are on composition or composition and cloth bodies. These dolls may have wigs and glass eyes (the oldest examples have black nonpupal eyes). Most wanted are those resembling geishas, children, and especially those like the old Thomas Nast Santa engravings show. Parts, wigs, and original clothing are also purchased. A photo is appreciated and will be returned. No cloth or rag-type dolls are wanted.

I also collect and buy **old, pre-1960 Santas and Christmas decorations. No lights (window or tree), fences, or large items are wanted.**

Jean Shields
1685 Berkshire Dr.
Vineland, NY 08360

I am interested in **Tiny Tears clothes and accessories**, due to owning several naked dolls. I am a new collector and am not really sure what all is out there. I would like items to be in good condition. Another interest is **Queensware by Wedgwood**.

Beverly Searcy
1801 Spillman Rd.
Morning View, KY 41063
606-356-2847

We Pay

Plastic Bed	**30.00+**
Sunsuits	**5.00-15.00**
Dresses	**5.00-20.00**
Underwear, Bonnets, Shoes	**3.00-5.00**
Miscellaneous Items	**5.00-50.00**
Ephemera Items	**5.00-20.00**

I am a private collector, collecting older dolls that I can afford and newer ones as I can get them. Since 1973 I have advertised for **frozen character dolls by E.F.C.G.** To date, I now have 37 different characters out of 100 possible. I also have 9 duplicates.

These are 3½" tall, all bisque, frozen with molded-on clothes and hair. The faces are all the same or nearly the same. The molded hair and clothes distinguish the various characters. Dolls are marked E.F.C.G. 1958 (the only year they were made). Sometimes marks may be undistinguishable without this information.

I will pay $35.00 each for those I don't have or I will trade doll for doll from my duplicates (Wilbur Wright, Bo-Peep, Shirley, Matthew and Luke from the Bible, and Dionne Quints Annette, Yvonne, and Emily). Dolls that are especially desired are Ed Sullivan, Roy Acuff, and Queen Elizabeth.

Frances Goodson
25354 Whitaker Rd.
Abingdon, VA 24211
540-475-3937

Door Push Plates

I collect **advertising porcelain door push plates** that were used on entrance doors to grocery stores, drugstores, and any store in general that sold manufacturers' products. They were attached to screen doors where you normally reached out to push the door in or out. The push plate was colorful and advertised the company's product; it often carried the words 'push' or 'pull' as well. Size of the plates varied, but the average was 4x7". These were made of enameled steel (more commonly called porcelain). Some examples that exist are: Red Rose Tea, Tetley Tea, Salada Tea, Chesterfield Cigarettes, Dr. Caldwell's Pepsin Syrup, and Vick's.

I buy according to condition. Please send photocopy or photo with a description for a price quote. **I will pay $75.00 to $125.00** for nice additions to my collection. I pay the postage.

Betty Foley
129 Meadow Valley Rd., #11
Ephrata, PA 17522
717-738-4813

Dresser and Vanity Sets

We are buying old dresser sets in mint or near-mint condition. Of special interest are sets in the original boxes. We purchase celluloid, porcelain (especially Limoges), silver, and silverplate. The more pieces to a set, and whether or not the pieces are signed will affect price. We also purchase feminine items such as **old perfume bottles, vanity purses, compacts, carryalls, and old mesh and beaded handbags**. We are a dealer, so we must purchase at a price that can be marked up for resale. We do purchase in volume.

Grandma's Memories
1827 Shoal Run
San Antonio, TX 78232
phone or fax 210-490-5988

Dresser and Vanity Sets   **We Pay**

Celluloid, 10 pieces in box...75.00+
Porcelain, 5 pieces (including lids as pieces)...........................75.00+
Limoges, 5 pieces (including lids as pieces)..........................125.00+
Silver (EX brush, hand mirror & comb) ....75.00+
Silverplate (EX brush, hand mirror & comb) ....40.00+

Egg Timers

I am interested in purchasing **figural egg timers**. These were produced mainly during the 1930s to the late 1950s. Figural timers are usually 3" to 5" in height and can be found in a wide array of designs and shapes. Chickens, dogs, and pigs were popular animal forms; people dressed in career and vocational uniforms (chefs, housemaids, sailors); and people in native costume were also produced.

To find a timer with the sand tube still intact is a plus but not a requirement for the timer to be considered acceptable and in good condition. Since most timers are china or bisque, damaging cracks, severe chips, and noticeable repairs render the piece almost valueless. Timers missing their sand tubes are recognized by a hole either going through the stub of a hand or arm or some part of the back of the figure.

Prices below reflect amounts paid for timers in excellent to mint condition with intact sand tube. All timers will be considered. All inquiries will be answered.

Jeannie Greenfield
310 Parker Rd.
Stoneboro, PA 16153

We Pay

Boat Captain, nautical outfit, no marks.......................................**20.00**
Boy Talking on Telephone, wears nickers & tam, Japan **35.00**

Chimney Sweep, dressed in black sweep outfit, w/ladder slung over shoulder, marked Germany **40.00**

Chef, holds lg fish in front of him, timer goes through fish from mouth to tail, Japan **45.00**

Clown, brightly colored clothes & face, Japan **25.00**

Country Girl, timer in both hands to her left side, dog at her side, Japan **25.00**

Dutch Boy, wears brightly colored native costume, Japan..........................**30.00**

Indian Chief, kneeling, wears full headdress, marked Germany **35.00**

London Bobby, wears English police uniform, Japan **25.00**

Rooster, beige & brown w/red wattle and comb, timer goes through mouth to back of head, marked Germany **30.00**

Fast Food Collectibles

We are looking to buy **McDonald's®** toys and memorabilia from the 1960s through the early '80s and older **Burger King, Burger Chef** items. We are primarily looking for mint or near-mint condition in older toys, manager and owner-operator items, store openings, conventions, and items depicting Archie, Speedy, or Slash Arch designs. We also buy collections of older items (no items from the past five years please). If you have any items as listed, please write, call, fax, or e-mail:

Bill and Pat Poe
220 Dominica Cir. E.
Niceville, FL 32578-4068
904-897-4163 or fax 904-897-2606
e-mail: McPoes@aol.com or ANEM34@prodigy.com

We Pay

1976 Remco McDonaldland Dolls, MOC only, ea..............................**up to 25.00**

1976 Remco McDonaldland Train Set, MIB, ea ....**up to 100.00**

1989 Sea World of Texas Sunglass, MIP or NM, ea...........................**up to 5.00**

1990 Barbie & Hot Wheels, Test Market, MIP, ea **10.00**

1988 Super GT Matchbox, MIP, ea ....**up to 5.00**

1988 Doozers, Fraggle Rock Test Market, MIP or NM, ea.................**up to 10.00**

1988 Black History, Vol. #1 & #2, & Happy Meal Boxes, ea ....**up to 25.00**

1986 Story of Texas, KTVV Austin & KPRC Houston, including map of Texas, any/all, M or NM, ea..**up to 25.00**

1985 My Little Pony or Transformers, NM or MIP, ea **10.00**

1986 Construx Happy Meal Toys, MIP only, ea...................................**up to 10.00**

Glass Knives

I need just a few, rare glass knives to complete my collection. The color, and size where indicated, are important because some of the same-pattern knives are fairly common in a different color or size. However, small variations in knife length (for example, $\frac{1}{8}$" to $\frac{1}{4}$") are insignificant because knife edges sometimes have been ground down to eliminate or reduce nicks. I would rather not buy knives with cracks, very deep gouges, or broken-off chunks; but nicks are acceptable. Original boxes would be nice, but are not required. Please send a self-addressed stamped envelope, or a fax or e-mail address.

Adrienne Esco
4448 Ironwood Ave.
Seal Beach, CA 90740
310-430-6479 or fax 310-598-1585
e-mail: escoebliss@earthlink.net

1986 Metrozoo Happy Meal Toys, NM or MIP, ea ....**up to 15.00**
Telephone, Ronald McDonald, sitting w/crossed legs, lg, NM, ea ...**up to 100.00**
Telephone, Ronald McDonald, standing, sm, NM or better, ea.........**up to 50.00**
McDonald Clocks, older ones, M or NM, ea......................................**up to 50.00**
Big Mac, Red Cube Radio, NM or better, ea ....**up to 25.00**
1979-1981 *McDonaldland Fun Times Magazines & Comics*, NM, ea....**up to 5.00**
1977 Milwaukee Brewers 'M' Baseball Cards, NM, per set of 30......**up to 50.00**
1974 San Diego Padres 'Round' Baseball Cards & Baseball Holder ...**up to 100.00**
1982-1990 Hard Bubble Counter Displays, NM..............................**up to 100.00**
Any Older McDonald's Items With Archie, Slash Arch, or Speedy, NM or
better ....**up to 50.00**
McDonald's Snoopy Doll, stuffed plush..**up to 10.00**
McDonald's Garfield Doll, stuffed plush w/green- or red-striped shirt ....**up to 25.00**
1989-1990 German McDonald's BMW-Taxi, HO scale car................**up to 10.00**
McDonald's Test Market Pooh Bear, Tigger & Eyore, stuffed plush, M ....**up to 25.00**
1979-1982 Happy Meal Containers or Boxes, M................................**up to 10.00**
Most Any Unique or Odd McDonald's Old Items Always Wanted....**up to 50.00**

World's largest collector of **Big Boy** memorabilia is buying all unusual and older items with the Big Boy logo. This could include ashtrays, salt and pepper shakers, menus, matchbooks, nodder heads, china, counter displays, children's lamps, employee items and awards, cookie jars, buttons, puzzles, games, lunch pails, comics — just about anything else with the Big Boy logo. children's lamps, employee items and awards, cookie jars, buttons, puzzles, games, lunch pails, comics — just about anything else with the Big Boy logo. I do not buy duplicates unless I can upgrade my collection. Items must be in good or better condition (no reproductions). I do not buy any vinyl banks or trading cards. The older the item, the better. I will pay shipping charges. For my highest buying price, send me 2 or 3 photos of the item and include a complete description as to age, condition, size, colors, and where it came from (if possible).

Steve Soelberg
29126 Laro Dr.
Agoura Hills, CA 91301
818-889-9909

Big Boy   We Pay

Ashtray, figural, green or maroon **300.00**
Bank, ceramic, full-color glaze..**300.00**
China or Glassware, w/logo..**20.00+**
Comic Book, Bob's Big Boy #1 ....**100.00**

Counter Display, plaster, 18" **1,000.00**
Counter Display, papier-mache, 14" **1,000.00**
Employee Awards & Trophies, ea .... **100.00+**
Promo Items, Buttons, Jewelry, Pins, Pamphlets .... **10.00+**
Decals or Anything Unusual w/Big Boy Logo .... **10.00+**
Hamburger Wrappers, early .... **10.00+**
Lamp, ceramic figural w/shade **1,500.00**
Matchbooks .... **10.00+**
Menu #1, showing original location **100.00**
Other Menus, early only .... **100.00+**
Nodder/Bobbin' Head Dolls **800.00**
Cookie Jar, ceramic, 1994 edition **400.00**
Transistor Radio **200.00**
Ashtray, white ceramic w/Big Boy figure on rim **200.00**
Lunch Pail, metal **200.00**

Figurines and Flower Frogs

Always buying **figural flower frogs (and matching bowls, if available).**
Some figures sit on a plain base (mound) with holes through to the bottom.
Other bases resemble hollow twigs or branches (mostly with birds perched on
top), rocks (with turtles, frogs, etc.), leaves with flowers, etc. — in other
words, things compatible to the figure. Most are open on the bottom or have
substantial openings for the water to enter.

Also always buying **miscellaneous utilitarian figural items (sugars and
creamers, teapots, pitchers, etc.).** Please, no damaged or repaired items.
Please describe or send photo along with price.

Nada Sue Knauss
12111 Potter Rd.
Weston, OH 43569
419-669-4735

I am interested in child-like figures that resemble the Hummel look-a-like
children, but they are imposters! (However, they are good imposters and can
pass for Hummels from a distance.) The figures **must have 'Designed by Erich
Stauffer** on the bottom and a style number; some numbers will be preceded by
an S or a U. Some of these figures will also have two crossed arrows on the
base and some will still retain their maker's sticker: 'Arnart Imports,' from

Japan. Originally a paper label was on the front of each figure giving a title to each boy or girl and/or its activity such as 'Farm Chores,' 'Music Time,' etc.

Most especially I'm looking for an angel figure as well as the figures of four nuns that I'm aware of. I'd also like the small perfume bottle girls, china animals, and a rectangular wall plaque of a clipper ship, Great Republic; all will have 'Erich Stauffer on the base.

Depending upon the uniqueness of the figure's activity and the uniqueness of its props (goose, dog, rooster, chicken, doll, etc.), I will offer $3.00 to $4.00 per inch tall but perhaps up to $5.00 per inch tall for those items mentioned. I'd pay $15.00 to $20.00 for the wall plaque; postage is extra, of course.

I'd need a good, overall description of the figure and its condition, number, height and base measurements, paper title, and asking price. Of course, there is nothing like a photo, if one is available. No need for a SASE; if I can use it, I will respond quickly. Thank you for your interest.

Joan Oates (CB)
685 S Washington
Constantine, MI 49042
616-435-8353

I am interested in buying **animal figurines made by the Chic Pottery of Zanesville, Ohio**. This company also made figural planters and creamers. As information on this company is very scarce, I will describe the characteristics of the figures I have. Figures are hollow-molded white clay with only minimal painted details on white ground with a glossy glaze. Even with light detailing of only one or two colors and simplicity of form, each small figure has a distinct personality of its own. All my pieces are unmarked, however from research I know several marks were used. I am interested in hearing from anyone who has more information about this company and its products. Items wanted must be perfect with no chips or cracks. As there are so many unmarked figurines, please send a photo to help with identification along with SASE.

Linda Holycross
1202 Seventh St.
Covington, IN 47932

I am a serious collector of **Roselane Sparklers**. These are small, stylized animals and bird figures made in the '50s in California. **I will pay $10.00 to $30.00** each depending on size for these figures. Please call or write.

Shirley J. Diimig
Rt. 4, Box 3145
Galena, MO 65656
417-272-8484

We are buying **Royal Bayreuth figurals and scenic polar bears** to include: Santa Claus; rabbits, squirrels, kangaroos, tigers, and most animal pieces; flowers such as roses, poppies, pansies, oak leaves, orchids; corn; and clowns. Most desirable are the water and milk pitchers, hatpin and toothpick holders, and candlesticks. One piece or a collection wanted. Prices vary by rarity.

Richard and Dorothy Earle
1830 SE 7th St.
Pompano Beach, FL 33060
914-562-8139 or 954-946-3284

I am looking for **nearly all figures of ladies, men, and madonnas**. I will buy almost any kind (**no toy dolls**) in ceramic, porcelain, or glass. Letters answered and photos returned. Please include your phone number.

Other items wanted include: **beaded bags, typewriter ribbon tins, veterans of foreign wars key chain license plates, compacts, salt dips and spoons, Clarice Cliff, sprinkler bottles, match safes, hair jewelry pictures, Wave Crest, opera glasses, and eye wear.**

Kayla Conway
4500 Napal Ct.
Bakersfield, CA 93307
805-833-0291

	We Pay
Baccarat	35.00+
Corday	50.00+
Cybis	50.00+
Florence	25.00+
Lladro	75.00+
Murano	35.00+
Royal Dux	80.00+
Sabino	50.00+
Val St. Lambert	35.00+

I am collecting **birthday angels by the National Potteries Co.** (Cleveland, Ohio). They were manufactured in Japan circa 1950s. I have one that says 1956 on the bottom. They came in both boy and girl versions and they hold something in theme with the month — **not** flowers of the month or jewels of the month.

They are about 7" in height (height varies somewhat) and are high-gloss finished porcelain. They have numbers stamped on the bottom along with a letter. However, the letter varies and I believe them to be referencing productions. I am not interested in any damaged or repaired angels. I am willing to pay up to $25.00 for each of the numbers of the ones I need.

Dorothy Selzer
1415 Erin Ln.
Waukesha, WI 53188-4969
414-521-9211

Birthday Angels by National Potteries Co.   **We Pay**

Girl, May #1365 ....25.00
Girl, September #1369 ....25.00
Boy, January #1917 ....25.00
Boy, February #1918 ....25.00
Boy, March #1919 ....25.00
Boy, April #1920 ....25.00
Boy, May #1921 ....25.00
Boy, November #1927 ....25.00
Boy, December #1928 ....25.00

I am looking for **two Lenox carousel horses**. The first is **Pride of America**, produced by Lenox in 1991. The figure is a white bisque porcelain horse on a hardwood base that is decorated in a patriotic theme in red, white, blue, and gold. The saddle is blue with white stars and has a red-and-white striped sash draped under it. Having 24K gold ornaments and hooves, it stands 8" high. It originally sold for $152.00.

The second figure is the **Carousel Circus Horse** produced in 1993. This is a palomino (gold colored with a white mane and tail) also made of bisque porcelain but is decorated with mauve flowers and blue and purple feathers around a pink saddle with a lavender sash and bow around the neck. It also has 24K gold ornaments and hooves and stands 8" high on a hardwood base. Originally it sold for $152.00. I will pay original price or higher depending on condition.

I am also looking for another figure by Lenox. He is called **The Prince**. He is an accessory to the legendary Princess Collection. He is a brunette that stands approximately 10" high. Dressed in a blue tunic with a mauve shirt, white tights, and brown boots, he wears a knife in his belt and holds a hat in his hand at his hip. He reaches out with a bouquet of flowers in his other hand. He wears a full-length purple cape trimmed in gold. Sold originally in the 1990s, I will pay the issue price of $156.00 or higher depending on condition.

Jacqueline Tal
1004 SW 95th St.
Oklahoma City, OK 73139
405-691-2414 or fax 405-692-0667

We Pay

Lenox, The Prince, porcelain figure...**156.00+**
Lenox, Pride of American, porcelain carousel horse ....**152.00+**
Lenox, Carousel Circus Horse, porcelain carousel horse.......................**152.00+**

Wanted to buy: **figural hand objects in glass, china, or pottery.** Items must be in mint condition only. Please call or write with description and price wanted. Photos are helpful.

Elaine A. Toth
P.O. Box 132
Lahmansville, WV 26731
304-479-8159 (after 5 pm)

Wanted: **bisque and china bathing beauties and nudes.** These may be with or without wigs. No Japanese items wanted. Other wants include **dolls, other figurines, compacts, and compact purses.**

Lori Landgrebe
2331 E Main
Decatur, IL 62521
217-423-2254

We Pay

Bathing Beauty, w/wig...**200.00+**
Compact/Purse Combination, before 1940 ....**200.00+**

We have need of certain **DeGrazia figurines, plates, ornaments, and the Cocopah Girl figurine**, which was issued for the Hummel Club.

Dills Desert Place
1006 N Vuena Vista Ave.
Farmington, NM 87401
595-325-0110

Wanted: **Brother Juniper figurines**. These are small male religious figures made by Publishers Syndicate Shatford Company in the 1950s. Each figurine has a little printed message. **I pay $20.00 and up** depending on the figure.

Joy DeNagel
132 E Somerset Ave.
Tonawanda, NY 14150
716-836-3841 (best time 10 pm EST)

I am interested in purchasing **quality retired Pendelfin rabbit figurines and display pieces made prior to 1970**. Quality and condition are extremely important. Please send picture and/or description along with price desired. I will respond to all inquiries.

George Sparacio
P.O. Box 791
Malaga, NJ 08328
609-694-4167 or fax 609-694-4536

Fire-Fighting Collectibles

For twenty-six years I have been a fireman. I have seen many changes and advancements during my career. In spite of that fact, the fire department remains a service that is steeped in tradition and rich in history. Even though fire fighting is a 'macho' thing as viewed by many, there remains a certain romance that lingers from the past. Many present day practices and traditions can be traced to the past easily.

So, it is easy to see why fire department antiques and early fire extinguishing devices are my passion. Of special interest are the early glass bottles embossed 'Fire Grenade' with the manufacturer's name. These Victorian extinguishers had names like Magic, American, Hart's Lightening, Harkness Fire Destroyer, Hardens Star, Eddison's Electric Fire Extinguisher — I could go on. The bottles were very decorative and made in clear, aqua, amber, green, and blue.

I also look for fire department-related antique advertising items, giveaways like letter openers, pocket knives, paperweights, thermometers, pens, calendars, cigar cutters, ashtrays, match safes, mirrors — anything FD related.

Larry Meyer
4001 Elmwood Ave.
Stickney, IL 60402-4146
708-749-1564

Fire-King

We like **all unusual Fire-King. We do not buy white, white with gold trim, or peach lustre.**

April and Larry Tvorak
HCR #34, Box 25B
Warren Center, PA 18851
or
P.O. Box 126
Canon City, CO 81215

We Pay

Batter Bowl, turquoise blue	35.00-150.00
Batter Bowl, white w/red band	20.00
Batter Bowl, fruit design	20.00

Bowl, basketweave, turquoise blue ....**35.00+**
Bowl, teardrop, jad-ite, depending on size **12.00-45.00**
Bowl, mixing; swirl, jade-ite, 5" **20.00**
Bowl, splashproof, jade-ite, depending on size............................**15.00-25.00**
Any Jade-ite Sheath of Wheat Piece...**8.00+**
Any Ivory Jane Ray Piece ....**8.00+**
Demitasse Cup & Saucer, jad-ite...**40.00**
Butterdish, jade-ite base w/clear lid...**30.00**
Casserole, Philbe, ivory ....**50.00+**
Serving Pieces for Anniversary Rose, Honeysuckle or Gamebird, ea........**5.00+**

I am buying **Fire-King mixing bowl sets and range top sets** in the following patterns. There are three of us collecting these sets. Please help and please make sure all sets are in very good condition. Phone and if there is no answer, please leave a message and your phone number and I'll call you back.

Pat Miller
16609 Sabillasville Rd.
Sabillasville, MD 21780
301-271-3420

4-Piece Mixing Bowl Sets   **We Pay**

Apple ....**up to 75.00**
Modern Tulip ....**up to 75.00**
Kitchen Aid ....**up to 100.00**
Black Dot, 8 1/2 in bowl...**up to 20.00**
Stripe...**up to 100.00**
Modern Tulip Bowl, 9½" **22.00**

4-Piece Range Top Sets   **We Pay**

Apple Salt & Pepper Shakers, pr ....**up to 30.00**
Modern Tulip Salt & Pepper Shakers, pr............................**up to 25.00**
Kitchen Aid Greaser ....**up to 30.00**
Kitchen Aid Salt & Pepper Shakers ....**up to 30.00**
Black Dot Greaser ....**up to 30.00**
Black Dot Salt & Pepper Shakers ....**up to 30.00**
Stripe Greaser ....**up to 30.00**
Red Dot Greaser ....**up to 30.00**

Fire-King

We specialize in **all Fire-King. We do not buy any white or white with gold lines.** We do buy all other colors and patterns, including gray, turquoise, blue, azurite, jade-ite, Game bird, Anniversary Rose, Homestead, and Honeysuckle. We also buy **kitchenware and novelties.** If you want to make some money, give us a call. We are known for treating our customers as fair as we can and giving them the best deal we can. We pay for all shipping. Please note that these prices might change, so at least contact us to get an offer.

Two of a Kind
115 E Main St.
Delphi, IN 46923
765-563-6479 or 765-742-1412

Jade-ite   We Pay

Ashtray	5.00-10.00
Bowl, Teardrop (Swedish Modern), 4-pc set	60.00
Bowl, Colonial Rim; 3-pc set	30.00
Bowl, Restaurant Ware, flanged	16.00
Cup & Saucer Set, demitasse; Jane Ray	25.00
Cup & Saucer Set, demitasse; plain	15.00
Skillet, 2-spout	30.00
Soup, flanged, Jane Ray	18.00
Plate, bread & butter; Jane Ray	18.00
Grease Jar	15.00
Pie Plate, juice saver	90.00
Pitcher, ball style	Call or Write
Any Sheaf of Wheat Piece	10.00

Miscellaneous Fire-King   We Pay

Nipple Cover, Sapphire Blue	75.00
Bowl, mixing; Kitchen-Aide, 4-pc set	75.00+
Butter Dish, jade-ite or ivory	20.00
Grease Jar, Kitchen-Aide	25.00
Fire-King Casserole Cookbook, 1944	18.00
Batter Bowl, turquoise	100.00
Salt & Pepper Shakers, w/good lids, pr	18.00

Fishing

We are collectors of **old fishing equipment and paraphernalia. All must be pre-1950** and in good to excellent condition. We are interested in single pieces or whole 'tackle boxes.' We can buy from photos; but UPS on approval is best way — we will pay immediately or return at our expense.

Sam Kennedy
212 N 4th St.
Coeur d'Alene, ID 83814
208-769-7575

We Pay

Wood Spear Fishing Decoys	**10.00-100.00**
Old Gigs, w/handles or w/o handles	**20.00+**
Wood Lures, w/glass eyes, ea	**5.00+**
Wood Tackle Boxes	**20.00-100.00**
Trout Creels	**40.00-200.00**
Bamboo Fly Rods	**20.00-200.00**
Fish Nets	**2.00+**
About Anything Else	**15.00-50.00**

I am a serious collector of **glass fishing floats**. I am currently looking to buy any European glass floats with embossed markings on the glass. This marking will be located on one of three spots. Either on the sealing button, the top of the glass or on the side of the glass. Listed below is a sample of what I will pay for the following floats. This by no means is everything that exists. If your float is not listed below, chances are I need it and will negotiate a fair price with you. Thank you.

Stu Farmsworth
P.O. Box 847
Wilsonville, OR 97070

Mark & Location of Mark	We Pay
Made in Germany, seal button	**25.00**
Made in Norway, seal button	**38.00**

Extra Portugal, side & top of glass **28.00**
Portugal Domar, side of glass **55.00**
F.A.L.E.S., seal button **32.00**
Made in England, top of glass...**40.00**
Made in England, side of glass **35.00**
British Made, top of glass **38.00**
Fortex, side of glass...**30.00**
G, top of glass **15.00**
P.C.F., seal button **15.00**
Embossed Anchor, top of glass..**55.00**
Embossed Anchor, seal button **65.00**
Neversink, top of glass...**35.00**
Made in Czechoslovakia (red), top of glass..**100.00**
WD, top of glass **20.00**
3 over-lapping fish, top of glass...**125.00**
L.T., side of glass..**22.00**
OH Jones Hartford Conn, side of glass **80.00**
Societa Art Vetraria Altare, side of glass..**100.00**

I buy **fishing-related items made before 1970**. Specifically wanted are advertising items and displays. Lures made of metal, glass, wood, and plastic are wanted. Send a detailed listing with manufacturer's name and model numbers if available along with item's condition. Items must be mailable.

Art Pietraszewski, Jr.
60 Grant St.
Depew, NY 14043
716-681-2339 (5 pm to 10 pm)

We buy **pre-1960s wooden lures, lure catalogs, tackle displays, and related items** including cardboard and wooden boxes, sinkers, reels, etc. Items must be in good condition or repairable; no repaints wanted. While price depends on age, condition, and needs, we pay 50% to 60% of book value (White, Lawson, Luckey) plus a bonus for collections.

Englewood Antiques
52020 Townshop Rd.
Fall Creek, WI 54742
715-877-3468

Collector buying **old fishing and hunting items**, including but not limited to:

Rods	Game Calls
Reels (especially Kentucky reels)	Catalogs
Lures	Wooden Duck Decoys
Creels	Spearing Decoys
Duck Calls	

All manufacturers wanted; free estimates provided in exchange for the opportunity to purchase.

Bob Walstrom
2235 Nancy Pl.
Roseville, MN 55113
612-487-6687

As an old-time collector, I will pay the following prices for **quality tackle in excellent condition**. The listings are mostly Heddon but I also buy most other manufacturers' tackle. Rare lure colors will add to the price. Sorry — no plastic or repaints wanted. Call weekday evenings.

Harold Ruth
332 R Ave.
Paton, IA 50217
515-968-4544 or 712-336-3335 or 712-336-5500

Heddon   We Pay

Black Sucker	**925.00**
Bottlenose Tadpolly	**275.00**
Moonlight Radiant	**2,000.00**
Sharkmouth Minnow	**350.00**
Wood River Runt	**30.00**
400 Killer	**325.00**
730 or 740 Wood Punkinseeds	**60.00+**
800 or 900 Swimming Minnow	**275.00**
700 Muskollunge Minnow	**550.00**
700 Muskolunge Minnow	**550.00**
3000 Spin Diver	**250.00**

Musky Lucky 13	75.00
370 Musky SOS	275.00
Bat Wing Ice Decoy	500.00
4-15 or 4-18 Reels	1,000.00
3-30 Reel	200.00
Dowagiac Reel	200.00
#40 Reel	225.00

Other Companies

We Pay

BC Milam #2 Reel	750.00
Black Sambo in Barrel	30.00
Centerhole Creels	100.00+
Creek Chub Pikie Minnow	5.00+
Creek Chub Sinful Sal	75.00
Creek Chub Gar	225.00
Granger, Heddon, Winchester, or South Bend Cross Built Split Bamboo Fly Rods	100.00+
Meek & Milan #2 Reel	800.00
Meisselbach #780	90.00
Pflueger Mustang	10.00
Pflueger All-In One Minnow	250.00
South Bend Bass-O-Reno	5.00
South Bend Truck-O-Reno	300.00
Winchester Minnow, 3- & 5-hook	250.00+
Winchester Reels, ea	65.00+
Wooden Lure & Reel Boxes	100.00+
Wright & McGill Bass-O-Gram	150.00
Tackle Catalogs, pre-1940, ea	30.00+

Flags of the United States

My first collecting love is early vintage U.S. national flags. As long as your flag is an authentic 'period' example and contains fewer than 48 stars, I'm interested. If it's an especially old or unusual piece, all the better!

I also seek other obsolete flags of U.S. origin in the form of political banners, military colors, U.S. government flags, etc. WWI Liberty Loan flags, Depression-era NRA flags, and banners of Civil War veterans groups are all within my collecting turf.

I rarely ever pass up a Stars and Stripes with printed words or an inscribed message over the stripe field; likewise for flags of hand-stitched construction. I would urge anyone concerned about the condition of their flag to get in touch anyway. My offers are very fair and you may be pleasantly surprised!

Ideally, a full-view snapshot plus a direct Xerox construction detail of your flag will help expedite negotiations; ortherwise, please furnish written specifications and a basic line drawing. Either way, your inquiry **will** receive a reply...that's a promise!

Bob Banks
18901 Gold Mine Ct.
Brookeville, MD 20833
301-774-7850

Vintage U.S. National Flags   We Pay

13 Stars (Centennial era), hand-stitched..150.00+
15-21 Stars, all hand-stitched construction..1,200.00+
23-28 Stars, all hand-stitched construction..800.00+
32-35 Stars, hand-stitched in row pattern ....500.00+
32-35 Stars, hand-stitched in Great Star pattern ....800.00+
32-35 Stars, printed parade flag, muslin or silk ....150.00+
36-39 Stars, all-sewn construction in row pattern ....180.00+
36-39 Stars, all-sewn construction in wreath pattern.............................250.00
40-44 Stars, all-sewn construction in row pattern ....80.00+
40-44 Stars, printed parade flag, muslin or silk ....25.00+
45-47 Stars, all-sewn construction in row pattern ....40.00+
45-47 Stars, printed parade flag, muslin or silk ....10.00+

Other Obsolete Flags of U.S. Origin   We Pay

Political Flags, Banners & Bandannas, 19th century..............................150.00+
Political Flags, Banners & Bandannas, 20th century................................30.00+
U.S. Army/Navy Flags, Guidons & Pennants, 19th century...................100.00+
U.S. Army/Navy Flags, Guidons & Pennants, 20th century....................25.00+
Exposition/Commemorative Flags, 19th century ....65.00+
Exposition/Commemorative Flags, 20th century ....20.00+
U.S. Government Programs (NRA, War Loan, etc), sewn.........................40.00+
U.S. Government Programs (NRA, War Loan, etc), printed.....................20.00+
American Social Movements Flags & Banners, sewn..............................40.00+
American Social Movements Flags & Banners ....15.00+

Folk Art

We are buyers of **older pre-1950 folk art**. Highest prices paid for highly visual and more unusual pieces. Feel free to send photos along with pricing — they will be returned.

Sam Kennedy
121 N 4th St.
Coeur d'Alene, ID 83814
208-769-7575

We Pay

Whirly Gigs	100.00+
Weather Vain	35.00-500.00
Old Painted Signs	50.00-1,000.00
Trade Symbols	100.00+
Mechanical Wooden Toys	100.00-3,000.00

Furniture

We buy quality **Victorian and turn-of-the-century furniture** — the fancier, the better. Oak, walnut, and rosewood are preferred although we also deal with mahogany. Items needing even major repair will be considered but unless the item is of exceptional quality, we do not normally purchase painted or upholstered items. Prices paid will depend on rarity, style, condition, type of wood, need, and location. Examples of prices paid for quality items in fair to good condition are given here. We also pay a finder's fee for referred items purchased.

Englewood Antiques
52020 Townshop Rd.
Fall Creek, WI 54742
715-877-3468

We Pay

Sideboards ....800.00-1,400.00+
Cheval Mirrors ....500.00-900.00+
Victorian Easels ....100.00-300.00+
Bonnet Chests ....450.00-700.00+
Lingerie Chests...400.00-700.00+
Wardrobes ....1,200.00-2,000.00+

Gambling

We are buyers of **old gambling paraphernalia — with a special interest in the days of the old West**. We buy almost anything that relates. We can buy from photos.

Sam Kennedy
212 N 4th St.
Coeur d'Alene, ID 83814
208-769-7575

We Pay

Old Cards, pre-1930...10.00-100.00
Dice, ivory, ea ....5.00+
Poker Chips, w/names, ea ....25¢-1.00
Poker Chips, ivory, ea..1.00+
Racks of Old Poker Chips 20.00-100.00
Roulette Tables...500.00+
Sleeve Cheaters ....10.00+
Pocket Pistols & Knives 20.00-150.00
Chuck Luck Cages...100.00+
Gambling Wheels...50.00-1,000.00

I buy **gambling chips** (ivory, pearl, casino, or composition poker types, etc.), **small gambling equipment** (faro, keno, poker, etc.), **playing cards, gambling ephemera** (catalogs, books, movie lobby cards, cigar box labels, etc.), and **other old items which are gambling related or have gambling-related images** (match safes, lighters, watches, etc.). I can buy one item or an entire set or collection. References furnished on request. I reimburse for postage on items sent for inspection (call first).

All items except for casino chips and catalogs should be from before World War II. In general, I do **not** want (1) gambling toys (e.g., plastic roulette wheel); (2) chips that are plain with no design (except mother-of-pearl chips); (3) plastic chips (except Catalin) and chips with interlocking rims; (4) bridge-sized playing cards (i.e., the narrow, 2¼" wide decks); and (5) large, heavy items (coin-op machines and furniture-like gambling equipment).

It is a good idea to send pictures and photocopies. Please indicate color, quantity, and condition of chips. For playing cards, be sure to include a photocopy of the ace of spades and joker and indicate the completeness and condition of cards and their box. Call first if you like.

Robert Eisenstadt
P.O. Box 020767
Brooklyn, NY 11202-0767
718-625-3553

We Pay

Chip, ivory, engraved w/nonconcentric design, 1½" dia, ea	**25.00+**
Chip or Marker, mother-of-pearl, engraved w/nonconcentric design, at least ⅛" thick, ea	**20.00**
Chip, Catalin, marbelized red, dark green and yellow, 1½" dia, set of 100	**30.00**
Chip, engraved or inlaid clay composition, per 100 quantity	**25.00+**
Chip, embossed clay composition, any except Jockey on Horse design, per 100 quantity	**15.00**

Games

I am interested in buying hand-held games or 'pocket puzzles.' These games are typically round and have moving parts or beads inside that are moved or shaken into place. I am very interested in games made in Germany or that are advertising related.

Old Kilbourn Antiques
Phil Helley
629 Indiana Ave.
Wisconsin Dells, WI 53965
608-254-8659

Basketball Puzzle	30.00
Black Man, w/red tie	70.00
Borden's Elsie the Cow	70.00
Coronation Puzzle	40.00
Eaton's Santa Claus in Toyland	50.00
Elephant in Suit	30.00
Ferris Wheel Scene	80.00
Hanging Chinaman	100.00
Indian Chief	25.00
Man & Gator	40.00
Native on Ostrich	60.00
Newltolland Hayliner	20.00
Paris Battle Scene	75.00
Soccer Player	20.00
Texaco (repro)	5.00

Do you have any great old **board games** in your shop or attic you'd like to sell? I'm interested in quality American board games from the late 1800s through the 1940s by companies like McLoughlin, Milton Bradley, Parker Brothers, or Selchow & Righter. I also buy games of smaller companies like Singer, Ives, Bliss, Ottman, and Geo. B. Doan & Co.

Large, colorful lithographed covers with fancy boards and pieces are favorites, especially on historical topics like Civil War, inventions, explorations, early sports, politics, railroads, and travel by airplane, balloon, automobile, or steamship.

I am also very interested in early real estate-themed games, like Landlords, Finance, Fortune, Business, Inflation, Easy Money, pre- and post-1935 Monopoly and deluxe Monopoly sets.

You'll often find Rook, Pit, Flinch, Touring, Bingo, Beano, Lotto, Checkers, Backgammon, and other more common games. I wouldn't be interested in those unless they are distinctive in some way. Call or write, let me know what you have and what you are asking for your great games. Photos preferred. There are a wide variety of games and a wide variety of prices I am willing to pay for them — based on rarity, subject, completeness and condition.

Pat McFarland
P.O. Box 161
Averill Park, NY 12018
518-674-8390

	We Pay
The Landlord's Game, by Parker Bros	500.00+
The Landlord's Game, by Magie	1,000.00+
Game of Business, by Magie	1,000.00+
Game Company Cagalogs, all years	25.00+
Handmade Landlord's/Monopoly (w/provenance)	Top Prices Paid
Monopoly, 1935 marked Trademark only	100.00+
Deluxe Monopoly, pre-1940	250.00+
Baseball, team identified, pre-1920	200.00+
Civil War Era Games	200.00+
George S Parker	25.00-200.00+
Parker Bros, pre-1900	25.00-200.00+

Glass Knives

I need just a few, rare glass knives to complete my collection. The color, and size where indicated, are important because some of the same-pattern knives are fairly common in a different color or size. However, small variations in knife length (for example, ⅛" to ¼") are insignificant because knife edges sometimes have been ground down to eliminate or reduce nicks. I would rather not buy knives with cracks, very deep gouges, or broken-off chunks; but nicks are acceptable. Original boxes would be nice, but are not required. Please send a self-addressed stamped envelope, or a fax or e-mail address.

Adrienne Esco
4448 Ironwood Ave.
Seal Beach, CA 90740
310-430-6479 or fax 310-598-1585
e-mail: escoebliss@earthlink.net

	We Pay
Aer-Flo (Grid), amber	200.00+
Aer-Flo (Grid), forest green	200.00+
Dagger, crystal, hand painted	80.00+
Miniature Thumbguard, crystal, 6" to 6½"	125.00+
Plain Handle, pink, 8" to 8½"	125.00+
Ribbed Thumbguard, crystal	150.00+

Glassware Other Than Depression Glass

I am buying **early American flint and non-flint pressed glassware**. Some items of particular interest are listed below.

Calvin L. Hackeman
8865 Olde Mill Run
Manassas, VA 22110
703-368-6982

Balder   **We Pay**

Salt & Pepper Shakers, pr	.45.00+
Sugar Bowl, w/lid	.20.00+
Toothpick	.20.00+
Water Pitcher	.25.00+

Dakota (Corn & Berry)   **We Pay**

Cruet	.45.00+
Salt & Pepper Shakers, pr	.45.00+
Spooner	.30.00+
Sugar Bowl, w/lid	.40.00+
Water Pitcher	.50.00+

Hawaiian Lei (non-flint) by Higbee   **We Pay**

Banana Stand	.50.00+
Bread Tray	.25.00+
Candlesticks, pr	.75.00+
Castor Set	.100.00+
Champagne Glass	.35.00+
Compote, octagonal	.40.00+
Compote, square	.50.00+
Compote, round, w/lid	.30.00+
Cruet	.45.00+
Cup & Saucer Set	.20.00+
Goblets, except cordials, ea	.30.00+
Honey Dish, square, w/lid	.30.00
Ice Cream Set	.100.00+

Glassware Other Than Depression Glass

Mug..**25.00+**

Plate, square ....**20.00+**
Platter..**35.00+**
Punch Bowl..**85.00+**
Punch Cup..**25.00+**
Sugar Lid..**15.00+**
Syrup..**75.00+**
Water Pitcher...**50.00+**
Any Piece in Color or Carnival...**Call**

New Hampshire (Bent Buckle)   We Pay

Bisquit Jar, w/lid..**60.00+**
Carafe..**45.00+**
Celery Vase..**25.00+**
Compote, lg ....**35.00+**
Custard Cup ....**10.00+**
Lemon Cup...**10.00+**
Milk Pitcher...**60.00+**
Plate...**10.00+**
Spooner ....**15.00+**
Sugar Bowl, w/lid..**20.00+**
Water Pitcher, bulbous, 3/4-gal...**70.00+**
Water Tumbler...**15.00+**
Wine, flared...**20.00+**
Any Piece w/Ruby Stain...**25.00-200.00+**

New Jersey   We Pay

Butter Dish, on high standard ....**50.00+**
Cake Stand ....**40.00+**
Compote, w/lid ....**40.00+**
Plate, dinner; 8"..**10.00+**
Salt & Pepper Shakers, pr ....**25.00+**
Syrup..**70.00+**
Water Bottle ....**40.00+**
Water Goblet ....**25.00+**

Wine Goblet ....**30.00+**
Water Tray..**30.00+**
Water Tumbler...**25.00+**

Teepee   We Pay

Stemware, other than champagnes ....**10.00-20.00+**
Wine Decanter/Carafe...**35.00+**
Water Pitcher...**45.00+**

Virginia (Galloway)	We Pay
Basket	60.00+
Bowl, rectangular	20.00+
Celery Vase	40.00+
Compote, w/lid	50.00-90.00+
Champagne Glass	40.00+
Cracker Jar	100.00
Egg Cup	20.00+
Jelly Dish, w/handles	15.00+
Lemonades, ea	20.00+
Mug	20.00+
Pickle Castor	50.00+
Pitchers, other than medium tankard, ea	40.00-60.00+
Plate	15.00-25.00+
Rose Bowl	20.00+
Salt Dip	15.00+
Salt & Pepper Shakers, pr	25.00+
Sugar Shaker	25.00+
Waste Bowl	20.00+
Water Bottle	25.00+
Water Goblet	45.00+
Water Tray	50.00+

Punch Cups (pressed glass)	We Pay
Big Diamond	25.00+
California (Beaded Grape)	20.00+
Connecticut	20.00+
Dakota, etched or plain	20.00+
Florida Herringbone	20.00+
Florida Palm	15.00+
Illinois	20.00+
Lion's Leg	25.00+
Louisiana	25.00+
Maine	15.00+
Maryland	15.00+
Mississippi (Magnolia)	25.00+
Missouri	20.00+
Nebraska (Bismark)	15.00+
Nevada	15.00+
New Jersey	25.00+
Ohio	20.00+
Oregon (Beaded Loop)	20.00+
Tennessee	20.00+
Texas	15.00+
Utah (Twinkle Star)	15.00+

Glassware Other Than Depression Glass

Vermont, any color .... 20.00+
Late Washington .... 15.00+
Early Washington .... 25.00+
Wyoming (England) .... 20.00+

Other Patterns   We Pay

Carolina Water Tumblers, ea .... 15.00+
Illinois Candlestick, ea .... 25.00+
Loop & Petal Compote/Vase, canary, flint .... 200.00+
Other Colored Flint Pieces (candlesticks to salts), ea .... 20.00-250.00+

Collector wanting to buy Heisey **Greek Key and Heisey baskets**. Only buying mint-condition glass. Also will consider other patterns.

Betty Brewer
2629 Possum Trot Rd.
Troy, TN 38260
901-538-9945

Shell Pink was made by the Jeanette Glass Company. It is a creamy pink milk glass made from 1957 to 1959. The only thing that ties the patterns together is the color!

April and Larry Tvorak
HCR #34, Box 25B
Warren Center, PA 18851
or
P.O. Box 126
Canon City, CO 81215

We Pay

Lazy Susan 120.00
Cake Plate, flat 85.00
Cookie Jar w/Lid 125.00
Butterfly Cigarette Box 75.00
Grape Octagonal Dish 25.00
Punch Bowl w/Base 100.00
Punch Ladle, pink plastic 15.00

I collect **Manhatten** pattern pressed glass made circa 1903 through 1907. I am interested in buying a syrup pitcher, soda straw holder, and water pitcher.

Elna Hall
206 Juniper
Mansfield, TX 76063-1815
817-473-6403

Tiffin glass wanted: etched serving pieces, candlesticks, poppy vases, and unusuals. Please enclose SASE for reply!

Shirley Baker
673 W Twp. Rd. #118
Tiffin, OH 44883
419-447-9875

Golf Collectibles

Golf has many forms of memorabilia from ancient clubs to tiny little items used to mark the ball on the green. Tokens, medals, and even wooden nickels have been used by many golf courses, tournaments, and other related businesses.

Norm Boughton collects **ball markers in any form** from early struck pieces that resemble coins to the fancy and not-so-fancy pieces with the little prongs made in both metal and plastic. He also collects **all forms of medals, tokens, and wooden money relating to golf** and his postcard collection is mainly from New York state but is expanding to include both the courses from the rest of the world as well as humorous golf postcards.

Norm Boughton
P.O. Box 93262
Rochester, NY 14692
716-292-5550 or fax 716-292-6513

Golf Collectibles

National Golf Day Medals **3.00-30.00**
Tokens ....**25¢-10.00**
Wooden Nickels...**25¢-10.00**
Postcards, New York state courses...**1.00-25.00**
Postcards, golf course scenes ....**50¢-5.00**
Postcards, humorous **1.00-15.00**
Books About Golf..**2.50-50.00**

Metal Ball Markers   We Pay

PGA, US Opens, prior to 1960 ....**2.50-25.00**
LPGA or PGA Tournaments, prior to 1960...**2.00-15.00**
Major Tournaments, after 1960 ....**2.00-10.00**
Advertising Markers **1.00-10.00**

Plastic Ball Markers   We Pay

Tournaments ....**50¢-5.00**
Courses ....**25¢-5.00**
Advertising...**10¢-1.00**

I am buying wood-shafted golf clubs. Clubs should have wood shafts and **not** coated steel shafts. If unsure if club shafts are wood or coated steel, use a magnet. Also I am interested in other items relating to golf, preferably those made prior to 1940.

Aurthur H Vanderbeek
15 Pearl St.
Rouser Point, NY 12979
518-297-6146 (April to November)
or
58 Jennifer Cir.
Ponce Inlet, FL 32127
904-761-5433 (November to March)

Wood-Shafted Putters...**17.00+**
Irons...**15.00+**
Woods..**20.00+**

Graniteware

I am always looking for **quality swirl graniteware in all colors** (blue, cobalt blue, green, brown, and red). Especially wanted is anything in 'old' red swirl, even if it is only a pie pan. Also wanted are **unusual gray pieces. Rarer items wanted include creamers and sugars, butter churns, salt and pepper shakers, muffin pans, cream cans, syrup pitchers, and butter dishes.**

Daryl
P.O. Box 2621
Cedar Rapids, IA 52406
319-365-3857

Hallmark Collectibles

I am searching for Hallmark ornaments and am especially interested in finding the Nostalgic Houses and Shops ornaments that were made from 1984 through 1991. Below is a listing of ornaments in which I am interested and their original retail value. Please include a good description and price when writing about your item.

Deana Jones
745 State Rte. 2151
Melber, KY 42069

Date, Ornament Name, Hallmark No.	We Pay
1993, Room for One More, 875QX538-2	8.75
1991, Peanuts, 1st Edition, 1800QLX722-9	18.00
1991, Starship Enterprise, 2000QXL719-9	20.00
1991, Nostalgic Houses & Shops, 8th Edition, Fire Station, 1475QX413-9	14.95
1990, Nostalgic Houses & Shops, 7th Edition, Holiday Home, 1475QX469-6	14.75
1989, Nostalgic Houses & Shops, 6th Edition, US Post Office, 1425QX458-2	14.25
1988, Five Years Together, 475QX274-4	4.75
1988, Nostalgic Houses & Shops, 5th Edition, Hall Bro's Card Shop, 1450QX401-4	14.50
1987, Nostalgic Houses & Shops, 4th Edition, House on Main Street, 1400QX483-9	14.00

1986, New Home, 475QX274-6 ....**4.75**
1986, Nostalgic Houses & Shops, 3rd Edition, Christmas Candy Shop, 1375QX403-3 ....**13.75**
1985, Nostalgic Houses & Shops, 2nd Edition, Old-Fashioned Toy Shop, 1375QX497-5 ....**13.75**
1984, Nostalgic Houses & Shops, 1st Edition, Victorian Doll House, 1300QX448-1 ....**13.00**
1984, First Christmas Together, any ....**Write**

Halloween

I am buying Halloween jack-o'-lanterns and papier-mache candy containers such as witches, pumpkin people, cats, etc. Also wanted are Halloween postcards, invitations, party books, games, hard plastic toys, decorations (mint-condition only), nut cups — anything Halloween except masks and costumes. The price I pay depends on condition, size, rarity, and age. Photos are required; I can not buy sight unseen. I buy Halloween all year around.

Jenny Tarrant
Holly Daze Antiques
4 Gardenview Dr.
St. Peters, MO 63376
314-397-1763

American Jack-O'-Lanterns   **We Pay**

With Paper Insert, 4", NM..**55.00-65.00**
With Paper Insert, 5", NM..**65.00-75.00**
With Paper Insert, 6", NM..**80.00-90.00**
With Paper Insert, 7", NM...**90.00-100.00**
Without Paper insert, 4", NM **45.00-55.00**
Without Paper Insert, 5", NM **55.00-65.00**
Without Paper Insert, 6", NM **70.00-80.00**
Without Paper Insert, 7", NM **80.00-90.00**
Cat Lantern With Insert, NM **85.00-95.00**

German Jack-O'-Lanterns   **We Pay**

With Insert, 3", NM..**50.00-60.00**
With Insert, 4", NM..**65.00-75.00**

With Insert, 5", NM...**85.00-95.00**
With Insert, 6", NM...**100.00-125.00**
Without Insert, 3", NM...**40.00-50.00**
Without Insert, 4", NM...**55.00-65.00**
Without Insert, 5", NM...**75.00-85.00**
Without Insert, 6", NM...**95.00-110.00**
Cat Lantern, w/face, 3"...**150.00-175.00**
Cat Lantern, w/o face, 3"...**130.00-150.00**
Cat Lantern, w/face, 4"...**200.00-220.00**
Cat Lantern, w/o face, 4"...**170.00-190.00**

American Toys or Candy Boxes   We Pay

Witch or Cat, hard plastic, Made in USA, 3"......................**7.00-10.00**
Cat, hard plastic, Made in USA, 4".................................**10.00-15.00**
Scarecrow, hard plastic, Made in USA, 5".........................**18.00-25.00**
Cat w/Pumpkin, hard plastic, Made in USA, 5"...................**30.00-35.00**
Jewelry Pin, hard plastic, Made in USA, sm **10.00-15.00**

German Candy Containers   We Pay

Cat on Box, papier-mache, 3", NM..................................**65.00-75.00**
Witch on Box, papier-mache, 3", NM **85.00-95.00**
Pumpkin Man on Box, papier-mache, 3", NM...................**75.00-85.00**
Cat, papier-mache, head removes, 4", NM.....................**125.00-150.00**
Witch, papier-mache, head removes, 4", NM **200.00-225.00**
Pumpkin Man, papier-mache, head removes, 4", NM......**150.00-175.00**
Cat on Pumpkin, papier-mache, 5", NM **150.00-175.00**
Witch on Pumkin, papier-mache, 5", NM.......................**200.00-225.00**
Pumpkin Man on Pumpkin, papier-mache, 5", NM.........**170.00-195.00**

Miscellaneous Halloween Items   We Pay

Postcards, ea, EX...**8.00-10.00**
Postcards, ea, M **10.00-12.00**
Dennison Bogie Books, ea **25.00-35.00**
Dennison Party Books, ea **20.00-28.00**
Bridge Tallys or Invitations, ea **2.00-4.00**
German Diecuts, 7", M...**25.00-35.00**
German Diecuts, 15", M..**45.00-55.00**
Board Games, by Beistle **25.00-45.00**
Boxed Games, by Milton Bradley......................................**45.00-65.00**
Other Games ....**Write**
Noisemakers, metal, M **10.00-15.00**
Nut Cups, crepe paper, sm, ea, M **8.00-10.00**

Halloween

I am buying the following **early Halloween postcards in excellent condition**: no bends, creases, or rips as well as writing, postal usage, soils, or stains on picture sides. Please send a picture (a black and white photocopy is fine), a description of the item, and the condition. I also buy **early lanterns, figural candles, candle holders, and chocolate molds**. I am also interested in turkey and Christmas chocolate molds.

Debbie Yates
P.O. Box 440
Norcross, GA 30091-0440
770-232-9799

Halloween Postcards   We Pay

Tuck Publisher, Series 150, any other than witch flying on broom	**10.00**
Tuck Publisher, Series 150, witch flying on broom	**15.00**
Tuck Publisher, Series 160	**20.00**
Ellen Clapsaddle, picturing objects or animals	**10.00**
Ellen Clapsaddle, picturing children, unsigned	**15.00**
Ellen Clapsaddle, picturing children, signed	**25.00**
Ellen Clapsaddle, w/moveable part, signed	**60.00**
John Winsch Publisher, full color	**45.00**
Hold-to-Light Halloween	**60.00**

We want to buy **all types of old Halloween items from the 1880s through the 1950s!** We especially like German papier-mache candy holders, such as witches, black cats, pumpkin characters, and vegetable people. We also want papier-mache Halloween lanterns (cat heads, pumpkins, etc.) with tissue paper faces, as well as celluloid Halloween toys. Other items we want are:

Toys, hard plastic, from the 1940s through 1950s
Noisemakers, tin with wood handle & Halloween scenes

Clicker, tin with Halloween themes
Early Composition Pumpkin People
Dennison Catalogs (Halloween decorations)
Halloween Postcards, pre-1920
Jack Pumpkinhead Material From *Wizard of Oz* Stories
Any Other Unusual Old Halloween Items

Sample prices are listed below. We answer all letters. See other wants listed under Christmas in this book.

Bob and Diane Kubicki
R.R. #2
W Milton, OH 45383
513-698-3650

We Pay

Book, *Jack Pumpkinhead of Oz*, old version ....**30.00+**
Candy Container, composition vegetable man, 8" ....**100.00+**
Candy Container, composition black cat, removable head, glass eyes, 4"...**65.00+**
Candy Container, composition black cat in dress, removable head, marked
    German **225.00**
Candy Container, papier-mache witch, German ....**175.00+**
Clicker, tin w/Halloween theme ....**2.00+**
Lantern, papier-mache black cat w/paper face ....**45.00+**
Lantern, pumpkin head w/tissue face, 6" ....**45.00+**
Lantern, German papier-mache pumpkin, 4" ....**65.00+**
Noisemaker, tin w/Halloween theme & wood handle ....**7.00+**
Noisemaker, ratchet-type w/composition pumpkin man ....**75.00+**
Postcard, vegetable people, dated 1911 ....**5.00+**
Pumpkin, composition, w/vegetable People, German, lg ....**285.00+**
Pumpkin Man in Top Hat, composition, 4" ....**45.00+**
Tambourine, German paper & wood pumpkin face ....**55.00+**
Toy, clown on wheels, hard orange plastic ....**12.00+**
Toy, witch on motorcycle, hard plastic ....**25.00+**
Toy, black cat on pumpkin, celluloid, 3" ....**55.00+**
Toy, pumpkin car w/witch & black cat, 4" long ....**100.00+**
Trade Catalog, Dennison's (Halloween decorations), 1920s **12.00**

We purchase **Halloween and Nightmare Before Christmas items**. Some
prices are listed here. Call us.

Chris Russell & The Halloween Queen Antiques
Pamela E. Apkarian-Russell, The Halloween Queen
P.O. Box 499
Winchester, NH 3470
603-239-8875

We Pay

Novelty Figure, hard plastic, Rosen (witches, cats, etc.), ea.............**10.00-60.00**
Figure, celluloid, Halloween or Christmas, ea **25.00-150.00**
Dennison Company Bogie Books, ea..**35.00+**

Nightmare Before Christmas Doll, any, depends on character **25.00-300.00**
Twelve Faces of Jack, in original case..**1,800.00**
Jack O'-Lantern (also lanterns as cats, devils, etc.), papier-mache...**20.00-400.00**
Halloween Costumes (character collectibles), in box, ea..................**5.00-200.00**
Candy Containers (witches, ghosts, veggie people), depending on rarity, con-
    dition, image, etc...**25.00-2,000.00**
Halloween Postcards, depending on rarity.......................................**1.00-300.00**
Spoon, sterling, Salem Witch souvenir items, showing the witch **40.00**
Rouge Jar, Salem Witch souvenir items **175.00**
Other Salem Witch Souvenir Items Wanted ....**Call or Write**

I am looking for **Halloween decorations from the '50s and '60s** such as
noisemakers, papier-mache pumpkins, candy containers, and decorations.
Please include a good description, condition, and price when writing about
your item.

Deborah Summers
3258 Harrison
Paducah, KY 42001

I'm collecting **1950 and pre-1950 Halloween items** such as papier-mache
pumpkins, cats, witches, etc., also plastic candy containers. Prices are given
for good-condition items. Other items than those listed are also wanted.
Please describe fully.

Other wants include **Halloween, dogs (definite breeds), buttons and
sewing (antiques or interesting), 1904 St. Louis World's Fair items (no clear
glasses or plates), Pepsi, Bakelite, Barbie dolls and clothes made before 1969,
teddy bears (early jointed mohair in good condition), Santa (old only), and
papier-mache character nodders of the 1950s.**

Gwen Daniel
#1 Charlestown Plaza
St. Charles, MO 63303
314-978-3190
e-mail: gdaniel@mail.win.org

We Pay

Pumpkins, papier-mache, sm...**40.00+**
Pumpkins, papier-mache, med...**60.00+**

needs range all the way back to the 1500s, although it is not often a map of that vintage turns up at a garage sale. What you may encounter will be some late 19th-century atlases; for which I can pay upwards of $50.00 apiece, depending on the atlas. More recent atlases, from the 1930s to date are not yet sought after by collectors and may not even be worth the cost of shipping them on approval. The same goes for supplemental maps issued by the National Geographic Society; I am not able to buy any — unless they date from 1920 or earlier. Recent AAA maps also do not have any collector value.

Testimony to the increasing interest in road maps is a recently formed organization, the Road Map Collectors of America, and a colorful new book, *Hitting the Road: The Art of the American Road Map*, by Doug Yorke and John Margolies. There are also more general map organizations, including IMCOS (International Map Collectors Society), AMMC (American Map Memorabilia Collectors Society), IMTA (International Map Trade Association), and PAC (Print and Advertising Collectors Association). Various hobby publications also exist, including *Mercator's World* and *Paper Collectors Marketplace*, for which I write a regular column on map collecting. I shall be happy to forward information on any or all of the above if you would kindly send me a SASE and let me know which organization and publications you are interested in.

The Internet has also become a good place to explore the wonderful world of maps, and there are a number of sites for you to visit. Many can be reached from the site I maintain; please see the URL below.

The subject of maps is vast...but it does not have to be confusing. The appeal of maps is universal; people are drawn to them by their simple practicality, by their power to evoke an intoxicating blend of romance and adventure steeped in nostalgia, and the continuing human need to satisfy our insatiable curiosity.

Charles Neuschafer
New World Maps, Inc.
1123 S Broadway
Lantana, FL 33462
561-586-8723
e-mail: charlieneu@aol.com
URL: http://pages.prodigy.com/maproom

Marbles

I am a marble collector who needs help finding old, **handmade marbles from the turn of the century and I'm looking for machine-made marbles**

made in the 1920s through 1940s. Photos are helpful; send them — call or write. I will consider marbles that are old and in good to mint condition. Other wants include **Van Briggle pottery, end-of-day glass, and carnival glass.**

David Smith
1142 S Sprint St.
Springfield, IL 62704
217-523-3391

We Pay

Handmade Marbles, ea	**1.00-150.00**
Comic Marbles, Bimbo, Moon, etc., ea	**10.00-50.00**
Machine-Made Marbles, ea	**50¢-10.00**
Marbles w/Figures Inside	**10.00-100.00**
Marbles in Original Boxes or Bags	**3.00-50.00**

———

Collector paying current book price for **pre-1940 glass marbles in mint or near-mint condition.** Sulphides, cat's eyes, clearies, Chinese checker (game), or clay marbles are not wanted. I will buy handmade or machine-made marbles as long as they are not ordinary or common. If you ship marbles for my offer, please include your telephone number. I will provide you with references if you ask. I look forward to hearing from you!

Yvonne Holmberg
7229 Pine Island Dr., NE
Comstock Park, MI 49321-9534
616-784-1715

———

We buy **marbles and marble-related items.** This includes individual marbles, original boxes, tournament trophies and medals, toys, games, and literature. We can use **anything related to marbles, the game of marbles, and the history of marbles.**

Stanley and Bob Block
P.O. Box 51
Trumbull, CT 06611
203-261-0057

Match Holders and Match Safes

I am an advanced collector interested in purchasing **quality pocket match safes**. I collect all categories with emphasis on figural, enameled, fancy, and unusual pocket match safes. I am interested in one item or an entire collection. I am also seeking **any related printed material** including catalogs, advertisements, patents, etc., **produced prior to 1915**. I respond to all inquiries. Listed below are a few of the items I am interested in buying.

George Sparacio
P.O. Box 791
Malaga, NJ 08328
609-694-4167 or fax 609-694-4536

We Pay

Agate Types, ea	**75.00+**
Baden Powell, figural	**225.00+**
Billiken, figural, sterling	**350.00+**
Chamberlain, portrait	**200.00+**
Cigar, figural, enamel band	**450.00+**
Daniel Boone, figural, brass	**250.00+**
Domino, figural, vulcanite	**50.00+**
Enameled, ea	**125.00+**
Fire or Firemen Motif, ea	**125.00+**
Figural, most types, ea	**125.00+**
Niello, on silver, Russian	**150.00+**
Oriental, figural type, brass, ea	**175.00+**
Pig, figural as running, brass	**155.00+**
Portrait of Famous Person	**150.00+**
President Grant, portrait	**275.00+**
Sentry House, enameled sterling	**600.00+**
Stanhope Peep-Eye, any type, ea	**100.00+**

Matchcovers

I collect matchbooks with the striker on the front and preferably unstruck. **I Pay 2¢ to 5¢ each per piece, depending on condition.** Categories of interest include matchcovers showing pizza, pigs, roosters, suns, stars, and dollar amounts on covers. Also those that are 240-strike. Somewhere out there is someone who has collected these over the years and they are just collecting dust. I would like a letter describing quantity, condition — and would appreciate an enclosed SASE. I reply to all inquiries with serious offers.

Billijo Piper
9836 Gunpowder Rd.
Florence, KY 41042
606-525-0422

Militaria

We buy **anything military** — from the Roman Empire to Operation Desert Storm. We buy small items like dog tags and big items like tanks! We are 30-year veterans of military collecting and dealing. We buy uniforms, flags, helmets, equipment, guns, daggers, hats, shoes, documents, medals, jewelry, boats, jeeps, armored personnel carriers, etc. We specialize in WWI and WWII, German, U.S., and Japanese items — but we buy all militaria.

Take a photo of the item and send along whatever history you know about it. This will help in determining the value of the item. Call me or drop me a line, I will be glad to give an estimate on any military items. We will give free estimates over the phone, but the best thing to do is send a picture of the item. We will be happy to talk with anyone about military items.

Kathleen Miller
Kat's Militaria
906 Chambers Ridge.
York, PA 17402
717-840-4156

We are collectors interested in purchasing items used by our **Revolutionary War soldiers and British (redcoat) memorabilia** as well. Musket balls to muskets, buttons and belt plates to uniforms — list what you have along with your asking price for an immediate response. Any items listed without an asking price will be reviewed and returned with either an offer or decline of purchase, depending on if we already have the item(s). All offers are based on rarity and condition. Photographs are extremely helpful, so as to determine the condition of the item. Please enclose a loose stamp with inquiries, we'll take care of the envelope.

Please note that we refuse to purchase any item that was recovered in breech of any State or Federal Antiquities Law or Federal Preservation Laws. Examples of this would be items found without a permit on state or federal parks and protected archaeological sites. Send inquiries to:

Minuteman Treasures
P.O. Box 705
Pine Plains, NY 12567-0705

I specialize in buying German military relics from WWII and earlier, but also buy military relics from Japan, Italy, the U.S., and other countries if the items are from WWII or earlier. Prices paid for items are based on the condition and rarity of an item. I buy from single items to entire collections. Write or call describing what you have, or ship insured for my offer. Prices shown below are a general guide, some items may be worth less, others are worth more.

John Telesmanich
P.O. Box 62
E White Plains, NY 10604
914-949-5519

We Pay

Badges	**20.00-300.00**
Belt Buckles	**20.00-250.00**
Books	**10.00-75.00**
Cloth Insignia	**10.00-200.00**
Daggers	**150.00-3,000.00**
Hats	**100.00-500.00**

Militaria

Helmets	50.00-2,000.00
Magazines	5.00-20.00
Medals	20.00-1,000.00
Postcards	5.00-50.00
Swords	200.00-1,000.00
Uniforms	200.00-1,000.00

Advanced collector is seeking **all items related to the French Foreign Legion, Devil's Island**. Original items only are wanted; I am not interested in reproductions or items originating from the souvenir workshop of Puyloubier (a veterans' home). Please note that I prefer not to make offers and would greatly appreciate photocopies or detailed descriptions. SASE requested. Prices are negotiable and contingent on age, size, condition, etc. I am also interested in **all items related to the Shanghai Volunteer Corps-Police, China (U.S./French/White Russian/Warlords/Gunboats), International Brigade (Spain), military kukris, Animal Rescue-Heroism, and truant officers.**

Gene Christian
3849 Bailey Ave.
Bronx, NY 10463
718-548-0243

We Pay

Artwork, oil, ea	**100.00**
Artwork, watercolor, ea	**50.00**
Banners, rectangular, ea	**500.00**
Banners, triangular, ea	**150.00**
Certificates, ea	**30.00**
Dioramas, ea	**150.00+**
Documents, ea	**25.00**
Dolls, ea	**50.00**
Figurines, ea	**100.00**
Handcrafted Items, ea	**50.00**
Plaques, lg, ea	**50.00**
Service Books, ea	**75.00**
Toy Soldiers (old), ea	**20.00**

Collecting war souvenirs has introduced me to a considerable amount of history. As time goes on, few people will remember what everyone went through during that time, nor realize there's value to an old German or Japanese sword, etc. This stuff is worth money to me! I buy most anything military from WWII. This includes German, Japanese, Polish, etc., helmets, daggers, swords, medals, uniforms — also U.S. Airforce leather flight jackets and squadron patches.

For my offer, please describe and photograph (copy is okay) what you have or mail insured for my offer. Be sure to include your phone number. Do not clean or polish your souvenir, as this could hurt the value. Typical buying prices are listed here. Turn your attic relics into cash, call or write.

Dick Pankowski
P.O. Box 22
Greendale, WI 53129
414-421-7056

We Pay

Helmets, German or Japanese	**50.00+**
Swords	**100.00+**
Metals	**5.00+**
Badges	**5.00+**
Patches	**5.00+**
Daggers	**50.00+**
Knives	**50.00+**

I am interested in buying the following military items: **Civil War Springfields, Colt 1860 Armies, any Civil War memorabilia, all types of German WWI and WWII edged weapons, swords, bayonets, and daggers**. Other military-related items will also be considered. Photos and descriptions of items would be helpful when you reply.

J. Salmon
104 Lakeview Dr. E
Egg Harbor Township, NJ 08234-7814
609-927-9641

I am looking for **Civil War, German, and Japanese military items**. Special wants include edged weapons, swords, helmets, medals, hats, papers, I.D. cards, postcards, original photos, equipment, antique black powder weapons, and flintlock (antique) pistols. Please send detailed description, price, and photocopies if possible.

Dora Lerch
P.O. Box 245
Garnerville, NY 10923
phone or fax 914-761-8903

I have been collecting **Japanese Samurai swords and fine quality military items** from the U.S. and Europe for 30 years. I would be interested in any Japanese swords and WWII or earlier German daggers regardless of condition. Also I'm collecting U.S. knives and militaria. I will, upon receiving SASE, try to give a free appraisal as to the collector value of your item(s). Note that some rarer items may command higher prices.

Thomas Winter
817 Patton
Springfield, IL 62702
217-523-8729

We Pay

Samurai Swords & Daggers	**up to 2,000.00**
German SS Daggers	**up to 1,000.00**
Regimental Flags	**up to 500.00**
Medals, Badges & Pins	**up to 350.00**
Uniforms, Helmets & Hats	**up to 700.00**

Milk Bottle Caps

I am interested in buying old **milk caps that fit on top of glass milk bottles**. I want all milk caps to be different and am interesting in Washington and Oregon states only. **I am paying 10¢ to 20¢ each** for these milk caps in good condition. Please send photocopy of them. Thank you.

Louis Ruzicko
Rt. #1, Box 90
Walla Walla, WA 99362
509-525-5525

Motion Lamps

We buy **animated motion lamps** made from the 1930s to the early 1960s. The lamps are heat activated which causes a shade to revolve and create a moving picture. It is important that all pieces are included with the lamp and that it is free from scratches and heat damage. The following list is only an example of available lamps. Other wants include **Josef Originals and Hawaiiana.**

Jim and Kaye Whitaker
Eclectic Antiques
P.O. Box 475, Dept. WB
Lynnwood, WA 98046
206-774-6910

We Pay

Econolite, Niagara Falls	**35.00-45.00**
Econolite, Antique Cars	**60.00-65.00**
Econolite, John Bull/General Trains	**65.00-70.00**
Econolite, Water Skiers	**100.00-110.00**
Econolite, Hopalong Cassidy, Roto-Vue Jr	**200.00-250.00**
Econolite, Carousel, Roto-Vue Jr	**65.00-75.00**
L.A. Goodman, Forest Fire	**40.00-45.00**
L.A. Goodman, Ship/Lighthouse	**55.00-60.00**
L.A. Goodman, Santa/Reindeer Over Rooftops	**110.00-130.00**
Scene in Action, Moon Over Lake	**100.00-120.00**
Scene in Action, Ship/Lighthouse	**75.00-85.00**

Motion and lava lamps from the 1940s and '50s are wanted. Must be in good working order with no warping from its bulb's heat. Nature scenes, campfires, waterfalls, forest fires, and Smokey Bear lamps are desired. **I am paying from $15.00 to $35.00** for these moving lamps depending on age and condition.

C.E. Nolte
2979 S 15 Pl.
Milwaukee, WI 53215

Motorcycles

Collecting motorcycles is a relatively new hobby. Generally speaking, enthusiasts are young and old, most are mechanically oriented. We appreciate the artistry involved in the manufacture of pre-1970 motorcycles. I am interested in purchasing **motorcycles and related items from 1895 to the late 1970s**. I will consider any American or European make (no Japanese). I like original (not repainted) motorcycles best — but I will consider all, running or not running, incomplete or only parts, in any condition. Also wanted are sidecars, scooters, unique home-built motorcycles, and steam motorcycles built prior to 1970. The following is a partial list of makes I would be interested in buying.

Ariel	Indian
BMV	Matchless
BSA	Norton
Crocker	Royal Enfield
Cushman	Simplex
Excelsior	Triumph
Harley Davidson	Whizzer

I also buy new or old stock parts, tools, used parts, clothing, memorabilia, etc. Since there are a great many related items I am interested in, I can only give a general list.

Service Manuals	Kidney Belts
Repair Manuals	Boots
Dealer Literature	Breeches
Advertising Items	Scarf Hats
Posters	Riding Caps
Photographs	Gloves
Tank Badges	Jackets
Lapel Pins	Uniforms
Oil Cans	Tool or Saddle Bags

I will buy large collections or will broker the same or will buy only one piece. I have years of experience, and references are available. If writing, please send a complete description of the item (including its age and condition) and a picture, if possible, along with a SASE. Please feel free to call for information.

Bruce Kiper
Ancient Age Motors
2205 Sunset Ln.
Lutz, FL 33549
813-949-5060

Wanted and paying cash for any **motorcycle parts, toys, pieces, old photos, frames, wheels, motors, gas tanks, front ends, speedometers — anything — even if broken or rusted**. Makes include American-made Harley, Pope, Thor, Thiem, Evans, Crocker, Racycle, Ace, Indian, Excelsior, Henderson, Arrow, Pierce, Cleveland, Merkel, Flying Merkel, Miami, Minneapolis, Marsh-Metz, Metz, Schickel, Yale, Franklin, Nera-Car, and Miller.

Items wanted include old riding hats, jackets, any state motorcycle licenses or license plates, dealer signs, clocks, advertising or dealer display items, lighters, match books, old catalogs, sales brochures, paint chip books, oil cans — any sizes, anything, any old motorcycle items! Thank you!

Tom Wilhelm
P.O. Box 534
Salisbury, NC 28145
704-647-0806

We Pay

Award	25.00-50.00
Bike Ring	50.00-80.00
Book, paint chip	100.00+
Button, FAM	25.00-75.00
Front End	300.00-500.00+
Gas Tank	50.00-150.00+
Harley-Davidson Enthusiast, bound, ea	40.00-75.00
Hat	20.00-75.00+
Headlight, old	35.00+
Leather Key Case	15.00-25.00
Leather Dressing	25.00-40.00
License Plate	20.00-50.00
Match book	5.00-15.00
Motorcycle Emblem	10.00-50.00+
Oil Can	15.00+

Patch, old	15.00-50.00
Patch, FAM	200.00+
Pennant, cloth	50.00+
Pin, Harley-Davidson, old	75.00+
Pin, Harley-Davidson silver wings	60.00+
Pin-Back Button	25.00-50.00
Sales Book, old	50.00+
Sign, metal, old	200.00-300.00
Sign, porcelain, old	200.00-500.00
Striping Colors, ea	10.00-35.00
Tie Clip	35.00+
Watch Fob	40.00+
Watch Fob, FAM	100.00-200.00

Murano Glass

Murano glass has been produced on the island of Murano (off the coast of Venice) for centuries. Scores of designers each produced a wide variety of items: vases, bowls, decanters, animal and human figurines. So there is a plethora of items in a wide variety of techniques. Most Murano pieces will exhibit bold colors and/or gold inclusions. Murano is mouth blown; therefore pieces may be similar in subject matter and color yet no two pieces will be identical. Therefore you can find more artistic renditions of the same piece. Murano is rarely signed but often labeled. Murano pieces should be color photographed and all damage and/or repairs noted, as well as any signature or label. We do not buy ashtrays, clowns, or lighters.

William Tabler
2554 Lincoln Blvd. #555
Marina del Rey, CA 90291
818-755-4565

We Pay

Abstract, stylized bird w/metal feet & legs	400.00+
Harlequin Figurine	300.00+
Murrine Vase	250.00+
Murrine Bowl	300.00+
Murrine Decanter	300.00+
Murrine Platter	275.00+
Lion, Tiger, or Elephant Figurine	325.00+

Starfish or Seashell-Shaped Bowl, w/gold inclusions ....250.00+
Patchwork Vases, Bowls & Decanters ....350.00+

Music Boxes

I am a private collector interested in purchasing **all types of antique musical boxes, phonographs, radios, etc.** I also pay finders' fees for assistance in locating these pieces. I pay top prices and guarantee a fast response to your correspondence.

John S. Zuk
106 Orchard St.
Belmont, MA 02178
617-484-4800 (home) or 617-349-0652 (office)

We Pay

Cylinder Musical Boxes...500.00+
Disc Musical Boxes..750.00+
Wooden (carved) Whistling Figures...500.00+
Mechanical Singing Birds..250.00+
Wind-Up Phonographs, 78 rpm ....50.00+
Cylinder Record Phonographs w/Horns ....200.00+

Music Memorabilia

I would like to buy **New Wave and Punk Rock items from 1975 through 1983**. I'm looking for records (picture discs, 45 rpm records with picture sleeves, EP records, bootlegs, and rare stuff), promotional novelties such as DEVO plastic hair, clothes, etc., and some posters.

I am desperately seeking the soundtrack to *Ladies and Gentlemen: The Fabulous Stains*. Also wanted is the original *Valley Girl* soundtrack and a *Bow Wow Wow* EP (with C30., C90., C90., Go!). I am interested in many groups so give me a call or write!

Barbara Brecker
76 Sicard St.
New Brunswick, NJ 08901
908-246-1589
AOL: SalandRei@aol.com or Internet: Davidgr@instbbs.camba.com

We Pay

Fabulous Stains Soundtrack	**30.00**
Other Records	**Call or Write**
Novelty Items	**Call or Write**

Musical Instruments

I buy **used electric/acoustic guitars and amps**. I prefer them to be American made and all original. But I will buy others. If the instrument is in the original condition and has very little play wear, I offer up to 75% of book value on most quitars. Any condition is okay, but it must be from normal play wear. I have some interest in banjos, mandolins, and lap steels. I'm wanting to buy Fender, Gibson, Martin, Gretsch, Epiphone, National, Kay, Guild, Danelectro, Silvertone, Rickenbacker, Airline, Hofner, Harmony, Vox, Sunn, Marshall, Musicman, Ampeg, and others.

Billy J. Burdette
1516 Bluebird Ln.
Anderson, SC 29621
864-375-0689

I collect **saxophones** — antiques as well as those from the '30s, '40s, and '50s. They may be silver, brass, or gold in color in any condition. The following manufacturers are the ones that I am looking for: **Conn, King Martin, Buescher & Selmer (Paris)**. The name is always on the bell. I am interested in all sizes except the C melody. Call if you do not know the difference and I will explain. Please call or write.

David Reed
841 W Main St.
Madison, OH 44057
216-428-6666 (after 6 pm)

Type	We Pay
Soprano, straight or curved	**175.00-225.00**
Alto, straight or curved	**100.00-150.00**
Tenor	**150.00-200.00**
Baritone	**200.00-300.00**
Bass or Larger	**Much More**

I buy and sell **antique and used band instruments**. I have customers worldwide waiting to buy the good ones. Price guides are available free by request with SASE. You've seen many old horns out there. Some may be quite valuable. Now you can know what to buy and where to sell it.

I have nineteen years experience in the business of specializing in restoring old brass instruments, and I have been building replicas for the last thirteen years. Written appraisals are available for a small fee, and verbal evaluation of your latest find is just a phone call away.

These are some **examples of items that I have purchased in the past year**:

Selmer Balanced Model trumpet, '50s vintage, excellent condition, $800.00

Conn Perfected Wonder cornet, circa 1910, gold-plated w/extra engraving, very good condition, $275.00

Conn double-bell euphonium, five valves, 1928, silver plated, excellent condition, $1,200.00

Boston Three Star cornet, circa 1885, silver plated, very good condition, $500.00

Aug Pollman E-flat cornet with rotary valves, circa 1875, German silver, excellent condition, $750.00

Stratton rotary valve cornet with bell over the shoulder, circa 1865, very good condition, $1,500.00

Fiske E-flat tuba, circa 1855, German silver, good condition, $900.00

Unsigned 8-key bugle, circa 1850, good condition, $950.00

Robb Stewart, Brass Instruments
140 E Santa Clara St., #18
Arcadia, CA 91006
818-447-1904

Napkin Rings

I buy napkin rings for my personal collection. I am partial to figural phenolic resin or Catalin napkin rings of the '30s through the '50s; many of these are colorful animal shapes or cartoon characters. Chipped and cracked ones are purchased, but prices are much less. Late Victorian or Edwardian ornate and figural rings must be complete and napkin holder-castor sets must have matching glass parts. Condition of silverplating affects value. Unusual modern handcrafted rings are desirable, too. Please describe all defects.

Margaret L. Bryan
189 S Fairfield Dr.
Dover, DE 19901-5756

We Pay

Phenolic Resin, chick, common type	22.00
Phenolic Resin, Scottie dog, seated or standing	36.00+
Phenolic Resin, animal (fish, rabbit, elephant, etc)	50.00+
Phenolic Resin, cartoon character (Popeye, Disney, etc)	65.00+
Victorian, figural w/original plating	125.00+
Victorian, figural w/worn plating	65.00+
Victorian, figural w/replating	65.00+
Victorian, figural needing minor repair	30.00+
Unusual Vintage or Sterling	15.00+
Unusual Modern, Craft & Novelty	5.00+
Fiesta Ware, sleeping Mexican boy	40.00
Commemorative, picturing buildings, etc	5.00+
New York World's Fair Trilon or Perisphere, 1938, ea	100.00
Columbian or St. Louis Fair, ea	40.00+
Buyer's Choice Carolers, Nativity	45.00+

Nippon

Eager to buy excellent, quality Nippon pieces. Best prices paid for large vases, urns, relief, moriage, coralene, and novelty items. No cracks, chips, or heavily-worn items wanted, please. High prices paid. Send photo for our review and we will return. We pay all shipping charges.

H. Browning
13281 Heather Ridge Loop
Ft. Myers, FL 33912

Noritake

I am buying **Deco Noritake**. I especially want figural lady pieces, lamps, powder puffs, and large figurals. I am the president of the Long Island Nippon Collector's Club and an active member of the Japanese Porcelain Collector's Club. I have a large group of friends and acquaintances who are also looking for specific pieces and will make contacts for you. I am only interested in pieces that are in excellent condition and that are clearly marked Noritake. I do not follow the price guides and will pay much more or less depending upon rarity and condition. I am not interested in dinnerware.

Timothy Trapani
145 Andover Pl.
West Hempstead, NY 11552
516-292-8355 (after 4 pm EST)

Noritake (Deco)	We Pay
Powder Puffs, Deco women	150.00+
Figural Lamps	700.00+
Gemini Bowls	700.00
Lady on a Chair Box	1,000.00+
Lady Figural Bowls & Dishes	175.00+
Indian Princess	900.00+
Deco Punch Bowls or Sets	400.00+

North Dakota Collectibles

We live in a small rural community in southwest North Dakota and are interested in buying **items originating in North Dakota, South Dakota, and Montana prior to the 1950s.** Wanted are souvenir items with town names (especially North Dakota towns of Bowman, Rhame, Marmarth, Scranton, Reeder, Amidon, Haley, and Griffin).

Items of most interest with these names are souvenir glassware items in red, green, blue, or white; advertising mirrors; and crocks. No alcohol or tobacco promotional items are wanted please. We also buy **Dakota Territory memorabilia, small artifacts or calvary items, books by North Dakota or regional authors, pottery by Messer (see Pottery in this book), and old salt and pepper collections.**

We pay from $10.00 to $100.00 for most items with no cracks or chips. Please send a photo or a detailed description. We will try to pay your asking price, or we will make you an offer.

Stan and Carrie Soderstrom
15 First St. SW
Rt. 2, Box 300
Bowman, ND 58623

We Pay

Advertising Mirrors	8.00+
Cavalry Items	5.00+
Dakota Territory Memorabilia	5.00+
Messer Pottery	40.00+
Salt & Pepper Sets	5.00+
Souvenir Glass, clear or colored	10.00+

Outboard Boat Motors

I collect all **toy metal outboard boat motors.** These may be electric, tin windup, steam powered, or gas powered. Most of these motors were made in Japan from 1955 to 1970 by KO. I want nice, clean motors with no repaints or chipped paint. No plastic motors are wanted. I will pay 10% extra if you have the original box. Also wanted are gas-powered race cars.

Richard Gronowski
140 N Garfield Ave.
Traverse City, MI 49686-2802
616-491-2111

We Pay

Evinrudes, 40 HP or 75 HP, ea **125.00**
Gale Sovereign, 60 HP **200.00**
Gale, 30 HP or 35 HP, ea...**125.00**
Johnsons, 40 HP or 75 HP, ea **125.00**
Oliver, 35 HP..**200.00**
Mercury, black, 100 HP **200.00**
Mercury, MK 55, MK 800, MK 78 or MK 75, ea **125.00**
All Other Johnsons, Mercurys, Scotts, Evinrudes, Gales, ea.....................**75.00**
Sea-Fury **75.00**
Sea-Fury Twin..**150.00**
Fuji or Orkin, ea **125.00**
Tin Winups, ea..**75.00**
Generic's I.M.P, Langcraft, Yamaha, Super Tigre, Speed King, Sakai, New
Evince, Le-Page, Swank, Aristocraft, Etc., ea...**50.00**

Orientalia

Wanted to buy: **Orientalia**. Japanese cloisonne smalls are wanted in mint condition of the Meiji era, signed and wireless. Also sought are early Chinese snuff bottles in mint condition — no reproduction or glass ones wanted. Chinese Mandarine squares/badges (textiles) are wanted in good to mint condition dating from the 19th century or earlier. Kindly send photos, descriptions and your price.

Alan R. Glazer
36 College Ave. #B3
Somerville, MA 02144
617-776-4475

Paducah, Kentucky Collectibles

I am buying Paducah, Kentucky collectibles. The Bauer pottery company began here, Coca-Cola and other bottlers were based in the area, and early whiskey crocks were marked 'Made in Paducah.' Postcards, paper collectibles, calendars, Irvin Cobb memorabilia, and old advertising are of special interest to me. If you will send a photo or detailed description, SASE, and the value you want for your item, I will respond.

B.J. Summers
233 Darnell Rd.
Benton, KY 42025

Paint Boxes

Wanted: children's metal paint boxes from 1940 through the 1970s. Especially sought are those with interesting cover graphics and bright colors. Please include a good description, condition, and price.

Michael Summers
3258 Harrison
Paducah, KY 42001

Paper and Ephemera

We are strong buyers of **all types of paper collectibles that detail the history of the United States and North America** from all periods prior to the 1980s. Our prices paid depend on the scarcity of an item, condition, etc. The older an item, the better. Our needs include but are not limited to: old stock certificates, old bonds, old photos (even common-type family or individual shots), matchbook covers (especially sports related and pin-up girls), old calendars, labels (fruit crate, tobacco, liquor, etc.), old advertising (displays, ads, etc.), old political paper, pre-1980 non-sport trading cards, old letters (even family correspondence), and old posters (especially sports and entertainment). Let us know what you have. We strive to pay more. Listed below are some minimum buying prices for selected items.

Partin's Treasures
P.O. Box 3510
Morristown, TN 37815-3510

Paper Americana   We Pay

Fruit Can Labels ....1.00+
Cigar Box Labels, pre-1950 ....1.50+
Matchbook Cover, Cotton Club ....2.00+
Matchbook Cover, 1973 Sugar Bowl ....2.50+
Coca-Cola 1980 Calendar, Olympics...3.00+
Coca-Cola Playing Cards, pre-1980 ....8.00+
Coca-Cola Display Sign, pre-1965 ....30.00+
Sheet Music, Abraham, 1942, Irving Berlin......................................5.00+
Movie Poster, The Alamo, 1967 ....15.00+
Movie Poster, Nevada Smith, 1966 ....10.00+
World War II Posters..8.00+
Coloring Book, JFK caricature cartoons ....20.00+
Playing Cards, Kennedy Family 1963...10.00+
Playing Cards, Marilyn Monroe, nude photos..................................12.00+
Pepsi-Cola Advertising Signs, pre-1965...12.00+
Postcard Photo Chalmers Motor Co., Detroit....................................5.00+
Stock Certificate, railroad, pre-1930 ....1.50+
Stock Certificate, coal mining, pre-1940..2.00+

Dear Friend — this is a list of mainly paper items that I always buy. If you have anything on this list please send me a brief description (title, condition, date, number) for my immediate offer. (If this is too much trouble merely pack everything up and mail for full payment, same day received!) I pay generously for everything I need and do repeat business with most sellers (since 1964). If required, bank and trade references are available, so deal in total confidence. If you have any questions, feel free to phone me anytime, night or day. Thank you.

Comic Books: 1900-1960s (these have mainly 10¢ and 12¢ cover prices, Giants 25¢), but I will consider higher-condition 1970s (15¢ and 20¢ cover price primarily). Duplicates are okay. Lesser condition comics have little value, but if pre-1960 send. If you are not sure about dates, or anything, don't worry about it; I'll appraise.

Big Little Books: 1933-1950. Those fat little books about 3" x 5" with titles like Flash Gordon, Dick Tracy, Tarzan, Buck Rogers, etc. Publishers were mostly

Whitman and Saalfield although there were others. Note: any with missing pages or covers have no value.

Sunday Comic Pages and Complete Comic Sections: 1960-1980s. Only complete sections are wanted; I'd like to know what strips, number of pages, condition, and date. Loose pages are harder to assess. Merely do the best you can, or quite simply: shoot the works to me and trust my generosity. (This has worked out very well.)

Walt Disney Books, Magazines, Comic Books, Etc.: 1928-1950s. All old Disney paper items are wanted. Publishes include David McKay, Whitman, Blue Ribbon, and others.

Pulp Magazines: 1930s-1940s. Those magazines printed on cheap paper with titles such as Doc Savage, The Shadow, Spider, G-8, air, horror, and spicy titles. (No others wanted.)

Song Magazines: 1920s-1960s. These were mainly words only with titles such as _Song Hits, Songs That Will Live Forever, 400 Songs, Hit Paraders_, etc. Anything with song lyrics (not music) is wanted. Lesser condition is acceptable on these.

Radio, TV, Cereal Premiums: 1930s-1950s. Items such as decoders, rings, pinback buttons, badges, booklets; characters such as Buck Rogers, Captain Midnight, Orphan Annie, Tom Mix; ads found in newspapers and other publications — all these and others wanted.

Cards (Gum, Candy, Sports): 1930s-1960s. Give company, date, condition or send.

Music (Popular, Jazz) Magazines and Books: 1920s to present.

Original Comic Book and Comic Strip Art

Books by L. Frank Baum, E.R. Burroughs; Pop-Up Books

Personality-Related Items: Including magazines, books, and toys relating to Marilyn Monroe, Elvis, James Dean, John Wayne, Shirley Temple, Superman, etc.

To speed delivery please indicate 'gift' on parcel and place a value of $20.00 or less on each parcel. Do not put invoice or letter in parcels. Please send via post office cheapest way (I'm in no hurry). Please pack well, with newspapers, as the mails can be rough.

A finder's fee will be paid to you if you put me in touch with a prospective seller. I do professional appraisals. For more information, please contact me.

I offer 100% satisfaction on all transactions. (I always have and always will.) I look forward to doing business with you. Incidently, Willowdale is a suburb of Toronto, which is 90 minutes from Buffalo or 3½ hours from

Detroit; for those with a truck full of items to sell and wish to bring them in personally, this is also okay with me.

Ken Mitchell
710 Conacher Dr.
Willowdale, Ontario
Canada M2M 3N6
416-222-5808

I am interested in buying **items circulated by William D. Pelley**. I will pay any reasonable price up to $200.00 for selected items from the following list:

Mimeographed Materials:
Christian Campaign Committee Bulletins, Circulars, 1936
The Councils of Safety of the Christian Party, Master Councillor's Address, #1-44, 1936
Scourge of Cords, 1938(?)
Councils of Safety Monographs, Post Booklets, 1938
Galahad College, Little Lectures, 1932
The Foundation for Christian Economics, Confidential Bulletin, #1-6, 1932-33
Twenty-Two Articles of Liberation, 1933
Pelley's Speeches to the Legion, 1938
Valiant Doctrine, The Blue Lectures, 1931-36
Valiant Doctrine, The White Lectures, #1-67, 1931-36
Valiant Doctrine, The Silver Scripts, 1931-36

Books, Pamphlets, Manuals:
Silvershirt Legion of America, member's manual, 1933-37
A Million Silvershirts by 1939, manual, 1938
The Hidden Empire, 1936
Dupes of Judah
The Key to Crisis, 1939
Jews Say So!

Serials:
New Liberator/liberation, May 1930-January 1941
Pelley's Weekly, August 1934-November 1936
Silver Legion Ranger, 1933-1934
Reality, October 1937-July 1939, July 1940
Roll Call, January-December 1941
Galilean, September 1941-March 1942

T. Vance Pollock
P.O. Box 1021
Kathleen, FL 33849
941-858-2961

Paper Money

We are major buyers of **all types and designs of large-size U.S. currency issued between 1862 and 1923.** Of particular interest are the 'home town' national bank notes issued by the U.S. government but bearing the name of the local national bank and signed by the bank cashier and president. A few examples are listed below. Please call or write on any notes not listed. Naturally, condition is very important. Prices listed are for clean, bright, undamaged specimens. Badly worn and damaged notes are worth less. Superb examples are worth much more.

Glenn G. Wright
P.O. Box 311
Campellsport, WI 53010
800- 303-8248

U.S. Large-Size Currency

	We Pay
1862 $1 U.S. Note	**100.00+**
1875 (or earlier) $1 National Bank Note	**100.00+**
1875 (or earlier) $2 National Bank Note	**300.00+**
1901 $10 U.S. Note	**150.00+**
1896 $1 Silver Certificate	**100.00+**
1896 $2 Silver Certificate	**175.00+**
1896 $5 Silver Certificate	**350.00+**
1899 $5 Silver Certificate	**125.00+**
1923 $5 Silver Certificate	**150.00+**
1891 $100 Silver Certificate	**2,000.00+**
1890 $100 Treasury Note	**5,000.00+**
1886 $5 Silver Certificate	**225.00+**
1875 (or earlier) $10 National Bank Note	**150.00+**
1875 (or earlier) $20 National Bank Note	**300.00+**
1882 $5 National Bank Note	**50.00+**
1882 $10 National Bank Note	**60.00+**
1902 $5 National Bank Note (red Treasury seal)	**50.00+**

1882 $20 Gold Certificate ....200.00+

Rare National Bank Notes, All Denominations   **We Pay**

Alaska...1,000.00+
Arizona Territory..1,500.00+
New Mexico Territory ....600.00+
Indian Territory..1,500.00+
Nebraska Territory ....2,500.00+
Colorado Territory ....1,000.00+
Utah Territory ....1,000.00+
Montana Territory...1,500.00+
Dakota Territory...1,000.00+
Oklahoma Territory ....1,000.00+
Wyoming Territory ....2,500.00+
Washington Territory..2,500.00+
Idaho Territory...2,500.00+
Puerto Rico...2,500.00+
Hawaii ....800.00+

Collector/dealer since 1965 of all **paper money and related items of the U.S. and Confederate States of America** wants to buy all state notes from the 1700s until the 1860s. Old bank checks and bonds are also wanted. Material we buy should be in nice condition; damaged or badly worn material has little value. Prices paid are subject to inspection. All materials sent are paid for within 48 hours or returned. We pay postage one way.

William J. Skelton
Highland Coin and Jewelry
P.O. Box 55448
Birmingham, AL 35255
205-939-3166, ext. 3

Miscellaneous & C.S.A. Items   **We Pay**

Bank Checks, pre-1900, w/Reserve stamps & vignettes, ea....................10¢-1.00
Macerated Money Items (made of old money ground up at the U.S. Treasury
   in Washington, DC, in early 1900s)..25.00-50.00
C.S.A. $500 Bill..50.00+
C.S.A. $100 Bill..10.00+
C.S.A. $50 Bill..10.00+
C.S.A. $20 Bill..5.00+
C.S.A. $10 Bill..5.00+

C.S.A. $5 Bill...**5.00+**
C.S.A. $2 Bill...**6.00+**
C.S.A. $1 Bill...**6.00+**
C.S.A. 50¢ Bill...**3.00+**

U.S. Currency, Large-Sized Type, Through 1923	**We Pay**
$1 Note	**10.00+**
$2 Note	**15.00+**
$5 Note	**10.00+**
$10 Note	**15.00+**
$20 Note	**25.00+**
$50 Note	**60.00+**
$100 Note	**120.00+**

We have over 20 years experience with **coins, paper money, and exonumia**. We are knowledgeable and reputable. Do not send your items until you speak with us. Send photocopies of your items, as this will help to determine condition. Condition is a prime factor in determining value. Whether it be Confederate, broken banks, fractional currency, large size, etc., we are interested. No foreign paper money from this century wanted.

Dempsey and Baxter
1009 E 38th St.
Erie, PA 16504

Paperweights

I am buying **figural advertising paperweights that are miniatures of what they advertise or are made out of the material that they advertise.** All paperweights must have the product name or manufacturer's name on them.

Don Friedman
660 W Grand, Apt. 4E
Chicago, IL 60610
312-226-4741

Paperweights

We Pay

Perry Superstile, NY (turnstile)..**100.00**
Ireland & Matthews Mfg. Co., Detroit (brass cuspidor) **35.00**
Coleman Lamp Co., Wichita, KS (Coleman lamp)...................................**60.00**
Lyon Bumper Metal Stamping Co., LI, NY (automobile bumper).............**75.00**
CT Ham Mfg. Co. (lantern)..**75.00**
Mueller (fire hydrant) **30.00**
Canada Cycle & Motor Co., Toronto (bicycles, skates or accessories) **75.00**
TA Cummings Foundry Co. (manhole cover)..**40.00**

———

I am interested in buying **antique glass paperweights**. I would like to buy the early type of weights that are round, domed, or mushroom shaped. Some of these weights may have facets cut on the surface. The subjects within the paperweights may be people, animals, fruit, butterflies, birds, flowers, or millefiori which are arrangements of slices of canes of glass which resemble tiny flowers. The weights I am interested in are often small, from 2" to 3½" in diameter. The base of the paperweight should be ground smooth or cut in a star pattern — no frosted bases please, also no advertising weights.

Please feel free to write with a description of your paperweight(s). Dimensions are helpful as are pictures and any history you may know. Condition is important; however, some scratches or small chips are inevitable on paperweights of this age. Please include your asking price with your correspondence.

Daria Canino
HC 73 Box 991
Locust Grove, VA 22508
703-972-1525

———

Collector desires antique (pre-1900s) glass paperweights: French, American, English, and Bohemian. Millefiori, flowers, and fruit designs are preferred. Also desire modern, artist-signed paperweights such as Stankard, Ysart, and Kaziun as well as modern Baccarat, St. Louis, and Perthshire limited edition paperweights. **Pre-1966 *Paperweight Collector Association (PCA) Bulletins* and other books desired**.

Private collector buying one paperweight or entire collections. On older paperweights, surface wear and minor chips to the base are not a problem. Please write or call first with description or photo together with your asking price.

Andrew Dohan
49 E Lancaster Ave.
Frazer, PA 19355
610-647-3310

We buy **antique French paperweights by Baccarat, Clichy, and St. Louis**. Prices depend on type and company. Also wanted are paperweights by U.S. maker **Charles Kaziun** (deceased). **We are paying from $200.00 to $3,000.00** depending on the individual paperweight.

Stanley A. Block
P.O. Box 51
Trumbull, CT 06611
203-261-0057

Pedal Cars

We are interested in buying any **pre-1967 pedal cars, boats, airplanes, etc.**, that are in clean to good, restorable condition. We will pick them up if within 100 miles or they can be shipped via UPS.

Other wants include **Van Briggle pottery, end-of-day glass, and carnival glass**.

David Smith
1142 S Spring St.
Springfield, IL 62704
217-523-3391

We Pay

Pedal Cars, Fire Engines, or Space Cruisers ....50.00-175.00+
Dump Trucks or Kidillacs ....50.00-175.00+
Pedal Boats or Airplanes ....50.00-175.00+

Pencil Sharpeners

I am looking for **pocket pencil sharpeners made of pot metal or Bakelite plastic**. I am especially seeking figural and comic character sharpeners. They can be marked U.S., Occupied Japan, Japan, German, or Bavaria. Paint and decals must be in good to mint condition.

Phil Helley
629 Indiana Ave.
Wisconsin Dells, WI 53965
608-254-8658

We Pay

Airplane, Bakelite	**29.00**
Armored Car, metal on rubber wheels, w/whistle, Japan	**60.00**
Charlie McCarthy, Bakelite	**36.00**
Cinderella, decal on Bakelite, round	**27.00**
Donald Duck, Bakelite	**40.00**
Dog, metal, German	**40.00**
Drummer Musician, metal, German	**30.00**
Indian Chief, metal, Occupied Japan	**45.00**
Magnifying Glass w/3 Kittens, metal, German	**55.00**
Mickey Mouse, Bakelite	**50.00**
New York World's Fair, Bakelite	**35.00**
Nude Boy w/Silver Cap, metal, German	**40.00**
Popeye, decal on Bakelite, rectangular	**32.00**
Scottie Dog, Bakelite	**16.00**
Tank, Keep 'Em Rolling, Bakelite	**30.00**

Pepsi-Cola

We buy **pre-1965 Pepsi-Cola advertising memorabilia** in excellent to mint condition. Areas of interest include calendars; tin, porcelain, cardboard, and paper signs; diecuts and window displays; festoons; light-up signs; playing cards; clocks; thermometers; trays; salesman's samples and miniatures; trucks and toys; etc. Our experience includes over ten years of collecting soda-pop memorabilia, editors for several antique and advertising price guides, and writers of a monthly column dedicated to soft drink collectibles.

As collectors we can offer top dollar for quality pieces and collections. Condition and rarity are important factors that must be taken into consideration when determining the value of an item. We are willing to travel to purchase items or pay for shipping and handling. Besides purchasing for our collection, we assist in determining the authenticity, age, and value of items at no charge. Please feel free to call us or write with your inquiries. A clear photograph is always helpful for a quick response.

Craig and Donna Stifter
P.O. Box 6514
Naperville, IL 60540
630-717-7949

We Pay

1941 Calendar, complete pad	**200.00+**
1951 Calendar, cardboard w/tear-off day pad	**400.00+**
1940 Sign, cardboard, self-framed, 24x34"	**250.00+**
1951 Sign, cardboard w/easel back, When Folks Drop In, 19x21"	**75.00+**
1948 Cut-Out Display, Girl in Window, cardboard, real curtains at window	**450.00+**
1945 Cut-Out Display, cardboard showing 4 fountain glasses, 12x18"	**200.00+**
1936 Sign, tin showing bottle, 11x49"	**300.00+**
1967 Sign, Say Pepsi Please, shows bottle & logo	**100.00+**
1950 Sign, More Bounce to the Ounce!, porcelain, 18x48"	**300.00+**
1950 Sign, Drink Pepsi-Cola Now!, celluloid, 9" dia	**100.00+**
1945 Sign, die-cut 3-dimensional tin crown, 31" dia	**175.00+**
1940 Glass Mirror Sign w/Thermometer, shows girl at bottom, 8x18"	**300.00+**
1954 Light-Up Sign, multi-purpose shadow box design, 19x9"	**200.00+**
1942 Thermometer, Bigger & Better, shows bottle, 16"	**175.00+**
1939 Serving Tray, Bigger & Better, Coast To Coast	**225.00+**
Toy Truck, friction powered, Japan, 9" long	**125.00+**
1945 Toy Hot Dog Wagon, plastic, 7x6"	**125.00+**
1955 Clock, Say Pepsi Please, neon light, 36" dia	**400.00+**
1961 Clock, Think Young—Say Pepsi Please!, double-bubble glass, 25" dia	**350.00+**
1940 Salesman Sample Cooler, 10x8"	**1,000.00+**
1940 Festoon, 7 pieces showing Pepsi & Pete	**900.00+**

Perfume Bottles

We purchase **perfume bottles of all types**: miniatures, Czechoslovakian crystal bottles, Baccarat, Lalique, DeVilbiss atomizers, and commerical perfume bottles. Commercial bottles are these that originally contained perfume when they were sold, such as Matchabelli Windsong in a small crown-shaped bottle. Commerical bottles should, if possible, have a label and the original box.

Monsen and Baer
Box 529
Vienna, VA 22183
703-938-2129 or 703-242-1357

Minatures   We Pay

Czechoslovakian, crystal, 2"...25.00+
Dior, Schiaparelli, Guerlain, or Coty.................................5.00+
Ceramic, metal crown top..40.00+

Atomizers   We Pay

DeVilbiss, 6"..100.00+
Volupte, 5"...75.00+
Lalique...300.00+

Lalique   We Pay

Apple for Ricci..100.00+
D'Orsay, black glass, Ambre d'Orsay....................................500.00+
Molinard Calendal Nudes..500.00+
Roger & Gallet Le Jade, green glass...................................1,500.00+

Commercial   We Pay

Vigny Le Golliwog..100.00+
Hattie Carnegie, bust of woman..100.00+
Ciro Chevalier, knight, black glass, in box...........................150.00+
Schiaparelli, Zut, woman's torso, in box..............................600.00+
Schiaparelli, Success, Fou, green leaf, in box.......................800.00+
Lucretia, Vanderbilt, blue glass, in box................................750.00+

Baccarat   We Pay

Elizabeth Arden, It's You, hand...800.00+
Houbigant, Buddha, in box..200.00+
Ybry, green square..200.00+
Ybry, purple or orange square...500.00+
Christian Dior, Diorissimo, in box......................................2,000.00+
Christian Dior, dog...5,000.00+

Peter Max Collectibles

I began collecting Peter Max **books and other illustrated items** in the mid-1960s. My collection has grown along with my respect and admiration for this wonderful artist. I buy clocks, dishes, books, prints, games, puzzles, clothing, jewelry, pillows, curtains, fabric pieces, magazines, toys — you name it! As with any collectible, condition is the most important consideration when figuring out a price. These amounts are only estimates.

Linda Cervon
10074 Ashland St.
San Buenaventura, CA 93004
805-659-4405 or fax 805-659-4776

We Pay

Dishes	10.00+
Clocks	15.00+
Clothing	10.00+
Magazine Art	2.00+
Toys, Puzzles, Games, Books	5.00+

Pharmacy Antiques

I buy **all types of pharmacy antiques** that would have been found in pharmacies and drug stores prior to the 1940s. I will buy anything and everything from one piece to an entire drug store. Some items I am looking for and the price I will pay are listed here.

Andrew E. Thomas
4681 N 84th Way
Scottsdale, AZ 85251-1864
602-947-5693 or fax 602-994-4382

We Pay

Patent Medicines	5.00-25.00

Show Globes	100.00-2,500.00
Drug Jars	10.00-100.00
Medicine Chests	25.00-250.00
Cabinets	100.00-1,000.00
Signs	10.00-500.00
Soda Fountain Items	10.00-750.00
Label Cabinets	100.00-500.00
Prescriptions	1.00-10.00
Prescription Files	10.00-50.00

Photographica

I am buying **Civil War original images** in the following formats: CDV's (carte de viste), tintypes (in or out of cases), ambrotypes, daguerrotypes, and the hard (gutta-percha) cases. Also wanted are **original Civil War papers, dug artifacts, guns, accoutrements, and autographs of notable Civil War generals** from the North and South. The price I pay depends on condition of the item, content of the image, and if the image is identified, etc. The better the condition and especially if it is identified to a soldier, the more I pay.

Shades of Blue & Gray
Dan Furtak
3543 S Ferguson
Springfield, MO 65807
417-887-0009
e-mail: DugSpring@juno.com

Images   **We Pay**

CDV's	up to 5,000.00
Tintypes	up to 5,000.00
Ambrotypes	up to 5,000.00
Daguerrotypes	up to 3,500.00
Albumins	up to 75.00+
Autographs	50.00-7,000.00

We purchase **all types of photo-related items**. We are in the market for cameras, lenses, tripods, toys, figurines — anything that relates to photography. Prices will vary due to the condition and working order of the items. Describe make, model, condition, and/or give a brief description. Also wanted are **items relating to Kodak, AGFA, Konica, Nikon, Canon, and Hasselblad. Items wanted include:**

Advertising Items
Ashtrays
Belt Buckles
Cameras (all kinds)
Candy & Gum
Cigarette Lighters
Clocks
Coasters
Compacts and Vanities
Containers
Dart or Pellet Shooters
Dishes or Tableware
Jewelry
Key Chains
Lights

Lenses
Masks
Music Boxes
Ornamental Items
Pencil Sharpeners
Photographs
Planters
Puzzles
Radios
Salt & Pepper Shakers
Stationery Items
Statues & Figurines
Soap
Vehicles
Viewing Devices

Harry E. Forsythe
3457 R.R. 40
Jacksonville, FL 32223

Pie Birds

I am interested in buying **old pie birds and old pie funnels** for my private collection. I answer all letters and phone calls and will pay postal charges. Depending on rarity, age, and condition, **prices can range from $25.00 to $100.00.** A few wants are listed here.

Wants include:
Fruit funnels: cherries, peach, apple (Japan, Our Own Imports sticker, possibly)
Bluebirds on nest pie vent
Castle-shaped pie funnel, white, from Scotland
Funnel marked 'The Gourmet Crust Holder and Vent Challis'
Funnel marked 'Delphine Crown China, England'
English funnels with advertising

Glass pie funnels, e.g., Phoenix Heat Resisting Glass
Rowland's Hygienic Patent Pie Funnel

Lillian Cole
14 Harmony School Rd.
Flemington, NJ 08822-2606
908-782-3198

I am an advanced pie bird collector buying **old pie birds**. I prefer old U.S.-made pie birds, but will buy English imports. Besides the ones listed below, I will consider other pie birds, as I belong to a Collector's Circle and have the want lists of many. The price paid depends on the rarity and condition and is negotiable. Entire collections will be considered. If the names are not recognizable, send a picture.

Linda Fields
158 Bagsby Hill Ln.
Dover, TN 37058
615-232-5099 (after 6 pm)

We Pay

Bluebird on a Nest	**150.00+**
Camark Cobbler Bird, any color	**100.00+**
Miniature T.G. Green Blackbird, 2¼"	**50.00+**
Donald Duck	**300.00+**
Josef Owl, white bow w/blue dots on head	**75.00+**
Josef Chick, pink	**75.00+**
Benny the Baker	**50.00+**
Rooster, decal on tail, marked MB	**40.00+**
Alaskan Puffin	**30.00+**
Duck, sm long neck, solid color	**40.00+**
Pearl China (S-Neck) Rooster, cream w/gold	**75.00+**
Pearl China (S-Neck) Rooster, black base	**75.00+**
Puffed Chest Canary, any color	**40.00+**
Shawnee (or Morton) Rooster, pink & blue or pink & green	**100.00+**
Barn Pottery Blackbird, 2-headed, yellow	**50.00+**
Clear Glass Rooster, Scotland, orange comb & waddle	**50.00+**
Clemenson Rooster, brown	**50.00+**
Brown & Orange Hen, marked White Dove	**40.00+**

Political

Political buttons of all kinds, new and old, are collectible, but the most desirable are the celluloid-coated pinbacks (cellos) produced between the 1890s and the 1920s. Many of these are attractively and colorfully designed, which enhances their value. Most buttons since then have been produced by lithography directly on metal discs (lithos).

Collectors generally favor presidential buttons — especially picture pins from 1960 or earlier. Jugates featuring presidential and vice-presidential candidates' photos are especially desirable; for example, James Cox-Franklin D. Roosevelt jugates from the 1920 campaign sell for up to $50,000.00! There are, however, numerous other specialties within the hobby, including state and local, third party, and 'cause' items.

Value depends on scarcity, historical significance, design, collector demand, and condition — buttons with cracks, gouges, deep scratches, and/or rust-colored stains (foxing) are not desirable. Reproductions exist, and many are marked as such, but some expertise is often needed to distinguish real from fake.

I will purchase quality items in any of the categories listed below if they are in nice condition. Send me a photocopy of whatever you have. If you wish, state your price; if not, I will make an offer. If I do not want to buy, I will give an informal appraisal. I will respond promptly to any all correspondence (include a reply postcard, please). The prices below are for picture pins only.

Michael Engel
29 Groveland St.
Easthampton, MA 01027
413-527-8733

Presidentials, 1896-1960 .... We Pay

McKinley, Bryan, T. Roosevelt, Taft, Wilson, sm picture buttons	5.00+
McKinley, Bryan, T. Roosevelt, Taft, Wilson, lg picture/jugate	15.00-20.00+
Parker, Hughes, sm picture buttons	5.00-15.00+
Parker, Hughes, lg picture buttons	100.00+
Parker, Hughes, jugates	100.00-500.00+
Harding, Coolidge, sm picture buttons	5.00-15.00+
Harding, Coolidge, lg picture buttons	100.00+
Harding, Coolidge, jugates	100.00-500.00+
Cox, picture buttons	100.00-200.00+
Cox, jugates	20,000.00-50,000
Davis, picture buttons	100.00-500.00+
Davis, jugates	1,000.00+
Hoover, Smith, picture buttons	5.00-20.00+

Hoover, Smith, jugates...100.00+
F.D.R, Landon, Willkie, picture buttons..5.00-15.00+
F.D.R, Landon, Willkie, jugates...15.00+
Truman, picture buttons...15.00+
Truman, jugates ....100.00+
Stevenson, Eisenhower, J.F.K...2.00-5.00+

Other Categories   We Pay

Third Party Candidates, pre-1960...10.00+
State & Local, pre-1920 ....up to 10.00
Woman's Suffrage..25.00+
Civil Rights/Vietnam..up to 10.00
Eugene V. Debs..75.00+

I am a collector and dealer in **political campaign collectibles of all types but in particular political campaign buttons/pins from all eras**. I will buy single pieces or entire collections. Please send photocopy of the item or (if too large to photocopy) a word description and the price you want for the item. I buy collections nation wide and offer top prices. While political buttons are my specialty, I'm also interested in political flags, banners, 3-D items, dolls, brochures, and other similar items.

Ronald E. Wade
2100 Lafayette Dr.
Longview, TX 75601
903-236-9615 (7-10 pm & weekends)

We Pay

Button, John Kennedy, Jack Once More in '64, 3½"................................**150.00**
Button, John Kennedy, Kennedy Election Night Staff, 3½"......................**300.00**
Button, William McKinley, Do You Smoke/That's What McKinley Promised, w/drawing of factory, 2"...**750.00**
Button, William Jennings Bryan, shows Bryan w/ear of corn..................**500.00**
Button, Theodore Roosevelt, w/drawing of him in Rough Rider uniform & For Vice President...**500.00**
Button, Me & Roosevelt for Lyndon Johnson..**1,000.00**
Button, Support the Collidge Administration w/Coolidge photo.............**450.00**
Button, John W. Davis & Vice President Candidate Bryan photo........**1,000.00+**
Button, Teapot Dome Scandal, 1920s ....**100.00+**
Buttons, Posters, Brochures, Postcards for Socialist Party Candidate for President, Eugene V. Debs...**100.00+**

Political

Button, Landon-Knox Out Roosevelt, photo...**500.00+**
Button, Harry Truman & Alben Barkley, photo.....................................**100.00+**
Button, Harry Truman & Alben Barkley, word..**15.00+**
Button, Lyndon Johnson, Civil Rights...**350.00**
Campaign Banner or Flag, Abraham Lincoln, w/name or photo.........**1,500.00+**
Whiskey Bottles w/Presidential Candidates' Photos..............................**100.00+**

Postcards

We purchase **postcards of all ages and types, good-plus condition only**. Complete collections, accumulations, single cards, old store stock, inventories — all are acceptable. Foreign, chromes, real photos, topicals, greetings, state views are purchased as well as top-of-the-line signed artists, poster art, Art Nouveau, Santa, and especially Halloween. Call us!

Chris Russell & The Halloween Queen Antiques
Pamela E. Apkarian-Russell, The Halloween Queen
P.O. Box 499
Winchester, N.H. 03470
603-239-8875

We Pay

Art Nouveau Cards by Alphonse Mucha **25.00-100.00**
Cards Depicting the Armenian Holocaust ....**20.00+**
Italian Artist-Signed Cards ....**5.00+**
Linen Cards of Black People..**1.00+**
Silk-Suited Santa Cards **15.00**
Winch Publishing Halloween Cards **35.00**
Real Photo Cards of USA Main Streets (depending on town).............**2.00-10.00**
Real Photo Cards of Black People ....**5.00+**
Real Photo Cards of Movie Actresses or Actors (Shirley Temple, Marilyn Monroe, Josephine Baker, Louis Armstrong, etc.)....................................**5.00-40.00**
Views of Tourist Sights (mountains, lakes, monuments or cathedrals), per thousand **5.00**
Views of Lg Cities (London, Paris, New York, Boston, etc.), per thousand ...**5.00**

I am buying **pre-1960 postcards from all southwestern states, particularly New Mexico**. I buy from five to five thousand and pay as follows depending on condition. Samples are welcome! No scenery wanted.

Fran Ryan
6504 San Blas Pl. NW
Albuquerque, NM 87120
505-839-4436

We Pay

1900-1920, ea	75¢-1.00
1920-1940, ea	50¢-75¢
1940-1960, ea	25¢-50¢

I collect **real photos on postcards (pre-1930) of small towns in Iowa, Nebraska, and Minnesota.**

Harold W. Ruth
332 R. Ave.
Paton, IA 50217
515-968-4544 or 712-336-3335 or 712-336-5500

We Pay

Street Scenes	8.00+
Business Interior Views	10.00+
Arnold's Port, Lake Okiboji, Spirit Lake	2.00-12.00

Wanted: **Prairie Du Chien, Wisconsin postcards from before 1950.** I pay $1.00 plus postage and insurance.

Checks Antiques
Janice Check
115 S Dousman St.
Prairie Du Chien, WI 53821
608-326-6014

I am a postcard buyer specializing in **Iowa postcards**. I pay top dollar for most Iowa cards. Towns and cities I'm most interested in include: Burlington, Mediapolis, Kingston, Huron, Sperry, Latty Dodgeville, Roscoe, Newport, Northfield, Linton, and Garland, Iowa. Please send me your list or call during business hours (CST). I will answer your inquiry.

Don Nelson
P.O. Box 426
Mediapolis, IA 52637
319-394-9143 (days) or fax 319-394-3045

I buy whole collections of old postcards — shoe boxes, postcard albums, and even full shipping crates. The more you have and the older they are, the better — 1940s and older U.S. cards preferred. Send me what you have in any quantity and I'll send you payment, including reimbursement for your UPS postage/insurance costs. If you are not completely satisfied, which is very rare, just return the payment within 7 days and I'll return the cards at my own expense and still reimburse for your postage! Fair value, prompt payment, convenient, and cost-free! References available.

Michael Johnson, The Postcard Guy
2040 Great Highway
San Francisco, CA 94116-1054
(415) 436-0203

Pottery

I am interested in buying most **Abingdon** pieces. Condition is important. I buy one item or a collection. I would appreciate pictures and mold numbers if possible.

Virginia Cramble
7340 Memory Ln.
Fridley, MN 55432
612-788-8162 (11 am to 5 pm) or 612-786-7303 (other times)

I am interested in pieces of **California pottery and Frankoma pottery**. California pieces can be from any company that was operating in the 1930s through the 1950s. Frankoma pieces need to be sculptures, miniatures, animals, hard-to-find glazes, and unusual advertising items.

I am also interested in any *Crockery and Glass Journal* from the 1930s through the 1950s that has advertisements or articles about glass and pottery companies. These do not have to be mint condition. **City directories from the same era** are needed.

Susan N. Cox
237 E Main St.
El Cajon, CA 92020
fax 619-447-0185

We Pay

Brayton Provencial Woman Cookie Jar	195.00
Brayton, Children's Series, boys or girls	80.00
Heidi Schoop Lamp, Tragedy & Comedy combination	195.00
Frankoma Buffalo, any glaze, old	300.00
Frankoma Sign, 1st edition, any glaze	450.00
Frankoma Medicine Man, older version, any glaze	175.00

I am interested in buying **old Fiesta for resale**. All pieces must be in mint condition — free of all chips, cracks, nicks, or other damage. Please send a list of pieces that you have for sale and your asking price. **Other dinnerware wanted for resale** includes:

Riviera
Harlequin
Coors Rosebud
Franciscan Starburst
Franciscan Apple (USA)
Franciscan Desert Rose (USA)
Franciscan Ivy
Other Hand-Painted Franciscan
LuRay
Bauer Ringware
Mexicana by HLC
Metlox California Provincial (Rooster)
Metlox California Freeform/Mobile & Contempra
Liberty Blue by Staffordshire
Vernon Kilns (no plaids)
Large Hand-Painted Picard Items (not dinnerware)

Neat Stuff
Carolyn Brooks
7808 Scotia Dr.
Dallas, TX 75248-3115
972-404-1951 or fax 972-404-1870

I buy **Fiesta in original colors** (dark green, yellow, dark blue, chartreuse, ivory, and red) with HLC ink stamp. I will pay more for unscratched, only slightly-used Fiesta pieces.

Clara Louthan
HC 64 Box 58
Coldwater, KS 67029
316-582-2850

Fiesta in Original Colors	We Pay
Nappy, 9½"	9.00
Nappy, 8½"	8.00
Tom & Jerry Mug	10.00
Cream Soup, w/handle	10.00
Soup Bowl	10.00
Salad Bowl	10.00
Fruit Bowl, 5½ or 4¾", ea	8.00-9.00
Dessert Bowl, 6"	8.00
Coffeepot	50.00
Tumbler, 5-oz	10.00
Plate, deep, 8¾"	10.00
Plate, 6" or 7", ea	2.00
Plate, 9"	3.00
Plate, 10"	12.00
Plate, compartment	12.00
Platter	20.00
Cake Plate	50.00
Chop Plate	8.00
Sauce Boat	8.00
Salt & Pepper Shakers, pr	6.00
Vase, 12"	50.00

I am buying **odd Fiesta Pieces** (lids, missing pieces, etc.) in order to supply a matching service. I pay 10% of current book price of entire item or each separate piece plus shipping. No items wanted with chips, cracks or repairs, please.

Kenneth D. Heston
P.O. Box 244
Marion, IA 52302
319-373-5065

I am interested in the **Weller Muskota line**. I buy good to mint condition flower frogs with no chips, hairlines, breaks, etc. I am particularly interested in the children and animals (no geese or fisher boys). I will pay UPS actual charges including any additional necessary insurance. Listed below is only a sampling of items I would like.

Robert L. Cox
237 E Main St.
El Cajon, CA 92020
fax 619-447-0185

We Pay

Muskota Dogs (2), on single base, 7½"	**700.00**
Girl on Stump (no doll), 8½"	**300.00**
2 Boys, 1 kneeling, 1 standing w/towel, 7"	**400.00**
Boy, standing w/towel, 6"	**300.00**
Kneeling Nude (no base), 3"	**200.00**
Girl, w/watering can, 7"	**250.00**

We are buying **pottery and china from the following list for resale**. Please send pictures and description of items, including any marks and your asking price. All pieces **must be in mint condition** — free of all nicks, chips, cracks, bruises, glaze crazing, or any other damage.

Blue Willow	Hull
Currier & Ives	Liberty Blue
Fiesta	LuRay
Franciscan	McCoy
Friar Tuck Monks	Memory Lane
Hall	Roseville

The Glass Packrat
Pat and Bill Ogden
3050 Colorado Ave.
Grand Junction, CO 81504

We live in a small rural town in southwest North Dakota and are interested in buying pottery made in North Dakota before 1965. Items may be marked **Dickota, Messer, Rosemeade, WPA (Ceramics Project, Works Project Administration), or UND (University of North Dakota, School of Mines)** and have paper stickers, incised, or ink-stamped marks. We also buy **Roseville, Shawnee, Red Wing, McCoy, Yellow Ware, and other pottery and stoneware**.

Items wanted include shaker sets, figurines, sugar/creamer sets, vases, knickknacks, flowerpots, and miscellaneous pieces. Items must have no chips or cracks. Send a photo of your item or collection, if possible, along with a good description and your asking price.

Stan and Carrie Soderstrom
15 First St. SW
Rt. 2, Box 300
Bowman, ND 58623

We Pay

Most Items, ea **20.00-100.00**

I am a collector of **Rumrill and Red Wing art pottery**. I am interested in purchasing one piece or entire collections. Of particular interest to me are nudes, animal planters, and Nokomis pieces for which I will pay top dollar. Pieces do not have to be in perfect condition. As founder of the RumRill Society, I am also interested in obtaining printed advertisements, catalogs, and correspondence with the Rumrill name. Call toll free or write.

Grancesca Gern
P.O. Box 2161
Hudson, OH 44236
1-888-RUMRILL (786-7455)

Wanted: **Red Poppy dinnerware made by Universal Potteries** of Cambridge, Ohio, and sold for years by Sears Roebuck & Company. The pattern has reddish-orange poppies (usually two poppies but sometimes only one) along with several other wild flowers. Pieces are trimmed with either a band of red or 22K gold.

We are just beginning our collection of Red Poppy and are looking for cups, saucers, plates, serving pieces, casseroles, etc. We buy only pieces in good condition. We don't buy chipped, cracked, or crazed pieces. We will reimburse actual shipping and insurance charges.

Ken and Barbara Brooks
4121 Gladstone Ln.
Charlotte, NC 28205
704-568-5716

Author of *Watt Pottery, an Identification and Value Guide,* published by Collector Books, I am a collector and dealer seeking **all Watt pottery pieces** decorated with hand-painted patterns. I pay top prices including your shipping expense and would be willing to work with you whether you are selling one piece or an entire collection. Either call or send a list and/or photos — I need to know the pattern, or description thereof; the mold number, if any, on the bottom of the piece; and the condition, including any chips, cracks, or discoloration.

Susan Morris
3388 Merlin Rd. Ste. #351
Grants Pass, OR 97526
541-955-8411
e-mail: smorris@cds.net

We are wanting to buy **Roseville, Shawnee, Watt, and Weller** pottery. We buy only pieces in excellent shape — no cracked, chipped, or factory-defective pieces wanted. **Items wanted include:**

Bowls
Candlesticks
Cookie Jars
Creamers
Figurals (birds, butterflies, animals)
Lamps
Jardinieres
Pitchers

Planters
Plates
Salt & Pepper Shakers
Sugar Bowls
Teapots
Vases
Wall Pockets

David W. Mayer
33 Mt. Vernon Pl.
Jamestown, NY 14701
716-487-1874

Precious Moments

Enesco's Precious Moments collectibles are becoming increasingly popular with collectors. Enesco first began production about 1978 of these figurines, bells, dolls, plates, and ornaments featuring children in various activities in soft pastel colors.

I am interesting in finding **figurines and dolls (no vinyl ones wanted)** to add to my collection. Especially wanted are original pieces, retired items, membership club pieces, and those with musical mechanisms. Figurines must be in mint condition with no chips, cracks, or repairs, with original box and papers. Please send a photo for identification, if possible, and describe marks on the base. Include your SASE for my reply. Listed below is only a very small sampling of figurines available. Please tell me about your items.

Patty Durnell
703 Tilton Rd.
Danville, IL 61832
217-443-4201

We Pay

Angel & Girl at Heaven's Gate, 'No Tears Past the Gate,' 1986 .... **15.00**
Baby Boy, w/dog & stocking, 'The Greatest Gift Is a Friend,' 1986............. **12.50**
Boy Banjo Player, 'Happiness Is the Lord,' 1984 .... **12.50**
Clown on Ball, 'Lord Keep Me on the Ball,' 1985 .... **12.50**

Commemorative Edition 5th Anniversary, 'God Bless Our Years Together,' 1984...**20.00**

Clown, w/dog & hoop, 'The Lord Will Carry You Through,' 1985............**15.00**

Premiums

I am interested in purchasing early items offered through **radio programs from the late 1920s to the 1950s. I am very interested in Superman, Green Hornet, Buck Rogers, Radio Orphan Annie, Tom Mix, and Space Patrol.** Major interests are giveaway ring premiums. Samples of prices paid are listed below. Please also see my listings in this book under **Cracker Jack and Pencil Sharpeners**.

Old Kilbourn Antiques
Phil Helley
629 Indiana Ave.
Wisconsin Dells, WI 53965
608-254-8659

Radio Premiums	**We Pay**
Babe Ruth Watch Fob	**50.00**
Buck Rogers Solar Scout Knife	**200.00**
Buck Rogers Solar Scout Uniform	**250.00**
Capt. Marvel Decoder, paper	**150.00**
Capt. Marvel Statuette	**500.00**
Capt. Video Saucer Ring	**150.00**
Green Hornet Secret Compartment Seal Ring	**300.00**
Jack Armstrong Lieutenant Whistle Badge	**170.00**
Operator #5 Skull Ring	**500.00**
Sgt. Preston Camp Stove & Tent	**450.00**
Space Patrol Cosmic Smoke Gun	**150.00**
Space Patrol Ring, plastic	**200.00**
Spider Ring	**750.00**
Superman Secret Compartment Ring	**600.00**

Premiums

I am buying **plastic cereal premiums and paper Funny Face items**. I'm also interested in **any character-related cereal boxes from the 1950s to 1970s**. The prices below are for mint-condition items.

Jim Rash
135 Alder Ave.
Egg Harbor Twp., NJ 08234-9302
609-485-7644 (answering machine)
609-646-4125 (nights, call collect)

Canadian Premiums
We Pay

Cap'n Crunch Nodders, plastic w/metal spring, ea	75.00
Hanna-Barbara Figures, green or orange plastic, 1", ea	50.00
Tigger Bowl Hanger	75.00
Wheelies (Aristocats, Fox & Hound, Etc.), ea	40.00

Freakies Premiums
We Pay

Cereal Bowl	75.00
Flip 'N Flies, ea	30.00
Goody-Goody Figure w/Fruit Basket	250.00
Goody-Goody Figure, rubber	30.00
Hamhose Figure, orange rubber	30.00
Hamhose Medallion	250.00

Funny Face Premiums
We Pay

Opened or Unopened Packs	Call
Goofy Grape 2-Handled Cups	100.00
Iron-Ons, 9x7", ea	20.00
Rare Pillows, Store Displays, Drink Stands	500.00+

Miscellaneous Premiums
We Pay

Cornelius Sugarcoat Walker	300.00
Moonstone Magnets, Tuneymoon or Bigbum, ea	40.00
M.C. Bicycle Spinner, Frankenberry or Chocula, ea	100.00
Monster Cereal Rings, ea	75.00
Quisp Magnaviewer	125.00
Quisp/Quangaroo 2-in-1 Cereal Bowl	300.00
Trix Rabbitt Cereal Bowl	50.00
Vulture Squadron Plane, Dastardly	100.00

I buy **cereal premiums from the '50s through the '70s**. Character items such as Quisp, Quake, and Yogi Bear are especially valued. Condition is important. Items must be complete and, if mechanical, in working order. Near-mint to mint condition items are preferred. Listed here are only examples of my wants. Please also see my listing under **Cereal Boxes** in this book.

Scott Bruce
10 Notre Dame Ave.
Cambridge, MA 02140
617-492-5004
e-mail: scott@flake.com

Cereal Premiums   **We Pay**

Cornelius C. Sugarcoat Walking Toy, 1958	**150.00-200.00**
Beverly Hillbillies' Elly May Doll, 1964	**50.00-75.00**
Gary Lewis' *Doin' the Flake* Record, 1964	**25.00-30.00**
Trix Rabbit Mug, Placemat & Bowl, 1964	**35.00-50.00**
Lovable Truly, inflatable, 1964	**75.00-100.00**
Tony the Tiger Cookie Jar (head), 1965	**50.00-75.00**
Quisp Propeller Beanie, 1966	**300.00-400.00**
Quake Cavern Helmet, 1966	**300.00-400.00**
Dr. Dolittle Medical Bag, 1967	**35.00-50.00**
Apple Jack Mug & Bowl, 1967	**35.00-50.00**
Yellow Submarine Rub-On Sheets, 1969	**25.00-30.00**
Quisp Bank, ceramic, 1971	**600.00-750.00**
Monster Cereal Squeeze Toys, 1980	**35.00-50.00**

Prayer Ladies

Prayer Ladies are china figurines made by Enesco. They have reddish-brown hair, a high-necked dress of pink, blue, or white with blue trim and a prayer on their apron. We **do not** buy napkin holders, salt and pepper shakers, or toothpick holders. We do buy other Enesco lines such as **Snappy the Snail and Kitchen Independence**. Please include large SASE with all correspondence. Prices listed are for pink ladies only.

April and Larry Tvorak
HCR #34 Box 25B
Warren Center, PA 18851
or
P.O. Box 126
Canon City, CO 81215

Kitchen Prayer Ladies, Pink   We Pay

Cookie Jar 125.00
Clothes Sprinkler 150.00
Bank...85.00
Crumb Sweeper...100.00
Planter 30.00
Bell..35.00

Prints

I am an avid **Maxfield Parrish** collector interested in prints, books, magazines, ads, and calendars. Please send a detailed description and a photo of your Parrish items along with your asking price. I will respond immediately to all offers.

Lisa Stroup
P.O. Box 3009
Paducah, KY 42002-3009

I am a private collector interested in purchasing **framed prints, posters, and photographs**. Below is just a partial listing of items I am looking for. Please write or call with your information. I pay top dollar, and guarantee a fast response to your correspondence. I also pay finders' fees for assistance in locating these items.

John S. Zuk
106 Orchard St.
Belmont, MA 02178
617-484-4800 (home) or 617-349-0652 (office)

We Pay

Maxfield Parrish, prints..100.00+
Maxfield Parrish, Edison Mazda calendars ....100.00+
Maxfield Parrish, magazine covers (Scribners, Life, etc.) ....25.00+
Stieglitz, black & white photos..100.00+
Ansel Adams, black & white photos ....100.00+
Man Ray, black & white photos..100.00+
Jules Cheret, posters..100.00+
Rene Penea, posters ....100.00+
Cassandre, posters..100.00+
Capiello, posters..100.00+

———————

We want to buy **prints and trade cards by N. Currier, Currier & Ives, C. Currier, Kurz & Allison, and McKenney-Hall**. No reproductions are wanted. Also **books relating to these publishers**. Fair prices paid promptly.

Rudisill's Alt Print Haus
John and Barbara Rudisill
P.O. Box 199
Worton, MD 21678
410-778-9290

———————

Yard-long prints are lithographs. The ones we collect show **lovely ladies dressed in fashions of the early 1900s to the late 1920s**. Although called yard longs, few actually were exactly a yard long, and some have been trimmed to fit into smaller frames. Various yard longs range in width from 6" to 11" with lengths of around 27" to 37". Some have the artist's name on the front, and most have advertising and a small calendar on the back. A few of the companies whose advertising appears on the reverse of yard longs are Pompeian Beauty Products, Diamond Crystal Salt, Pabst Extract, Walk-Over Shoes, and Selz Shoes.

We collect only prints that are in excellent condition (meaning no highly visible creases, tears, or water stains). The colors must be bright and crisp, not noticeably faded. We prefer untrimmed, original-length prints with the original frame and glass.

The following are examples of specific yard longs we would like to find for our collection. There are many others not listed that we would also like to have.

Also wanted are **German die-cut and embossed calendar tops showing pretty ladies, and Art Deco picture frames** made of glass with reverse-painted geometric designs and metal corners that range in size up to 12x14". (An illustrated flyer is available on request.) See also **Boxes, Compacts, and Purses** in this book.

Mike and Sherry Miller
303 Holiday Dr.
Tuscola, IL 61953
217-253-4991

Yard-Long Prints   **We Pay**

1913 Pabst, signed Stuart Travis **100.00-150.00**
1914 Pabst, signed Alfred Everitt Orr **110.00-165.00**
1918 Selz, unsigned...**175.00-200.00**
1925 Selz, unsigned...**175.00-200.00**
1929 Pompeian, signed Bradshaw Krandall...............................**100.00-135.00**

———

I collect **prints and lithographs of children (particularly girls) by any artist prior to 1950 as well as Bessie Pease Gutmann prints**. The price I will pay depends on subject, condition, and artist.

Eunice Gentry
1126 Prairie Ave.
Cleburne, TX 76031
817-556-3746 or fax 817-556-9929

———

Purses

I buy a **variety of antique purses** from the 1920s and earlier. I especially want enameled mesh with bright colors, strong designs, and scenes. If there are rips in the mesh, I will still buy them. Beaded purses are another type I especially love. Damaged beaded purses are okay too. Small holes, ripped or missing fringe, or torn away from the frame or no frame at all is okay. I want multicolored abstract patterns or scenes of people, places, or any interesting motifs with as much detail as possible. I like big purses with tiny beads. I also buy the purse frames by themselves with some jewels or other fancy types. I love early purses too — Civil War era or before. I look for any type of unique or fabulous purse. Prices will vary depending on the condition and the motif of the purse. I also belong to a local purse club and would be happy to sell for you at my meetings.

Leslie Holmes
P.O. Box 596
Los Gatos, CA 95031
408-354-1626

We Pay

Beaded, multicolor	**375.00+**
Beaded, very early	**200.00+**
Damaged, depending on motif	**275.00+**
Damaged Mesh	**100.00+**
Enameled Mesh	**275.00+**
Purse Frames	**50.00+**
Brass Purses	**175.00+**
Tapestry	**150.00+**
Unusual Purses	**225.00+**

I am looking for **beaded bags that have scenes** — especially End of the Trail or Queen Mary. Also wanted are mesh bags in good condition. I prefer very old items. Other wants include: **compacts, eye cups, sewing items, stanhopes, typewriter tins, figural Victorian clocks (ladies, angels, and Deco girls).**

Kayla Conway
4500 Napal Ct.
Bakersfield, CA 93307
805-833-0291

Purses   **We Pay**

Beaded, w/scenes	**50.00+**
Bags w/Compacts	**50.00+**
Mesh	**35.00+**
Sterling	**150.00+**
14K Gold	**800.00+**

Other Wants   **We Pay**

Clarice Cliff	**Call or Write**
Sewing Items	**Call or Write**
Stanhopes	**Call or Write**
Sterling Silver	**Call or Write**

I am a leading buyer of **vintage beaded and mesh bags, handbag frames, needlework purses, and compacts** of the Victorian era through the 1940s. I especially like unusual and fancy purses with elaborate designs and pay good prices for them.

Enameled mesh bags should have either a bright floral design, birds, scenes, or celebrity faces. The design could be simple with jewels in the frame or the body of the bag. I also buy novelty designs such as those with a compact incorporated into the frame or the body of the bag. I buy purses with Mickey Mouse or The Three Little Pigs dangling from the frame. Beaded bags should have tiny glass beads with scenes of people, houses, castles, animals, mountains, rug motifs, or unusual subjects. Bags with fancy glass jeweled or enameled frames are wanted. I also purchase bags with watches imbedded in the frames or the body of the bag and metal or early plastic dance purses that may have glass jewels or tassels. I need vintage purse frames with holes for sewing that are not silver, with fancy enameling, glass jewels, or a pretty pattern.

I buy one item or a collection. If you think your bag is exquisite or one of a kind, I will probably be interested in buying it. For a good visual reference, consult my book, *The Best of Vintage Purses,* by Schiffer Publishing of Pennsylvania. I would buy any bag similar to those pictured in this book. Send photocopies or pictures with SASE and the price you are asking if possible. I also buy **glass beads, costume jewelry, compacts, ladies' accessories, vintage purse advertisements, and related trade catalogs.**

The Curiosity Shop
Lynel Schwartz
P.O. Box 964
Cheshire, CT 06410
203-271-0643

                                                                  We Pay

Vintage Purse Frame	**35.00+**
Mesh Bag, w/celebrity face	**250.00+**
Mesh Bag, w/scene	**100.00+**
Mesh Bag, w/compact	**125.00+**

Mesh Bag, w/glass jewels ....**100.00+**
Mesh or Beaded Bag, w/Disney character or World's Fair theme, ea.....**100.00+**
Bag w/Watch (as part of the bag)..**100.00+**
Dance Purse..**140.00+**

Do you have a gorgeous antique purse to sell? Does it have jewels, people, castles, gardens, flowers, roses, birds, cherubs on it? Perhaps it has a Persian rug design or Egyptian motif? Is it beaded, needlework, petit point, embroidered, painted mesh, or made of tapestry? Does it have a carrying chain or beaded strap? Is it in mint or excellent condition? If so, I'll buy it!

I also buy pretty jeweled 1920s vanity bags. These small, very fancy brass filigree purses are encrusted with beautiful colored jewels or pearls, and often contain a compact or lipstick. They have jeweled metal tassels and metal carrying chains or silk cords, and may be marked Trinity Plate inside.

If you have any old, tiny beaded, jeweled, or ornate purse frames with sewing holes or damaged purses (pieces okay too), I would be happy to have them for repair work.

Attention pickers! Let me know where you see a fabulous purse or item (call or write w/location, address, or phone), and if I buy it, I'll send you a cash thank you.

I'm interested too in **extraordinary antique lace clothing, gowns from Victorian era through 1920s, jeweled perfume bottles, jeweled dresser boxes, jeweled lamps, sultry boudoir dolls, and elaborate vanity items for ladies**.

Purses should date from the 1930s or earlier. Please send a photo or photocopy of items you wish to sell. Please state asking price!

Victorian Touch
Valerie Roberts
P.O. Box 4
Micanopy, FL 32667
352-466-4022

We Pay

Jeweled Brass Vanity Bag, jeweled tassel & metal chain, interior silk pockets **175.00**
Needlepoint w/Figures, ornate jeweled frame & clasp, chain, France **225.00**
Beaded Reticule, floral design, beaded tassle, drawstring **95.00**
Mesh Bag, aqua color design, ornate openwork frame, blue glass jewels ...**135.00**
Woven Tapestry Purse, brown w/flowers & bird, ormolu frame, 1900s...**155.00**
Fine Petit Point, woman standing by rosebush, jeweled handle w/chain...**165.00**
Cut Steel Beaded, jewel encrusted frame, muted carpet design, 9x16", mint condition...**275.00**
Beaded, rose garland, openwork frame w/flowers, chain handle.............**145.00**
Beaded Scenic, Venetian Canal, elaborate jeweled frame, lg, ca 1910s....**300.00**

Metallic Gold Thread, seed pearls & prong-set rhinestones, chain **85.00**
Rose-Colored Velvet, gold beads & sequins, pearls, purple jewels...........**115.00**
Beaded, unusual Egyptian design, celluloid handle, link chain, fringed....**165.00**
Cut Steel Beaded, colorful pattern, ornate net fringe, jewel encrusted, or chain
    handle **285.00**

    We collect **metal mesh purses painted with multicolored designs**. Most were made by the Whiting & Davis Co. (W&D) or the Mandalian Manufacturing Co. in the 1920s and early 1930s.

    We are not interested in all painted mesh bags. We do not want purses that could be described as plain. We're looking for bags with striking designs, unusual features, or ornate frames. Purses with excessively worn, faded, or damaged paint are not candidates for our collection. Minor wear and a few separated links are acceptable, and the more unusual the purse the more forgiving we tend to be.

    One style of mesh purse with an unusual feature that we particularly look for is the vanity bag. Mesh vanity bags combine a purse and a compact and were made in a variety of different styles. Some have the compact made into the corner or center of the purse frame. Other purses, including many made by R&G, have a round frame with a mesh bag attached below and the compact mounted on top. One Whiting & Davis model, the 'swinging compact' mesh vanity bag, has a compact attached to the purse frame by a metal bar allowing the compact to swing out from the purse.

    Below are just a few examples of bags we're trying to find. There are many other bags with similar features we'd like also to add to our collection. Request our illustrated want list.

Sherry and Mike Miller
303 Holiday Dr.
Tuscola, IL 61953
217-253-4991

Painted Metal Mesh Purses   **We Pay**

Child's Size (2x3" to 3x4")..**50.00-75.00**
Child's Size (2x3" to 3x4"), figural design on mesh **75.00-125.00**
Purse w/Art Deco 'Moderne' Geometric Design (5x7") **100.00-150.00**
Purse w/Ornate or Unusual Frame (5x8")....................................**125.00-175.00**
Purse w/Betty Boop or Mickey Mouse...**350.00+**
Mandalian Purse, painted swans or deer.....................................**150.00-200.00**
Mandalian Purse, elaborate florals design & painted frame (5x10") ...**175.00-225.00**
R&G Vanity Bag, w/cloisonne lid & octagonal top **300.00-350.00**
W&D Purse, snow-covered log cabin scene **150.00-200.00**

W&D Purse, painted dragon (5x7")..**300.00-350.00**
W&D Corner Compact Vanity Bag...**350.00+**
W&D Swinging Compact Bag ....**350.00+**

Radios

Decades before the chip made lap-top computers a reality, the transistor mobilized radio put top sixty musical sounds into shirt pockets. At a pricey $49.95 for Christmas shoppers of 1954, the Regency TR-1 was soon competing with more colorful and less expensive mini-tube sets by Emerson and toy-like crystal models with names like Pee-Wee and Rocket.

I collect **miniature plastic radios of the 1950s and early 1960s.** Early sets are recognizable by the civil defense triangles on the fequency dial. Primitive sets, often presents to children, can be more valuable than the sets used by adults. Cosmetic condition is more important than a radio's working condition in determining value. A photocopy of the front of a little radio and description of any cracks or scratches will do. The following is just a tiny sampling of the hundreds of radios I hope to purchase.

Mike Brooks
7335 Skyline Boulevard
Oakland, CA 94611
510-339-1751 (evenings)

We Pay

Crystal Sets, including Disasteradio, Pee-Wee, Rocket, Others ....**50.00+**
Early Transistor Sets, earphone sound only..**50.00+**
Emerson Mini-Tube & Transistor Series 747, 838 or 839.........................**75.00+**
Mantola & Mitchell Models...**300.00+**
Regency TR-1, pearlescent colors..**500.00+**
Raythson Transistorized T-100 ....**300.00+**
Sony TR-55..**1,000.00+**
Solar Pocket Radios ....**100.00+**
Toshiba, various models..**50.00-200.00**

Wanted: **radios made of wood and plastic**. The wooden ones I am interested in are mostly made before 1960. All types of upright models and table models are wanted. I am also interested in **plastic models from the '30s, '40s, and '50s**. The thicker Bakelite and marbelized ones are the ones I'm mostly interested in, but will purchase others. The best way to sell your radio(s) is to send me a photo along with the model number and don't forget the price. I am also interested in the tubes that went in radios (OIA, 99, WD11, WD12, etc.). Other interests are **crank phonographs**. Send list along with your prices to:

Jim Allen
420 S 46th St.
Lincoln, NE 68510
402-483-5789

Railroadiana

I buy the following tall **globe lantern frames and globes** which are marked with the embossed (raised) letters. All such items must be old and in excellent condition. The globes must be at least five inches tall with an extended base (lip) on the bottom. Higher prices paid for colored globes with these embossed markings. Will also pay top dollar for other marked brass top lanterns and/or embossed extended gases from other railroads.

I am a private collector and will pay top dollar for most types of **brass locks with embossed (raised) railroad or express markings**. This includes heart-shaped locks, round 'push key' locks, and Keen Kutter locks. All such locks must be old and in excellent condition — normal wear from light use is acceptable. The following are examples of the prices I pay for specific locks.

Bill Cunningham
3629 Candelaria
Plano, TX 75023
214-596-9646

Lantern Frames	We Pay
AT&SFRR, w/steel top	300.00+
AT&SFRR, w/brass top	650.00+
CB&QRR, w/brass top	500.00+
CRI&PRR, w/brass top	550.00+
Santa Fe Route, w/steel top	200.00+

UPRW, w/brass top ....650.00+
UPRR, w/brass top ....600.00+
UPRW-U, w/brass top ....650.00+
UPRW-SP, w/brass top ....650.00+
Union Pacific, w/brass top ....450.00+

Lantern Globes   We Pay

AT&SFRR ....650.00+
AT&SF ....500.00+
CB&QRR ....300.00+
CRI&P ....450.00+
CRI&PRR...600.00+
UPRW ....650.00+
UPRR ....600.00+
UPRW-U...650.00+
UPRW-SP ....650.00+
Union Pacific...300.00+
Santa Fe Route ....200.00+

Round 'Push-Key' Locks   We Pay

AT&SFRR 500.00
D&RGRy Ice House Lock..800.00
D&RGYCo Water Service 800.00
F&CCRR 1,000.00
RGWRy Train Box Lock..900.00
RGWRy Water Service 900.00
RGWRy Ice House Lock 900.00
Santa Fe System 700.00
WF&Co's Express 800.00

Heart-Shaped Locks   We Pay

AT&SFRR 500.00
CMRY 800.00
D&RGRR, fancy back...700.00
L&NRR, fancy back 1,100.00
UPD&GRY, fancy back...1,200.00
UPRYCo, fancy back 1,000.00
WF&CO EX 700.00
Santa Fe System, fancy back 1,200.00

Keen Kutter Locks   We Pay

C&SRR 800.00
FW&DCRR 800.00

Railroadiana

FRISCO	500.00
MVRR	700.00
OSLRRCo	900.00
T&BVRR	1,000.00

The term railroadiana is meant to cover all collecting facets of the golden age of railroading. Depending upon the railroadiana collector's interest, items such as lanterns, tools, locks and keys, dining car wares (china, glass, silver, linen), advertising, timetables, signs, watches, and other items are eagerly sought.

Our particular area of interest is **authenticated patterns of dining car china**. We seek those pieces which have a top or side logo (design or mark) and/or a designated railroad back stamp. In addition, we seek to buy railroad station restaurant and eating housewares, examples of china and silver from street and electric railways, and also pieces from railroad-related ferryboat and steamship systems. This listing represents only a sampling of railroadiana items we seek to buy. We respond to all offerings by telephone or letter. Other interests include **Shelley and Buffalo Pottery** (see our listings in this book).

Fred and Lila Shrader
2025 Hwy. 199 (Hiouchi)
Crescent City, CA 95531
707-458-3525

Railroad China   We Pay

Alaska RR, various patterns, pieces & shapes	90.00+
Baltimore & Ohio RR, cups & saucers	75.00+
Butter Pats, most all railroads	25.00-75.00+
Children's Dishes, most all railroads	55.00+
Coffeepot, Union Pacific, various patterns & sizes	95.00+
Cup & Saucer, most all railoads	35.00+
Egg Cup, most all railroads, various sizes & shapes	25.00+
Great Northern Railway, various patterns, pieces & shapes	45.00+
Individual Creamer, w/handle or w/o handles, most all railroads	25.00+
Key System, most all pieces	50.00-100.00+
Northern Pacific (Yellowstone Park Line), most all pieces	45.00+
Pacific Electric, most all pieces	50.00-100.00+
San Diego & Arizona Railway, most all pieces	100.00+
Southern Pacific RR, various patterns, most all pieces	25.00-100.00+
Teapot, most all railroads, various sizes	95.00+
Western Pacific RR, Various patterns, most all pieces	25.00-100.00+

Glassware	We Pay
Carafe or Water Pitcher	35.00+
Cordial, w/railroad logo	25.00+
Juice Glass, w/railroad logo	7.50+
Wine or Water Stem, w/railroad logo	10.00+

Linens	We Pay
Blanket, w/railroad logo or name, wool	35.00+
Headrest, w/railroad logo or name	10.00+
Napkin, w/railroad logo or name	10.00+
Place Mat, w/railroad logo or name	10.00+
Tablecloth, w/railroad logo or name	10.00+
Towel, w/railroad logo or name	3.00-10.00+
Uniform, full or individual pieces, railroad designated	3.00-25.00+

Silver	We Pay
Butter Pat, top mark only, most all railroads	15.00+
Coffeepot, side mark, most all railroads	70.00+
Condiment Sets (shakers w/other items), most all railroads	45.00+
Creamer, side mark, most all railroads	30.00+
Flatware, place setting pieces, most all railroads	5.00+
Flatware, serving pieces, most all railroads	20.00+
Teapot, side mark, most all railroads	70.00+

The Little Falls Railroad and Doll Museum Ltd. is constantly looking for **dolls and railroad memorabilia** to enhance and expand the museum. We are looking for any railroad-related items, especially those that operated in Wisconsin and Eastern Minnesota. We are seeking paper goods, equipment, and old trains of any kind. We negotiate prices as a set price is usually impractical. We will trade some items, and as with dolls, we are able to give recognition for donations on a tax exempt basis.

We can be reached by phone, fax, or mail. All contacts will be answered.

The Little Falls Railroad and Doll Museum Ltd.
P.O. Box 177
Cataract, WI 54620-0177
phone or fax 608-272-3266

Razors

Serious collector interested only in **fancy handled straight razors**. Ornate sterling silver and aluminum handled examples are wanted. Carved mother-of-pearl, and celluloid examples with raised figural handles — especially those with color — are wanted. I'm also interested in seven day razor sets in their original boxes. The razors must be in excellent condition. The better the condition, the higher my offer. Send clear photograph or photocopy. **Do not send any razors**. I will pay $100.00 or more for a fancy handle straight razor that I need for my collection.

Russ Palmieri
27 Pepper Rd.
Towaco, NJ 07082
201-334-5829

Fancy-Handled Razors   **We Pay**

Mother-of-Pearl, carved 100.00-350.00
Aluminum, ornate 100.00-200.00
Sterling Silver, ornate..100.00-500.00
Celluloid, w/raised figure...100.00-500.00

I collect early **unusual safety razors, blade banks, mechanical blade sharpeners, and stroppers**, as well as shaving-related catalogs, instruction sheets and booklets, window and counter advertising, display materials, and manufacturer giveaways. I no longer collect the following brands: Rolls, Durham, Valet, Gillette, Kriss Kross, Twinplex, or Listerine.

Prices will vary depending on the particular item, its age and condition, as well as its container. But my price will reflect a collector's interest and not a dealer's — who might expect to pay less in order to be able to resell. The following are brand names of some early safety razors which might command prices in excess of $100.00 and in some cases several hundreds of dollars:

A-C Specialty	U-Magnet
Collins Wind-Up	Wanie
Dr Scott Electric	Witch
Fox	Wilbert
Home	Winner
Modern Deluxe	Yale
Mohican	Zinn

Lester Dequaine
155 Brewster St.
Bridgeport, CT 06605
203-335-6833

Records

Primarily as part of my research project to compile a discogrphy of **78 rpm kiddie records**, I am buying old children's records. They can be any label, any year. It is most important that they have their original sleeves, album covers, jackets, etc.; as I may eventually need to photograph them. The exceptions would be picture discs. In this case, the records alone can be photographed. In addition, most children's 78 rpm records without the original covers are not collectible, since most people want these items mainly for the artwork.

When sending me information on what you have, simply indicate the record label and record or album number(s). I will usually know the titles for the number supplied; I will contact you if I need further information. Also, describe the condition of the cover. I am not as concerned with the record condition unless it is missing, cracked, chipped, or otherwise unplayable. Occasionally I can use records without the sleeve (I may have an empty sleeve; need the information on the loose record for research purposes).

Since there is no price guide for 78 rpm kiddie records, I can not list how much I will pay except on an individual basis. I can say that most records go for $1.00 to $10.00 with a small percentage going higher, and in some cases for several hundreds of dollars. Recordings of famous figures (fictional and nonfictional) naturally are more desirable — basically because there is a crossover collectors' market.

Peter B. Muldavin
173 W 78th St.
New York, NY 10024
212-362-9606

Wanted: **78 rpm records with scarce and unusual labels**. The following are some scarce labels and special series — all of which are wanted, regardless of musical content or lack thereof. All are pre-1940, and should not be confused with more modern labels having the same or similar names. For illustrations of these (and many other) labels, see my booklet, *Shellac Shack's*

Want List of 78 RPM Records, and/or my book, *American Premium Record Guide*. Prices are minimums for the least desirable issues on each label; better issues will be bought at higher prices (sometimes multiples of quoted prices). Labels should be free of significant damage (writing, stickers, needle scratches, stains, tears, etc.), and the playing surface should be in nice, playable condition (some of the following will be bought at reduced prices, even if playing surface is impaired, if label is nice).

Also buying many other records on other labels and other eras: popular, dance bands, jazz, blues, hillbilly, celebrities, rock 'n roll, rockabilly, rhythm and blues, etc. No classical wanted unless on scarce labels. List must include label, record number, artist/band, and song titles. I will buy single records, collections, hoards, store stocks, and will travel if quality/quantity warrant.

Please note that that some of these labels may be confused with more modern, similarly-named labels, reissues/repressings that reuse original names, logos, etc.

L.R. Docks
P.O. Box 691035
San Antonio, TX 78269
210-492-6021 or fax 210-492-6489

78 RPM Records w/Scarce, Unusual Labels   We Pay

Ajax (Canada)	4.00
Aurora (Canada)	5.00
Autograph (Marsh Laboratories, Chicago)	4.00
Belvedere (Hochschild, Kohn & Co.)	4.00
Berliner (7", single-sided, embossed label)	8.00
Black Patti (Chicago Record Co.)	50.00
Blu-Disc (#T-1001 through #T-1009)	35.00
Buddy (six cities/companies mentioned on label)	20.00
Carnival (John Wanamaker, New York)	10.00
Chappelle & Stinette	10.00
Chautauqua (Washington, DC)	10.00
Clover (Nutmeg Record Co.)	3.00
Connorized	2.00
Dandy	4.00
Davega	2.00
Davis & Schwegler	5.00
Domestic (Philadelphia)	3.00
Edison (Needle Cut Electric)	6.00
Edison (Long-Playing 24-Minute)	10.00
Edison (Long-Playing 40-Minute, 12")	15.00
Edison (sample record, 12")	20.00
Electradisk	2.00
Everybodys	3.00

Flexo (small, flexible disc, by Pacific Coast Record Corp. San Francisco, or
Hollywood Film Enterprises) **6.00**
Golden (Los Angeles, not the children's record of circa 1950) **5.00**
Gramophone (7", single-sided, embossed label) **8.00**
Herschel Gold Seal (Northwestern Phonograph Supply) **5.00**
Herwin (St. Louis) **5.00**
Hollywood Record (California) **5.00**
Homestead (Chicago Mail Order) **4.00**
Improved (7", single-sides, by Eldridge R. Johnson) **8.00**
Marathon (7", by Nutmeg Record Corp.) **6.00**
Meritt (Kansas City) **25.00**
Moxie **10.00**
Mozart (St. Louis) **3.00**
National (Iowa City, Iowa) **2.00**
New Flexo (small, flexible disc) **5.00**
Nordskog (with motto: The Golden-Voiced Records) **6.00**
Odeon (American 'ONY' Series; not foreign/ethnic issues) **4.00**
Paramount (12000 and 13000 Series) **2.00**
Parlophone (American 'PNY' Series only) **3.00**
Par-O-Ket (7", embossed, not paper, label) **4.00**
Pennington (Bamberger & Co., New Jersey) **4.00**
Personal Record (By Columbia, '-P' Series) **2.00**
Phonograph Recording Company (San Francisco) **5.00**
QRS (Cover Recording Co., New York) **5.00**
RCA Victor Program Transcription **4.00**
RCA Victor Picture Records (early 1930s) **15.00**
Rialto (Railto Music House, Chicago) **10.00**
Stark **5.00**
Sunrise (Grey Gull affiliated, ca 1930) **3.00**
Sunrise (RCA Victor product, ca 193) **20.00**
Sunset (Made in California USA) **3.00**
Sunshine (St. Petersburg, Florida) **5.00**
Sunshine (Los Angeles, Calif.) **10.00**
Superior (Gennett affiliated, ca 1930-31) **4.00**
Timely Tunes (RCA Victor product) **5.00**
Tremont (American Record Mfg) **2.00**
Up-To-Date (ca 1925) **25.00**
Victor 23000-23041, inclusive **3.00**
Victor 23250-23432, inclusive **5.00**
Victor 23500-23859, inclusive **2.00**
V-38500-V-38631, inclusive **5.00**
Victor Pict-Ur-Music **3.00**
Yerkes **4.00**

Wanted to buy: **LP albums, 45 rpm records, and 12" singles of modern jazz and Black artists and groups from the 1950s through the '80s.** Any quantity wanted in excellent to never-played condition. We buy to sell and sell to buy! Send $25.00 for list of 6,000 records wanted or $15.00 for a catalog of records for sale (refundable with $25.00 or more purchase).

First Place Records
P.O. Box 3477
Texarkana, AR 75504
fax 501-772-0988

Highest prices paid for antique **Edison 78 rpm phonograph records, LP's and 16" transcriptions, old tube radios and TV's, phonographs, and sheet music.** We specialize in '20s, '30s, '40s, and '50s jazz, swing, blues, country and western, vocals, big bands, combos, personality, rock 'n' roll, rhythm and blues, 10" record sets, etc. Auction lists available upon request; want lists welcome.

John Marinacci
301 Murray Ave.
Bridgeville, PA 15017
412-221-4946 or 412-221-6763

Wanted: **new or used records.** One thing to remember when writing about records — condition is a big factor! I am currently buying all records **except** Christmas (Goodyear, Firestone, ect.), exercise records, Time-Life, Reader's Digest, etc. Old records are okay as long as they are playable. I pay more for picture records and Edison, Vogue, cylinder, Berliner, seven, and ten-inch records.

There are some records that are worth more. As an example, I pay $1.00 to $15.00 for records by the Monkees. And if a record comes without a cover, the price will be less. Please send a list of the records you have and I will get back with you as soon as I can.

Don O. Knight
1434 Hummell Valley Rd. SW
New Philadelphia, OH 44663

Salesman's Samples and Miniatures

I am starting a collection of **children's and salesman's sample sewing machines**. Pre-World War II machines are especially wanted. The machine should be in good condition without missing parts. Please call and/or send photograph. Prices offered will vary depending on condition.

I am also interested in purchasing cook stoves in good to excellent condition. I am just beginning this collection. Please call or send a clear photograph. Prices listed here are general depending on model and condition.

Jacquilyn Rubin
4133 Drosera Ave.
Mays Landing, NJ 08330
609-965-3039

Sewing Machines	We Pay
Casige	50.00-125.00
Smith & Egge Mfg. Co.	150.00-225.00
Any German Model Made Before WWII	50.00-175.00
Singer	75.00-125.00
Foley & Williams Mfg. Co.	150.00-225.00

Cook Stoves	We Pay
Arcade	85.00
Crescent	175.00
Eagle	85.00-375.00
Kenton	30.00-75.00
Little Giant	425.00
Rival	50.00-180.00
Triumph	130.00
Bing	400.00

Salt and Pepper Shakers

I buy **novelty salt and pepper shakers**. I buy from one set to an entire collection. I have been known to buy eight- to ten-thousand set collections. No collection is too large for me to handle. Price I am willing to pay per set depends on what is in the collection and the condition. Please contact me for details. I buy through the mail. Photos or videos are required. If the collection is large enough, I will drive to buy it.

The Salt and Pepper Man
Larry Carey
P.O. Box 329
Mechanicsburg, PA 17055
717-766-0868

We Pay

Advertising	20.00+
Black Americana	20.00+
Black Americana Condiment Sets	200.00+
Plastic Gas Pumps, no Esso wanted	25.00+
Comic Characters	45.00+
Nodders w/Figural Bases	75.00+
Miniatures	20.00+
Storybook Sets	30.00+
Condiments (salt, pepper & mustard) w/figural bases, particularly sets made in Germany & marked on the bottom	150.00+
Poinsettia Studios, Calif	25.00+
Goebel (Hummel), from Germany	25.00+
Fruit & Vegetables w/Faces	20.00+
Shawnee Pottery	20.00+
Rosemeade Pottery	25.00+
Messer Pottery, North Dakota	50.00+
People, Animals, Huggies, or Go-With Sets	1.00-20.00

I buy **many types of novelty figural salt and pepper shakers**. I concentrate on quality rather than quantity. I pay top dollar for high quality. I specialize in top-of-the-line items. Favored categories include recognizable characters and personalities (Felix the Cat, Ghandi, Martin and Lewis, Nancy and Sluggo, etc.); figural nodders (two shakers which rock back and forth inserted in a stationary base); Black Americana (Coon Chicken Inn, Luzianna Mammy, etc.); advertising figurals (Happy Homer, Hershey Bean Babies, Black Crow Restaurant, etc.); plastic gas pumps; condiment sets (pair of shakers and little covered mustard cruet with spoon, usually on a tray) in characters such as Popeye, Katzenjammer Kids, Pinocchio, Three Legged Man, etc.; Ceramic Arts Studio sets such as Disney or nursery rhyme characters; anthropomorphic sets (fruit and vegetable people, inanimate objects dressed as people);

nudes and naughties; baseball and sports related; German and Goebel sets; and figural lustreware sets. Price paid is determined by condition, desirablity, quality, and rarity. I don't buy nonfigural glass or wooden sets. There are hundreds more I want to buy besides what are listed here. Please supply description, price, and/or photos when offering shakers to me.

Judy Posner
May through October
R.D. 1, Box 273 HW
Effort, PA 18330
717-629-6583 or fax 717-629-0521
e-mail:Judyandjef@aol.com
or
November through April
4195 S Tamiami Tr. #183HW
Venice, FL 34293
941-497-7149 or fax 941-493-8085
e-mail:Judyandjef@aol.com

Shaker Sets   **We Pay**

Al Capp Shmoo, various	50.00-100.00
Black People, w/graduate caps	75.00
Ceramic Arts Studio Brown Bear, on all fours	150.00
Ceramic Arts Studio Camel	125.00
Cowboy Nodder	200.00-225.00
Disney's Tweedledee & Tweedledum	250.00
Fruit & Vegetable People	15.00-25.00
Fruit & Vegetable People, running	25.00-35.00
Fruit & Vegetable People, wire frame	25.00-35.00
Felix the Cat, Germany	250.00-350.00
Felix the Cat, Japan	150.00-200.00
Hershey Chocolate Bean Babies	100.00-125.00
Inanimate Objects, dressed as people	15.00-45.00
Little Black Girl in Bathtub	150.00
Little Black Sambo & Tiger	175.00
Man Feeding Squirrel Nodder	200.00-350.00
Mermaids, various	15.00-45.00
Mickey Mouse Condiment Set, Germany	250.00-350.00
Pinocchio & Jiminy Cricket	75.00-85.00
Popeye Condiment Set, lustreware	300.00-325.00
Sad Sack	95.00-125.00

Salt and Pepper Shakers

We are looking for **whimsical Japan and Occupied Japan figurines and salt and pepper shakers as well as occupied Japan elves** that have slender legs, frilly gold-trimmed collars and an almost vertical slanted eyebrow. These can be found in various poses, such as lying about or playing musical instruments. They have lily pads on their collars. An Occupied Japan Humpty Dumpty salt and pepper set is wanted such as found in Gene Florence's *The Collector's Encyclopedia of Occupied Japan* third series on page 107, first row, first set. Elves can be found on page 89 and on the third row. Anything Japan or Occupied Japan that is very whimsical and well made. We pay for shipping, handling, and insurance. Please call or write anytime. Pictures are very helpful.

Michelle Carey
2512 Balmoral Blvd.
Kokomo, IN 46902
317-455-3970
e-mail: mgcarey@netusal.net

We Pay

Occupied Elf	**15.00-20.00**
Occupied Frog	**18.00-22.00**
Occupied Elf w/Instrument	**18.00-22.00**
Occupied Frog w/Instrument	**20.00-25.00**
Humpty Dumpty Shakers in Occupied Japan	**75.00-80.00**
Musical Instruments w/Faces	**15.00-20.00**
Flower People	**15.00-20.00**
Any Anthromorphic & Whimsical Piece	**10.00+**

Plastic figural gasoline pump salt and pepper shaker sets that stand approximately 2½" tall are just one example of the many specialty versions of novelty salt shaker collectibles. Produced for and distributed free by service stations from the early 1950s through the 1970s, these miniature replicas of actual gas pumps were made for almost every brand of gasoline during that era. Brands representing those with the most service stations are the most common and are less desirable, such as Esso, Texaco, and Phillips 66.

I'm seeking to buy sets representing the gasoline brands listed below. Many may still be in their original boxes; others will be unpackaged. Write with your find, and I'll respond immediately to your inquiry. Also see my listing under **Thermometers** in this book. **Prices paid range from $10.00 to $85.00 a pair for these brand names:**

Aetna
APCO
Amlico
Ashland
B/A
Bay
Boron
CALSO
Carter
Clark
Cliff Brice
Comet
Crystal Flash
Derby

Dixie
Fleet-Wing
FS (Farm Service)
Frontier
Getty
Hancock
Hudson
Hi-Speed
Imperial
Jet
Keystone
Kayo
Leonard

Lion
MFA
Martin
Pan-Am
Paraland
Rocket
Site
Speedway 79
SOC
Tenneco
UTOCO
Vickers
Zephyr

Peter Capell
1838 W Grace St.
Chicago, IL 60613-2724
312-871-8735

Scales

We buy all types of coin-operated scales in any condition. Also incomplete scales and parts are wanted. Send a photo of scale along with serial and model numbers. We also buy all other types of scales. Prices are for complete working scales.

Bill and Jan Berning
P.O. Box 41414
Chicago, IL 60641
815-784-3134 or 815-895-6328

We Pay

Pace Scales ....**50.00-300.00+**
Rockola ....**40.00-200.00+**
Lollipop Scales ....**300.00-2,000.00+**

Public Scales	**50.00-300.00**
Pioneer	**300.00-500.00**
Watling Fortune Scales, sm	**100.00-300.00+**
Advertising Scales	**100.00-2,000.00+**
Ticket Scales	**40.00+**
Electronic Scales	**25.00-500.00+**
Hamilton Scales	**100.00-10,000.00+**

Schoolhouse Collectibles

Even though most all of us have some memento of our school days — yearbook, scrapbook, class picture, diploma, club pin, senior ring, letter, sweater, etc. — as a rule, schoolhouse collectibles are not something one would deliberately set out to accumulate without good reason! Being a professional educator, I have a very exciting reason. I plan to establish a school-related museum. Someone once said that 'school is a building that has four walls...with tomorrow inside.' I want to preserve some of those 'tomorrows' that have made us the great country we are today.

Education is essential to a free society. We associate certain items such as bells, books, and blackboards as being tools of educators. Just as educational methodology undergoes reformation, so does the educator's equipment. New innovative methods come and go; old equipment is replaced by the new. McGuffy's Readers were essential in the 1800s, just as computers are essential today. As you gather schoolhouse-related articles, let your imagination soar. Add to the list below; let me hear from you.

Kenn Norris
P.O. Box 4830
Sanderson, TX 79848-4830

We Pay

George Washington Print	**15.00**
Abraham Lincoln Print	**15.00**
Teacher's Hand Bell	**15.00**
Inkwells, desk	**8.00**
Inwells, molded	**5.00**
Dip Pens	**2.00**
Diplomas, Announcements	**3.50**
Yearbooks	**3.50**
Maps	**5.00**

Map Holders, oak 30.00
Photographs 1.50
Slates, single 12.00
Slates, double 24.00
Pencil Sharpeners, student 3.00
Pencil Sharpeners, class 7.00
Mounted Bells 50.00
Lunch Pails 5.00
War Bond Posters 10.00
War Bond Stamp Books 10.00
Wartime Booklets for Paper, Scrap, & Metal Drives 5.00
Marbles, jacks, Jump Ropes 5.00
Class Rings 15.00
Club Pins 2.00
FFA or FHA Articles 3.00
Athletic Equipment 5.00
Leather Football Helmets 50.00
Award Letters 3.00

Scientific and Technical-Related Antiques

I am buying the following scientific and technical related antiques:

Surveying instruments: pre-1910 compasses, transits, levels, etc.
Microscopes: pre-1900, large, elaborate or simple forms, etc.
Astronomy-related items: planetariums, globes, telescopes, navigational instruments, etc.
Medical instruments and curiosities: cased surgical sets, anatomical models, phlebodmy and phrenological items, quack medical devices, etc.
Precision and scientific instruments: associated with physics demonstrations, telegraphy, mining and assaying, exploration, pre-1900 motors, etc.
Calculating and computing devices: decorative and unusual forms only
Typewriters: decorative and/or unusual forms only
Photographica: daguerreotypes, cased and unusual photographs, unusual cameras

All related items: trade catalogs, early books and photographic images.

Dale R. Beeks
P.O. Box 117
Mt. Vernon, IA 52314
319-895-0506 or 800-880-5178

Scouting Collectibles

I collect **Boy Scouts of Canada items**. My main interest is District and Region badges but all Canadian scouting items will be considered. Of special interest is Canadian scouting in Europe; this is the scouting done on the NATO armed forces bases. My other scouting collecting interests are **World Jamboree items** preferably before 1963. Please write for a quick reply.

Frank D. Smith
33601 First Ave.
Mission, British Columbia V2V 1H3
Canada

Sewing Collectibles

Before the advent of the sewing machine, garments and household goods were made by hand. High-quality needlework tools were used by generations of needleworkers during the 18th, 19th, early 20th centuries. Tools were made of gold, silver, ivory, mother-of-pearl, and other fine materials as well as of wood, brass, leather, and silk. Forms of decoration including tartanware and transfer ware from Scotland, inlays of ivory and mother-of-pearl on horn and ivory, hand-engraved and carved decoration, embossed designs, and many others.

I am especially interested in **tools and work boxes of the 19th and early 20th centuries.** Figural pieces (tape measures, needlecases, etc. in the form of animals, buildings, flowers, birds, people, etc.) are of special interest as are items from the Victorian era. I buy single items, sets, and collections. Prices paid reflect the rarity, condition, age, and material of individual pieces and would be impossible to generalize here.

If you have any of the following items for sale or other hand needlework tools I may have omitted, I would appreciate hearing from you with a complete description and your asking price. I do not buy reproductions or broken tools.

Bodkins and Ribbon Threaders
Chatelaines (complete or individual pieces)
Crochet Ball Holders
Darning Eggs and Glove Darners
Emeries
Fitted Needlework Boxes
Hem Gauges
Knitting Needle Sheaths and Guards
Needle Books
Needle Cases
Needlework Clamps
Pin Disks
Pincushions and Pin Cubes
Scissors
Spool Knaves
Tape Measures
Tatting Shuttles
Thimbles, Thimble Holders, and Cases
Thread Containers, Winders, Reels, and Stands
Thread Waxers
Victorian Brass Needlecases and Tape Measures
Other Tools Wanted

Marjorie Geddes
P.O. Box 5875
Aloha, OR 97007
503-649-1041

Collector interested in buying **metal thimbles**. Please send description and price. Also buying **tape measures of any shape or material** with the measurements marked on fabric or ribbon. Please send description and price. If 'surprising' me by sending items on approval, please enclose return postage and insurance. If I buy the items, I will reimburse you. Thank you.

Bernie Biske
47529 Cheryl Ct.
Shelby Twp., MI 48315-4707

Thimbles and sewing items wanted include:

Antique thimbles — precious metals, ornate, commemorative, or dated
Thimble cases — leather, wood, bone, shell, or metal
Measures — spring-loaded tape in celluloid or metal figural or advertising case
Antique sewing kits — metal, ivory, bone, wood
Sewing birds — clamps with bird figures that have beaks that open to hold material, may have one or two pincushions, patent dates on wings (note: undated ones may be reproductions)

Authentic sewing birds are worth at least $100.00 to me. No plastic, aluminum, wood, or modern limited edition thimbles are wanted. **Thimbles, thimble cases, measures, and sewing kits** (depending on material, rarity, age, condition, and authenticity) **can be worth $10.00 to $500.00** to me. If you are ready to sell, contact me. Please send SASE for a reply.

Antique Dry Goods
Susan M. Deputy
P.O. Box 320
King George, VA 22485
540-775-5472

New collector looking for **figural celluloid tape measures**. I only have six, so I have a long way to go.

Daryl
Box 3621
Cedar Rapids, IA 52406
319-365-3857

Sewing Machines

Collector seeks **antique sewing machines, hand-crank, treadle, and toy sewing machines**. Hand-crank and treadle machines need to be pre-1875. Also I'm looking for catalogs, stocks, advertising leaflets, instruction booklets (no cut outs). Some machines where sold in huge numbers even before 1875; therefore, **I do not buy** machines manufactured by **Domestic, Howe, Standard, Singer** (except treadle machines driven by a flat leather belt), **Wheeler Wilson, and Willcox & Gibbs**. I do not buy any pressed steel toy sewing machines except Mary Pearl Pixie and Tabitha. Paying top dollar for machines in mint condition but will also buy items in need of repair or restoration. Description should include any information you can find on the machine such as manufacturer, patent dates, serial numbers, and overall condition. Willing to pay finder's fee. Other wants include **typewriters, calculators, pencil sharpening machines, and hand-powered vacuum cleaners (bellows type)**. Please call 1-800-942-8968 for immediate cash. The prices listed are just a few for machines in good and working order; there are many more.

Peter Frei
P.O. Box 500
Brimfield, MA 01010
800-942-8968 or fax 413-245-6079

We Pay

	We Pay
Blodgett & Lerow	**10,000.00**
Bartholf	**4,000.00**
Battelle	**7,000.00**
Beckwith	**800.00**
Bosworth	**4,500.00**
DW Clark, patented February 23rd, June 8th 1858	**2,000.00**
Fairy	**750.00**
Fetter & Jones	**3,500.00**
Hendricks, patented March 16th 1858	**2,000.00**
Little Monitor	**2,500.00**
Ne Plus Ultra	**8,000.00**
Novelty, patented August 27th 1867	**1,200.00**
Pratt, Lady's Companion	**5,500.00**
Singer Nr.1, base of sewing machine measures 12x12"	**3,500.00**
Stebbins	**4,000.00**
Woodruff	**4,500.00**

Shaving Mugs

I collect the following types of **shaving mugs and barber bottles:**

(1) Figural mugs in the shape of animals, people, birds, etc., with or without a shaving brush and matching figural handle

(2) Mugs and bottles which are covered with papier-mache imitation tree bark

(3) Clambroth mugs and bottles covered by an open-work silver-deposit design
(4) Mugs with photographs and names on the side
(5) Ceramic shaving soap pots with individual names

Prices for these items vary considerably throughout the country but I believe that my offers are among the highest. Check with me first.

Lester Dequaine
155 Brewster St.
Bridgeport, CT 06605
203-335-6833

Shoe Button Covers

I am always buying shoe button covers. Somewhat similar in appearance to today's blouse-button covers, shoe button covers were very popular from 1900 until 1925. They were created to brighten up the drab, usually dark colored buttons that were part of most women's shoes manufactured during the era. The buttons were necessary to secure the straps which gripped the ankles.

I have earned an excellent country-wide reputation for fair and prompt offers. That is why people send me their shoe button covers and I mail them a check or an offer (whichever the seller prefers). And, unless you are sending covers containing gold, silver or precious stones, there is probably no need to incur the high cost of insurance.

The prices which I pay are dependent on the condition, style, and rarity of the shoe button covers. While sets are preferred, I also purchase 'singles.' The availability of the original box can enhance the value by up to 20%. The following chart illustrated the prices which I typically pay.

Eugene R. Klompus
P.O. Box 346
Prospect Hts., IL 60070

We Pay

Set of 4, silver w/hand-etched design, unbranded, ca 1915 ....**15.00**
Set of 3, French manufacture, ca 1900 ....**20.00**
Set of 4, French manufacture, poor condition, ca 1895 ....**35.00**
Set of 2 (incomplete set), Frere brand, ca 1905 ....**4.00**
Single Cover, silver, etched scroll, ca 1920 ....**5.00**

Skookum American Indian Dolls

Serious collector interested in buying top quality Skookum dolls. The dolls must be in original excellent condition (without replacement parts). The older dolls have leather shoes, newer dolls have plastic shoes. The faces are papier-mache, not plastic. Original boxes are a plus but not a necessity. Send clear photocopy or photograph. **Do not send any dolls.** I will pay **$75.00 to $500.00** for a Skookum that I need for my collection.

Jo Ann Palmieri
27 Pepper Rd.
Towaco, NJ 07082
201-334-5829

Size	We Pay
12" Male Skookum	75.00+
12" Female Skookum	75.00+
15" Male Skookum	100.00+
15" Female Skookum	100.00+
20" Male Skookum	125.00+
20" Female Skookum	125.00+
Larger than 20" Male or Female Skookum	200.00 to 500.00

Silhouettes

Silhouettes on glass that were made from the 1920s through the 1950s are wanted. I am not interested in the newer ones. These are **convex or flat glass with painted-on silhouettes**. The silhouettes made on convex glass were of black, red, rose, blue, white, or yellow colors. Any color, shape, or size is wanted. **Related items** such as ashtrays, books with silhouette illustrations, china, lamps, jewelry or boxes, trays, wastebaskets, etc., **are sought as well**. I am also looking for **old catalogs, salesmen's samples, or anyone with information about Fisher** (they made pictures and trays with wildflower backgrounds). Other wants include **butterfly wing pictures and jewelry**. Prices will depend on condition and rarity. I will accept collect calls, but photographs or photocopies are very helpful.

Shirley Mace
P.O. Box 1602
Mesilla Park, NM 88047-1602
505-524-6717 or 505-523-0940
e-mail: Shmace@nmsu.edu

Silver, Sterling, and Silverplate

I am buying **popular patterns of silverplate flatware, hollow ware, etc.** I prefer pieces in excellent condition without monograms. I will pay for shipping and insurance. Below is a sample of some wanted pieces.

I am also buying popular patterns of **sterling flatware and hollow ware.** I prefer pieces in excellent condition without monograms, but will consider all patterns and conditions. I will pay for shipping and insurance. Some examples of patterns and companies are listed here. As prices vary, please call for my wholesale buying price.

Buttercup, Gorham	Grande Baroque, Wallace
Catus, George Jensen	Lucerne, Wallace
Chantilly, Gorham	Old Master, Towle
Eloquence, Lunt	Repousse, Kirk
Francis I, Reed & Barton	Strasbourg, Gorham

Other wants include: **Shawnee pottery, Regal china, Old McDonalds Farm (Regal), Watt pottery, Roseville pottery, Weller pottery, Rookwood pottery, Coors pottery, and sterling.**

Rick Spencer
Salt Lake City, UT
801-973-0805

We Pay

Alhambra, 1907, Anchor Rogers	2.00-75.00
Berkshire, 1897, 1847 Rogers	2.00-150.00
Berwick, 1904, Wm Rogers	2.00-150.00
Bride's Bouquet, 1908, Alvin	1.00-100.00
Century, 1923, Holmes & Edwards	50¢-60.00
Charter Oak, 1906, 1847 Rogers	2.00-200.00

Columbia, 1893, 1847 Rogers **1.00-150.00**
Eternally Yours, 1941, 1847 Rogers ....**50¢-75.00**
First Love, 1937, 1847 Rogers ....**50¢-75.00**
Floral, 1903, Wm Rogers **2.00-150.00**
Glenrose, 1908, Wm Rogers..**2.00-150.00**
Grenoble, 1906, Wm Rogers **2.00-200.00**
La Vique, 1908, 1881 Rogers **1.00-200.00**
Modern Art, 1904, Reed & Barton ....**75¢-125.00**
Moselle, 1906, American...**3.50-600.00**
Old Colony, 1911, 1847 Rogers ....**75¢-125.00**
Holly, 1906, EHH Smith **63.00-250.00**
Thistle, 1905, EHH Smith...**1.00-125.00**
Vintage, 1904, 1847 Rogers **1.00-200.00**

I've been **buying and selling silver (not silverplate)** for over 15 years and will always try to pay the most for your silver. To prove this is my policy, if you send your silver to me (remember to pack it securely and insure) I will send you my offer in the form of a check. If you accept, just cash the check; if you are not happy with my offer, just return my check, and I will return your silver plus your postage costs. So it costs you nothing to try — so far over 99% of my offers have been accepted!

The following is a brief listing of the prices that I will pay. Please keep in mind that these are minimums for bent or damaged pieces. I will pay more (often much more) for rarer, nicer, or more unusual pieces. See also my listing under **Coins** in this book.

B - 4 Your Time
Attention: Phil Townsend
15 Tabar Ave.
Lee, MA 01238

We Pay

Forks or Spoons, sm, ea..**1.00-50.00**
Forks or Spoons, lg, ea..**2.00-100.00**
Thimbles, ea..**1.00-50.00**
Salt & Pepper Shakers, pr **5.00-100.00**
Candlesticks, pr ....**5.00-1,000.00+**

Silver, Sterling, and Silverplate

MidweSterling is the biggest buyer of **used silverware (knives, forks, spoons, ladles, etc.) and hollow ware (trays, pitchers, tea sets, goblets, trophies, etc.)** nationwide. There are five types of metallic silverware and hollow ware: sterling, silverplate, stainless, pewter, and Dirilyte. Generally, if it is **sterling** it will be marked 'sterling' or '925' or '925/100.' The marks '800' or '900' or 'coin' mean it is respectively 80% or 90% or 90% pure silver. Sterling is 92.5% pure silver. Rarely is sterling not marked 'sterling' or '925.'

Generally, if it is **silverplate** it has a metal color of sterling but not the marks of sterling. Some common marks on silverplate are any word with 'plate,' 'Wm Rogers,' '1847 Robers Bros,' 'Holmes & Edwards,' or 'EPNS.' **Stainless** will have the look of stainless and be marked 'stainless,' '18/8' or only with the manufacturer's name. Virtually of no value are restaurant stainless, premium/promotion stainless, and stainless sold through low-end retail stores. **Pewter** is generally marked 'pewter' and **Dirilyte** (gold colored) is marked 'dirilyte.'

A combination of the following determines value: pattern, maker, condition, rarity, size, style, version of piece; and of course, supply and demand. Dented knife handles, pitted knife blades, monograms, and excessive wear all detract from silverware value. Dents, missing pieces, broken parts, and monograms all detract from hollow ware value.

MidweSterling also offers a repair service including knife reblading and garbage disposal damage repair. We perform a careful apprasial for maximum value to buy your merchandise. Pictures of hollow ware and photocopies of flatware front and back with trademarks are necessary if you do not know the pattern name. Listed here is a general model of values — most patterns will fall into this range. Fancier, heavier, older hollow ware is worth the most. Weighted or cement-filled sterling hollow ware is usually worth very little. **Note also that stainless, silverplate, pewter, or Dirilyte hollow ware is only valuable if very elaborate.**

MidweSterling
4311 NE Vivion Blvd, Dept WTB
Kansas City, MO 64119-2890
816-454-1990 (closed Wednesday, Sunday)
fax 816-454-1605

Most Patterns

	We Pay
Sterling Hollow ware, not weighted, per pc	**5.00-10,000.00**
Sterling Flatware, per pc	**5.00-50.00**
Sterling Souvenir Spoons, fancy, old, per pc	**10.00-200.00**
Stainless, Silverplate, Pewter, or Dirilyte Flatware, per pc	**5¢-5.00**

In the sterling silver market today, pieces are judged by age, quality, condition, and weight (although weight is not nearly as important as in prior years). I am interested in buying exotic and unusual pieces in silver, coin .800 to .900, sterling, and silverplate. Craftmanship from all periods is highly desired. Hand chasing and embossing, fine engraving, and full-figure and enameled objects, etc., are sought. Huge centerpieces, medallion heads, animal or human figures, silver compotes, tureens, and pitchers are wanted. I also have interest in presentation or commemorative pieces, pieces with historical or political provenance, or highly unusual pieces. We pay top dollar for:

Russian silver	Gorham Martele
Georg Jensen	Rococo Revival
Tiffany	Renaissance Revival style
Georgian-English silver	Applied and mixed metals
Victorian-English silver	Francis I
Elaborate silverplate	

Ann Marie Alexander Galleries
Fine Art and Antiques
P.O. Box 1002
Dania, FL 33004-1002
954-987-1485

Snowdomes

I am an advanced snowdome collector (I wrote the first book, *Snowdomes* and founded the newsletter and collector's club, *Snow Biz*). I want unusual items and am willing to pay for them. I collect **plastic snowdomes** from small, obscure tourist attractions, sites, towns; and advertisements or promotional domes for any type of product including (but not limited to) TV and radio stations, newspapers, hotels, restaurants, food products, political campaigns. Here are a few specific ones I happen to know about, but my wants are certainly not limited to this list. I don't care if they have water, as long as their plaques are very legible.

Nancy McMichael
P.O. Box 53310
Washington, DC 20009
202-234-7484

We Pay

Albany, New York State Capitol, plastic	**20.00**
Angel, figural, all plastic, 5"	**50.00-75.00**
Black Cat, figural, all plastic, 5"	**50.00-75.00**
The Bounty at Tahiti, plastic	**15.00**
The Bounty at Cape Horn, plastic	**15.00**
Boy Scout Jamboree, older plastic dome not new glass	**25.00**
Chrysler Building, plastic	**25.00**
Chrysler Building, glass, older	**75.00**
City Island, New York, plastic	**25.00**
Coney Island, plastic	**25.00**
Dogpatch USA, w/Daisy Mae & Lil' Abner, TV-shaped brown plastic	**15.00**
Elf, figural, all plastic, 5"	**50.00-75.00**
Dwarf, figural, all plastic, 5"	**50.00-75.00**
Flagship Hotel, advertising, plastic	**15.00**
Grim Reaper, figural, all plastic, 5"	**50.00-75.00**
Greek God, figural, all plastic, 5"	**50.00-75.00**
Howdy Doody, figural, all plastic, holds water ball in lap	**100.00**
Indian Chief, figural, all plastic, 5"	**50.00-75.00**
Kentucky Horse Farm, Louisville, Kentucky, plastic	**25.00**
Letchworth State Park, plastic	**25.00**
Lighthouse, figural, all plastic, 5"	**50.00-75.00**
Los Angeles Civic Center, plastic	**20.00**
Madison Square Garden, plastic	**25.00**
Monticello, NY, plastic	**20.00**
Owl, figural, all plastic, 5"	**50.00-75.00**
Palisades Park, N.J., plastic	**25.00**
Pine Creek Railroad, Allaire, N.J.	**30.00**
Playland, Rye, NY (might say Rye Playland)	**40.00**
Sarasota, Florida (or any tourist attraction in Sarasota)	**15.00**
South Fallsburg, NY, plastic	**25.00**
The Shell Factory, Ft. Myer, Florida	**25.00**
Tar Heels (from University of North Carolina), older plastic dome	**20.00**

I buy **souvenir, plastic location snowdomes from the late '60s through the present** that name a specific location on a plaque inside the dome. They can be any size and shape. I do **not** buy any dome with Lucite plaques that have scenes screened on them inside. While condition affects value, they need not be new or in mint condition and they need not have water or snow inside. I am particularly interested in domes from the Los Angeles area: amusement parts, tourist attraction, and other sites such as L.A. Civic Center, L.A. City Hall, Grauman's Chinese Theatre, etc.; Chinatowns; small, obscure amusement parks from all over; figural if they name a place and domes that sit on a pedestal or a calendar base. The more specific the site the better. I am very negotiable on prices and will pay shipping. I buy one or a collection. The minimum I pay is $5.00 a dome. I will answer all letters.

Chloe Ross
7553 W Norton Ave. #4
Los Angeles, CA 90046-5523
213-874-3044 (no early calls)

Soda Fountain Collectibles

We collect **early soda fountain material but especially paper items** which provide so much information about this wonderful business. Our interests range from trade catalogs, trade magazines, photos of early soda fountain interiors, straw dispensers, syrup dispensers, pottery root beer mugs, soda glasses marked with the product name, glass malted milk dispensers, mechanical shake makers, etc. We also own three of the marble soda fountains made in the 1870s and '80s. Someday a book about soda fountain history will result from all of this. Please note that condition is very important.

Harold and Joyce Screen
2804 Munster Rd.
Baltimore, MD 21234
410-661-6765 (after 6pm EST)

We Pay

Photographs, interiors of old soda fountains	up to 60.00
Soda Fountain Magazine, pre-1910	30.00
Soda Fountain Magazine, 1910-1919	25.00
Soda Fountain Magazine, 1920-1930	20.00
Soda Dispenser Magazine	15.00
Western Druggist Magazine, pre-1900	10.00
Trade Catalogs, pre-1900, per illustrated page	1.50
Trade Catalogs, after 1900, per illustrated page	1.00
Trade Catalogs, in color, pre-1940, per illustrated page	1.50
Straw Dispenser, Grape Smash, complete	900.00
Straw Dispenser, Bohemian	450.00
Straw Dispenser, opalescent swirl, any pattern, w/original lid	600.00
True Fruit Advertising, by J. Hungerford Smith Co.	Call
Root Beer Mug, Miners	125.00

Soda Fountain Collectibles

Root Beer Mug, Liquid Carbonic 90.00
Root Beer Mug, Pa-Poose 100.00
Soda Glass, Golden Orangeade..35.00
Soda Glass, Jersey Creme..35.00
Syrup Dispenser, Cardinal Cherry, w/original pump.........................1,100.00
Syrup Dispenser, Jersey Creme, w/original pump...............................700.00
Floor Model Mechanical Milk Shakers...800.00

Souvenir China

Wanted: **rolled edge 10" souvenir/historical plates from Staffordshire, England,** and imported by Rowland and Marsellus, Royal on, and A.C. Bosselman, as well any other souvenirs with scenes of cities or towns that have any of these importers' marks. We buy all unusual Rowland and Marsellus souvenir china. Their back-stamp mark may be written in full or be shown as R&M in a diamond. (R&M was a New York importer from Staffordshire, England.) Blue transfers on white are of cities, towns, or personalities and were produced from 1900 through 1930. Also wanted are **German white porcelain divided dishes that usually have a large gold or orange and red lobster handle.** Please write or call. All calls and letters answered.

David Ringering
1480 Tumalo Dr. SE
Salem, OR 97301-9278

We Pay

Rolled-Edge Plate...**50.00+**
Coupe Plate, 10"...**45.00+**
Fruit & Flower Bordered Plate, 9½" ....**35.00+**
Souvenir Plate, 9"...**25.00+**
Tumbler..**40.00+**
Cup & Saucer...**50.00+**
Vase ....**150.00+**
Pitcher ....**150.00+**
Miscellaneous Piece..**90% of book value**
Divided Lobster Dish, German ....**50.00+**
Souvenir Tumbler, German, metal w/North American scene ....**10.00+**

Sporting Collectibles

I buy sports tickets, sports books, programs, and other publications such as guides and annuals. Also wanted are pennants and other forms of memorabilia. Baseball, football, basketball, hockey, boxing — all sports — all items wanted.

Bob Adelson
13610 N Scottsdale #10
Scottsdale, AZ 85254
602-596-1913

Stamps

I am buying quantities of U.S. canceled stamps. They can be on paper. Please send an inquiry first if you have large quantities. Always include SASE for my response. I usually respond same day received unless I'm on vacation and mail usually is 3 to 5 days. I pay promptly.

Fred Susukida
4224 Waialae Ave.
Ste. 5-236
Honolulu, HI 96816

We Pay

U.S. Canceled Stamps (common variety okay), per thousand **1.00**
Foreign Stamps (on paper okay), per thousand **1.00**

Stanhopes

I am looking for all types of these little items with a peep hole and a scene of some type. I have many other wants such as sewing items, children's sewing machines, keychain licenses; contact me for specifics.

Kayla Conway
4500 Napal Ct.
Bakersfield, CA 93307
805-833-0291

We Pay

Binoculars	10.00+
Cars	10.00+
Cross	10.00+
Needle Case	40.00+
Toy TV	10.00

Stoneware

Decorated stoneware from West Virginia and Southwestern Pennsylvania with cobalt or manganese decoration on stoneware body (light to dark gray) decoration, the fancier the better are wanted; stencils are okay but free-hand designs are better. Especially wanted are figural pieces (dogs, lions, squirrels, etc.); urns; water coolers; pitchers; fence post tops; jars and jugs with people, animals, flowers, verses, and merchant listings; also pieces with fruit and odd splashes of blue. I am also interested in ledgers, billheads, etc., from potteries. Please enclose clear photograph and description along with SASE. No repaired jars please!

Wanted are items from these potteries:

A. Boughner, Greensboro, PA
Knox & Haught, Shinnston, WV
Blackshere & Beatty, Mannington, WV
Koon & Bro. Mannington, WV
Hogan & Woodyard, Mannington, WV
A. Conrad, Shinnston, WV
J.P. Parker, Jane Lew, WV
Thompson & Williams, Morgantown, WV
Hamilton & Jone, Greenboro, PA
Williams & Reppert, Greensboro, PA
Roger Lloyd, Palatine, WV
Knotts & Swidler, Palatine, WV
Richey & Hamilton, Palatine, WV
T.D. Harden, Palatine, WV
Boyers & Harden, Palatine, WV
Any Pottery Marked Marion Co. VA 1853, 1854
Jars Marked Rivesville, WV

Jars Marked Babbackville, WV
Jars Marked Cameron, WV

I am buying blue and white stoneware, embossed pitchers, butter and bread crocks, water coolers, mugs, rolling pins, cannister sets, etc. **I pay from 30% to 50% of book** depending on condition and blue and white contrast. I also want any **Homestead Grays, baseball memorabilia (postcards, photos), and anything related the the Homestead Brays versus the Grant Town Pirates.**

Rusty
P.O. Box 373
Grant Town, WV 26574-0373

Stove-Related Items

Being at the nationwide communication center of antique stove interests, I can provide free advice to would-be sellers about **stove-related items.** I'm not a collector, so won't pay top retail dollar, but if a *really desirable* pre-1935 item becomes available, I've occassionally paid a correct price for it as a discriminating and not very active picker. My main focus is on stove information items. Like my customers, I'm information hungry, not a condition snob. As long as all the pages are present and legible, I'm interested; even if all I get to do is rent the item to make a photocopy.

Clifford Brown
Antique Stove Information Clearinghouse
417 N Main St.
Monticello, IN 47960
219-583-6465 (phone is best **any** hour; keep trying)

Information Items   **We Pay**

Stove Manufacturer's Cookbook, 1910, 50 pages, w/illustrations.....**up to 15.00**
Stove Manufacturer's Cookbook, 1933, 100 pages, hardbound, thermostat illustration only ....**up to 7.00**
Stove Manufacturer's Catalog, 1890, 100 pages, Northern mfg........**up to 25.00**
Stove Manufacturer's Catalog, 1934, 50 pages, Southern mfg............**up to 6.00**
Stove Manufacturer's Operating Directions Card, 1914 ....**up to 4.00**
Stove Manufacturer's Trade Card, 1890, w/stove illustrations & operating directions ....**up to 4.00**

Stove-Related Items

Metal Trades Journal, such as *Stoves & Hardware Reporter*, ca 1900, ea, in quantity ....**up to 4.00**

Book, hardbound, 1890, such as *Kitchen Boiler Connections*............**up to 7.00**

Book, hardbound, 1941, *Fire on the Hearth*, by J. Peirce ....**up to 10.00**

Noninformative Items   We Pay

Base Burner, 1899, ornate, largest size, best grade, complete, unrestored, minor damage ....**up to 500.00**

Base Burner, 1926, plain, cheap grade, regardless of condition ......**Not Wanted**

Gas Range, 1915, 4 burners, long legs, window in oven door, complete, minor damage ....**up to 200.00**

Gas Range, 1927, 4 burners, long legs, 2-tone porcelain, ...**Not Wanted**

Portable Oven, 1895, sheet iron, embossed design, signed by the right manufacturer ....**up to 22.00**

Portable Oven, 1930, sheet iron, not embossed, unsigned, undesired manufacturer..**Not Wanted**

Stove Board, 1918, floral design, 95% not rusted............................**up to 20.00**

Stove Board, 1935, pseudo-wood grain, regardless of condition (a stove board is a sheet-metal-over-wood protector for under the stove)..........**Not Wanted**

I am buying **Round Oak stoves, advertising, and selected stoves.** The Round Oak factory was located in Dowagiac, Michigan. They advertised mainly with an Indian (Doe-Wah-Jack).

Advertising items must be in very good-plus condition. Chips, tears, water stains, etc., will subtract from the price. If you have a harder-to-find piece, I may consider buying a lower grade. Stove prices are for complete models in very good condition — they may be in need of new nickel, finials, or may need replating but must be complete with no damage. I can use Indians as finials with feathers missing for less.

Items not of interest include the sad iron and solid Indian finials as these are reproductions. Also I'm not interested in porcelain stove brochures or catalogs. There are items other than those listed that would be of interest — let me know what you have! If possible, please send photos of large items or photocopy smalls (postcards, trade cards, catalogs, etc.). Also give an accurate description of condition. I can pay more on quality items.

Greg Marquart
P.O. Box 8615
Benton Harbor, MI 49023
616-926-7080

Round Oak Advertising   We Pay

Litho, Dutch Boy or Standing Indian...**450.00+**

Calendar, 1914, w/standing Indian ....**300.00+**
Calendar, Indian & Dutch boy ....**180.00+**
Calendar, 1918, forward full pad ....**125.00+**
Cardboard Standee, Indian & stove..**500.00+**
Plate, dark green or brown...**75.00+**
Plate, other colors ....**100.00+**
Pocket Mirror ....**60.00+**
Watch Fob ....**125.00+**
Tin Sign...**200.00+**
Cuff Links, pr **60.00**
Stock Certificate **50.00**

Round Oak Stoves   We Pay

All 12" Models ....**500.00+**
Kate Lee, 16" or 18" ....**1,500.00+**

Finials   We Pay

Standing Indian..**75.00+**
Round Indian Logo ....**50.00+**
Others ....**25.00+**

Swanky Swigs

Swanky Swigs are small decorated glass containers (juice glasses) with small flowers, sailboats, animals, dots, stars, or checkers and they come in different sizes — anywhere from 3⅟₁₆" to 4¾". Kraft cheese spreads came in these containers and they date from the 1930s to the present. In most cases, I only need one each of the Swanky Swigs listed here.

Joyce Jackson
900 Jenkins Rd.
Aledo, TX 76008
817-441-8864

                                                                                      We Pay

Antique #1, 4¾", black, blue, brown, green or orange ....**20.00+**
Antique #2, 4⅝", orange, blue or black..**25.00+**
Band Pattern #5, 3⅛", red & black..**20.00+**
Bustling Betsy, 4¾", green or orange..**20.00+**
Checkerboard, 4⅝", white & green or white & blue................................**25.00+**
Checkers, 3⅛" ....**Call or Write**

Circles & Dots, 4¾", black or green ....**20.00+**
Cornflower #2, 4³⁄₁₆", dark blue, light blue or red....................................**20.00+**
Ethnic Series, 4⅝", Scottish, burgundy...**25.00+**
Ethnic Series, 4⅝", India, yellow ....**35.00+**
Fleur-de-Lis, 3⅛", black & red ....**Call or Write**
Kiddie Kup, 4¾", orange or black ....**20.00+**
Lattice & Vine, 3½", blue & white or red & white....................................**35.00+**
Provincial Crests, 4⅝", Canada, burgundy & red....................................**30.00+**
Star #1, 4¾", black or green..**30.00+**
Special Issues, 3½", red tulip #1 (Del Monte)...**60.00+**
Sportsman Series, 4⅝", Hockey, deep red **25.00**
Tulip #1, 3½", yellow ....**20.00+**
Tulip #1, 4⅝", black or yellow ....**20.00+**
Tulip #3. 4¾", dark blue or light blue...**20.00+**
Any Glass Marked 'Greetings From Kraft'......................................**Call or Write**

Syrocowood

We collect pressed wood items made by Syrocowood and other companies such as Ornawood and Durawood. We are especially interested in brush holders, thermometers, and Scottie-related items. We are looking for items in excellent condition.

Carole Kaifer
P.O. Box 232
Bethania, NC 27010
910-924-9672

We Pay

Brush Holders **10.00-25.00**
Thermometers **5.00-20.00**

Tiffany Lamps

I am buying **Tiffany lamps, shades, wall sconces — damaged or mint condition**. Any size, design, and/or color is desirable. The price I am willing to pay depends on all the above factors but an average price is listed below.

Reyne Hogan
2507 Observatory Ave.
Cincinnati, OH 45208
513-321-5141

We Pay

Single Gold Lily Shades	**500.00+**
Single Bell Shades	**500.00+**
Damascene Gold Shades	**2,000.00+**
Other Colors	**3,000.00+**
Leaded Shades	**5,000.00+**
Bases	**1,500.00**

I buy **small Tiffany pieces**. Small pieces as boxes, spoons, jewelry, etc., are wanted for my collection. Call or send your price list.

Other interests include: **pocket watches, Reddy Kilowat, Royal Doulton, Beswick, match safes, old autographed books, eye cups, law enforcement badges, sterling silver, sewing items, stanhopes, Clarice Cliff, and purses.**

Kayla Conway
4500 Napal Ct.
Bakersfield, CA 93307
805-833-0291

We Pay

Boxes	**1.00-50.00+**
Jewelry	**10.00-1,000.00+**
Spoons	**1.00-100.00+**
Other Smalls	**1.00-50.00+**

Tire Ashtrays

I'm interested in buying most tire ashtrays. I'm aware of about 800 different ones now, and a listing here couldn't do justice to what's available. Please send a complete description of tire lettering and condition. Please note any defects such as burn marks on the tire or incomplete (or missing) painted advertising imprints/stickers on the ashtray insert. Please contact me prior to shipping and provide a complete description in your first letter. I also have tire ashtrays available for sale, as well as *The Tire Ashtray Collector's Guide.* This guide details over 600 varieties and is available from me for $12.95 postpaid. I'll reply to all inquiries which include SASE.

Jeff McVey
1810 W State St. #427
Boise, ID 83702-3955

Tobacciana

I am buying **cigar advertising items** as shown in the listings below. All items must be in fine to very-fine condition. Please include a complete description — colors, dimensions, flaws, etc. — and if possible, a photo or photocopy of the item. All items **must contain cigar advertising**. In case of cardboard or tin signs and tin cigar containers, an **actual cigar must be shown**. It can be a single cigar, a box of cigars, a man smoking a cigar, etc. This requirement applies only to signs and tins. All other items need have only the cigar brand name. **Note:** I do **not** want wooden cigar boxes, cigar labels, or cigar bands.

The Cigar Man
Mike Schwimmer
325 E Blodgett
Lake Bluff, IL 60044-2112
847-295-1901

We Pay

Advertising Mirrors	25.00-75.00
Ashtrays	10.00-25.00
Change Mats, any material	15.00-50.00
Change Receivers, glass	35.00-75.00
Cigar Cutters, Piercers, or Trimmers	15.00-35.00
Cigar Box Openers	10.00-20.00
Pin-Back Buttons	20.00-50.00

Pocket Match Safes, Matchboxes, or Book Holders **15.00-75.00**
Pocket Pouches, leather, cloth, or metal..**5.00-15.00**
Signs, cardboard or tin, must show cigar......................................**10.00-150.00**
Signs, framed in glass, pre-1920 ....**75.00-250.00**
Tins or Cans, must show cigar **15.00-100.00**
Tip Trays or Serving Trays...**40.00-150.00**
Trade Cards or Business Cards...**4.00-8.00**
Other Unusual, Small Items..**Call or Write**

Tools

I collect and use **wood-working tools**. I'm currently trying to fill out a collection of Stanley planes. Also wanted are levels, rules, marking gauges, etc. Wooden molding planes always fit into my collection. **I will pay $100.00 and up** for planes needed to fill out my collection. Unusual tools are also wanted.

Write with description including size, shape, and any markings on plane or tool. Photos really help. All letters answered promptly. If calling, call evenings (PST).

David Barth
P.O. Box 81
Elk, WA 99009
509-292-2600

Toothbrush Holders

These figural holders were made depicting animals, people, storybook personalities, and Disney characters. They have been made of plastic, bisque, and ceramic materials and date from the 1930s. Please describe or send a photo. **I will pay $35.00 and up depending on the subject. I am also interested in clothes sprinkler bottles.**

Joyce Wolford
1050 Spriggs Dr.
Lander, WY 82502
307-332-5868

Toys

We specialize in **collectible memorabilia from the 1950s through today, but primarily '50s and '60s**. We are especially interested in buying character products. We are not limited to just toys; we will also buy board games, lunch boxes, movie and TV-character toys, comic books, comic strips, original art, toy soldiers, toy weapons, action figures, playsets, View-Master items, robots, space toys, non-sports cards, drinking glasses, cereal premiums, and so on. We are always interested in **original packaging, instruction sheets, and catalogs**.

Toy Scouts
137 Casterton Ave.
Akron, OH 44303
330-836-0668 or fax 330-869-8668

We Pay

Character Rings, 1940s	**Call**
Comic Books, 1930s-60s	**Call**
Doll, Batgirl Super Queen, Ideal, 1967	**1,000.00**
Doll, GI Joe female nurse, Hasbro, 1967	**1,000.00**
Figurine, Superman or Captain Marvel, wood, 1940s	**500.00-1,000.00**
Mad Scientist Laboratory Set, 1963	**2,000.00**
Gun, Lost in Space Roto-Jet, Mattel, 1966	**1,000.00**
Jewelry, MAD's Alfred E. Newman, 1960s	**100.00+**
Outfit, Captain Action or Spider Man, Ideal, 1967, ea	**1,000.00**
Outfit, MAD's Alfred E. Newman Straight Jacket, 1960s	**500.00**
Outfit Accessory, Batman Utility Belt, Ideal, 1966	**1,000.00**
Playset, Batman, Ideal, 1966	**5,000.00**
Playset, Justice League of America, Ideal, 1967	**10,000.00**
Model Kit, King Kong's Thronester, Aurora, 1966	**3,000.00**
Model Kit, Godzilla's Go-Kart, Aurora, 1966	**3,000.00**

As a collector of **Baby Boomer-era items (1948 through 1972)**, I am interested in an endless number of items and toys produced as promotions for TV shows. I am looking for **children's lunch boxes and thermoses, Beatles and Elvis items, rock 'n roll memorabilia, super hero and other character dolls or** items, robots and space toys, cap guns and sets, original boxes (even if empty), and much more. Any items relating to the following are wanted: Howdy Doody, Green Hornet, Beany and Cecil, Batman, Beatles, Brady Bunch, Jetsons, American Bandstand, Dark Shadows, Davy Crockett, Universal Movie Monsters, robots and space toys, Paladin, Munsters, Addams Family, Bonanza, Flintstones, Lost in Space, Space Patrol, Supercar, Star Trek, Star Wars series, Underdog, Rifleman, and many others. Price depends on the item. Any toys, character, advertising, or TV show-related items will be considered for purchase or trade.

Below is a listing of some of the items I am searching for and prices I am willing to pay for excellent-condition items. I would be paying a lesser amount for lesser-condition items. Mint-in-box items would be worth more to me. Please send photos if possible when sending an inquiry and a LSASE for a reply. I would like the opportunity to purchase your items. Thank you.

Terri's Toys and Nostalgia
Terri Mardis-Ivers
419 S First St.
Ponca City, OK 74601
405-762-8697 or 405-762-5174 (evenings)
fax 405-765-2657
e-mail: ivers@pcok.com

General Categories of Interest — We Pay

Miniature Boat Motors, metal, battery-operated, realistic forms w/Johnson, Evinrude, etc., printed on side	**70.00+**
Vehicles, versions of real cars, boats, etc., 8" or larger	**30.00+**
Promotional Model Vehicles, prior to 1980	**20.00+**
Other Vehicles	**Call or Write**
Cap Guns, through the 1960s	**15.00+**
Gun & Holster Sets, through the 1960s	**up to 200.00**
Dolls (Munsters, Beatles, Elvis, Addams Family, I Dream of Jeannie, Star Trek, Lone Ranger, Hopalong Cassidy, & so many more!)	**10.00-150.00**
Cowboy Character items (except paper) for Lone Ranger, Gene Autry, Bonanza, Rifleman, Roy Rogers, Tom Mix, and TV Show Westerns	**Call or Write**

Hopalong Cassidy — We Pay

Clothes Hamper	**200.00**
Chaps	**40.00**
Skirts	**30.00**
Guns	**40.00**
Holsters	**70.00**

Toys

Bicycle	**500.00**
Tricycle	**500.00**
Clocks, Dolls, Lamps, Bedspreads, Vinyl Flooring, Saddle, Figurines, Potato Chip Tin Can, Wallet & Other Items	**25.00+**

Elvis Presley Enterprises Items   We Pay

Scarves	**35.00**
Jewelry	**100.00**
Overnight Case	**100.00**
Doll, 1956	**300.00**
Guitar, 1956	**250.00**
Autograph Book	**200.00**
Wallet	**200.00**
Handbag	**200.00**
Shoes	**200.00**
Record Player	**200.00**
Scrapbook	**75.00**
Pillow	**20.00**
Many Other Items Wanted	**Call or Write**

Beatles Items, circa 1960s to '70s   We Pay

Kaboodle Kit	**200.00**
Brunch Bag	**200.00**
Record Player	**350.00**
Guitar	**150.00**
Shoes	**50.00**
Thermos	**60.00**
Hat	**20.00**
Drums	**200.00**
Lamp	**70.00**
Drinking Glass	**25.00**
Alarm Clock	**100.00**
Many More Items Wanted	**Call or Write**

Kiss & Monkees Items   We Pay

Guitar, Drums, Trading Cards, Radios, Toy Cars, Hand Puppets, Dolls, View-Master Reels, Lunch Boxes, Thermoses, Jewelry	**30.00**
Colorforms	**20.00**
Sleeping Bag	**45.00**
Tour Jacket	**50.00**
Record Player	**50.00**
Kiss Waste Basket	**30.00**
Kiss Make-Up Kit	**20.00**
Games & Many Other Items Wanted	**Call or Write**

I'm a Christian collector as well as 'picker' (I buy for different people who are collectors or resell items) with interests in **Baby Boomer collectibles of the 1940s through 1980s.** Many wants are listed below; I'm also interested in **clocks, watches, cookie jars, lamps, lighters, phones, and radios.**

Do not send anything without our agreeing on price. I only buy old items in undamaged condition. SASE is a must. Please send photo and price. I have been a collector/picker since 1971.

R. Gray
2047 Jeffcott St.
Ft. Myers, FL 33901
941-332-0153

We Pay

Annalee Animals	**up to 50.00**
Bobbin' Head Dolls & Nodders	**up to 20.00**
Breyer Horses & Animals	**up to 20.00**
China, w/Aunt Jemima or Little Red Riding Hood	**up to 50.00**
China or Ceramic Items, w/Care Bears, Garfield, Disney, etc.	**up to 20.00**
China, w/Western motif or railroad logo	**up to 25.00**
Figurines, animal & nursery rhymes, marked Wade, England	**up to 10.00**
Moon & Star Glassware	**up to 10.00**
Purses, plastic or Lucite	**up to 20.00**
Steiff Animals	**up to 50.00**
Taxidermy Items	**up to 50.00**
Toby Mugs	**up to 100.00**
Unusual or Gaudy Items, old	**Call or Write**
World Globes, w/black oceans	**20.00**
World's Fair Items, dated through 1964	**25.00**

I have a special interest in **character toys, cars, and items of the '50s through the '80s.** Categories of particular interest to me (but not limited to these) are listed here. In the diecast car line I am looking for Hot Wheels, Matchbox, Corgi's, and others. Items may be packaged or unpackaged but have no broken or missing parts.

Other interests include: **advertising, fast food collectibles, character drinking glasses, movie stars and TV memorabilia, View-Master reels, and Western memorabilia.**

Delores Lawson
Dee's Collectibles
Florida Twin Markets
U.S. Hwy. 441
Mt. Dora, FL 32757
407-298-4749

	We Pay
TV Characters	5.00+
Slot Cars	5.00+
Raggedy Ann & Andy	5.00+
Vogue Picture Discs	20.00+
Lunch Boxes	5.00+
Movie Stars	5.00+
Hotwheels & Matchbox Cars	2.00+

I want to buy **the very first Holiday Barbie doll in the red dress, the large Alien figure that was made in the '80s, and old one-piece rubber baby dolls that squeak that were usually made in the 1960s.** Other wants include **Hallmark Mayor's ornaments, Fenton glass made before the 1980s, and older Hot Wheels cars**.

G. Crinklaw
8118 N State Hwy. AC
Willard, MO 65781
417-742-3940

Let's face it — some people never grow up! Never having outgrown my childhood, I am still buying toys. I buy **all kinds of vintage toys** but am especially interested in lithographed tin, celluloid, and character toys. I also buy old board games, dolls, dollhouse furniture, etc.

Other interests include: **postcards, paper ephemera, Black memorabilia, advertising, Halloween collectibles, world's fairs, Christmas collectibles, and Valentines.**

Judith Katz-Schwartz
P.O. Box 6572
New York, NY 10128
212-876-3512

I am looking for **toys from the late 1950s through the 1960s**. I'm especially interested in toys and games that are TV related. I am also interested in science-fiction memorabilia from this time period. Please send a description of your item, including its condition, and your selling price.

Michael Summers
3258 Harrison
Paducah, KY 42001

Two Guys Toys, a major dealer in **Baby Boomer collectibles**, is operated by two guys, Keir Neubauer and Ira Brotman with extensive knowledge of toys from the 1950s through the 1970s. 'There hasn't been very much we haven't seen, collected, or sold over the last fifteen years of collecting and dealing in old toys,' notes Keir Neubauer, whose personal toy collection contains in excess of 30,000 items and runs the gamut from Aurora model kits to old cereal boxes. The toy collecting hobby has taken off over the last ten years as Baby Boomers want to recapture their childhood experiences. Toys from this era were generally of high quality, with excellent detail and features (such as shooting projectiles) that surely would not pass today's strict government standards. Top prices are realized for items in their original packaging with little play wear. We are especially interested in purchasing old store-stock toys, but any collection of one piece to thousands is desired. We pay fair prices for items, and will send payment by next day air. Don't sell too cheap, call the Two Guys! Any old toys wanted — call now!

Two Guys Toys
92 Kara Ln.
Feasterville, PA 19053
215-364-6685
610-649-5943

We Pay

GI Joe Action Soldier, in box	**125.00-175.00**
Captain Action Doll, in box	**150.00-250.00**
Captain Action Outfits, in box	**200.00-3,000.00**
Barbie Dolls	**25.00-5,000.00**
Aurora Slot Cars	**5.00-100.00**
Old Cereal Boxes	**Call**
Old Robots, battery operated	**100.00-1,000.00**

As a child I spent a lot of my time playing cowboys and Indians and soldier. Now as an adult I am trying to reclaim some of those fun times that I spent as a child. So I am collecting the toy guns I played with as a boy. I am buying character **toy guns, holsters, and machine guns from the '50s and '60s.** As an advanced collector, condition is important. But I will consider guns that are not in excellent or mint condition. Here are some examples of what I am buying and paying.

Ron Wright
P.O. Box 69
Burbank, OH 44214
216-624-3741

We Pay

Paladin, Have Gun Will Travel, guns	150.00+
Paladin, Have Gun Will Travel, holsters	150.00+
The Rebel, Johnny Yuma, gun & holster	300.00+
The Rebel, Johnny Yuma, scatter shot gun	250.00
Hopalong Cassidy, guns	100.00+
Gene Autry, guns	75.00
Mattel Shoot 'N Shell, sm	100.00
Mattel Shoot 'N Shell, .45 caliber	150.00
Tommyburst, machine gun	100.00

Wanted by collector: I seek **cap guns that have revolving cylinders from the 1950s and cast iron types** — the earlier the better. In **BB guns** I look for anything and everything except those with plastic parts or stocks. I will pay well for quality guns according to rarity; condition is also very important. Send photo and description and price to:

Terry Burger
2323 Lincoln St.
Beatrice, NE 68310
402-228-2797

Daisy BB Guns   **We Pay**

#1 Cast Iron Model	300.00-1,500.00
Cast Iron Heilprin	200.00-1,000.00
Double Barrel	200.00-800.00

Cap Guns	We Pay
Fanner 50	**50.00**
Early Cast Iron Types	**50.00+**
Animated Types	**300.00-3,000.00**

My wife and I are show and mall dealers. We specialize in toy **cap guns, BB guns, and cowboy gun and holster sets** featuring Hopalong Cassidy, Roy Rogers, Gene Autry, Matt Dillon, Wyatt Earp, etc. I will pay a fair price for good stuff. **I have paid as much as $500.00 to $600.00 for BB guns and $600.00 to $700.00 for cap guns.**

Paul D. Patchin
3425 Co. Rd. E-F
Swanton, OH 43558
419-826-8661

We buy, sell, trade: **Hot Wheels, Matchbox, Johnny Lightning, slot cars, Corgi, as well as car models, dealer promos, games, lunch boxes, Mego, GI Joe, toys of the '50s to '70s, and more.**

Todd's Toy Box
2084 Coral Ln.
Eagan, MN 55122-2007
612-452-6560

	We Pay
Hot Wheels, 1960s to 1970s	**5.00+**
Matchbox, 1950s to 1970s	**5.00+**
Models	**8.00+**
Slot Cars	**8.00+**
dealer promos	**20.00+**

I buy **Matchbox cars made from 1953 through 1969**. I will pay top dollar for most Matchbox cars with original boxes as listed in the price guide of the book, *Lesney's Matchbox Toys, Regular Wheels, 1947 through 1969,* by Charlie Mack and printed by Schiffer Publishing Ltd., copyright 1992. I am also interested in buying **Matchbox produced after 1969 and also all years of Hot Wheels, Johnny Lighning, and Aurora slot cars**. A color photo could be helpful. Please contact:

Richard Okula
P.O. Box 6393
Wolcott, CT 06716
203-879-6883

We Pay

#1 Road Roller, metal rollers **50.00**
#2 Dump Truck, metal wheels **50.00**
#3 Cement Mixer...**50.00**
#4 Tractor **50.00**
#4 Motor Cycle 'Triumph' **50.00**
#5 London Bus, metal wheels **50.00**
#6 6-Wheel Dump Truck **50.00**
#7 Milk Wagon **75.00**
#8 Caterpiller Tractor **30.00-65.00**
#9 Fire Truck...**25.00-50.00**
#10 Sugar Truck **40.00**
#11 Tanker...**50.00**
#12 Jeep, w/man..**50.00**
#13 Tow Truck..**35.00-50.00**
#14 Ambulance **20.00-55.00**
#15 Prime M&M Mover..**50.00**
#15 Refuse Truck **20.00**
#16 Trailer...**40.00**
#17 Austin Taxi..**50.00**
#17 Green Van...**50.00+**
#18 Caterpillar Bulldozer, w/man **50.00**
#19 MG Sports Car **75.00**
#19 Auston Racer **35.00**
#20 Stake Truck **50.00**
#21 Long Distance Coach...**50.00**
#22 Vauxhall Sedan **50.00**
#22 Pontiac **20.00**
#23 2-Wheel Camper...**50.00**
#24 Excavator, metal wheels **50.00**
#25 Dunlp Van **50.00**
#25 VW Beetle...**60.00**
#26 4-Wheel Cement Mixer **50.00**
#27 Low Loader...**85.00**
#28 Compressor Truck, metal wheels **50.00**
#29 Milk Truck..**50.00**

#30 Silver 6-Wheel Crane **35.00**
#31 Ford Wagon **50.00**
#32 Jaguar XK 140 ....**60.00**
#33 Ford Zodiac **50.00**
#34 VW Van **20.00-55.00**
#35 Horse Truck **50.00**
#35 Snow Truck **20.00**
#36 Austin A50 ....**50.00**
#36 Lambretta Motorcycle **60.00**
#37 Coca-Cola Truck...**50.00+**
#38 Refuse Truck **30.00**
#38 Vauxhall Wagon **25.00**
#38 Honda Motorcycle & Trailer **20.00**
#39 Ford Convertible **60.00**
#39 Pontiac Convertible...**30.00+**
#40 Dump Truck **50.00**
#41 D Type Jaguar **65.00**
#42 News Van **50.00**
#42 Studebaker Wagon **20.00**
#43 Hillman Minx...**50.00**
#43 Pail Loader **25.00**
#44 Rolls Royce..**25.00+**
#45 Vauxhall Victor **50.00**
#46 Morris Minor **50.00**
#47 Brook Bond Tea Van **50.00**
#48 Boat, metal or plastic **25.00-50.00**
#49 Half Track..**40.00**
#50 Commer Pick-Up **50.00**
#50 Tractor **20.00**
#50 Kennel Truck..**20.00**
#51 Cement Truck..**50.00**
#52 Maseati Racer **35.00**
#53 Aston Martin **50.00**
#53 Mercedes Benz ....**20.00+**
#54 Personel Carrier...**20.00**
#54 Ambulance **15.00**
#55 Army Amphibian **50.00**
#55 Police Car, blue **55.00**
#55 Galaxie or Mercury Police **20.00**
#56 Trolley Bus **55.00**
#56 Fiat 1500, red **50.00**
#57 Wolseley 1500 ....**50.00**
#57 Chevrolet Impala...**40.00**
#58 Airport Bus..**70.00**
#58 Pail Loader **20.00**
#59 Singer Van **60.00**
#59 Fairlane Fire Chief **50.00**
#60 Morris Pick-Up **20.00**

#70 Thames Van	**25.00**
#71 Army Water Truck	**30.00**
#71 Jeep Pick-Up	**20.00**
#71 Ford Wrecker	**20.00**
#72 Tractor	**25.00+**
#73 Refueler	**65.00**
#73 Ferrari Racer	**30.00**
#74 Refreshment Stand	**50.00**
#75 Ford Thunderbird	**85.00**

I am buying **antique mechanical toys**. I primarily collect tin wind-up toys but am also interested in friction and battery-operated toys. **Toys made prior to 1965** in good to mint-in-box condition are preferred. Listed below are some of the manufacturers that I am seeking.

Scott T. Smiles
848 SE Atlantic Dr.
Lantana, FL 33462-4702
407-582-4947

We Pay

Chein	**50.00+**
Lehmann	**250.00+**
Made in France	**100.00+**
Made in Germany	**125.00+**
Made in Great Britain	**50.00+**
Made in Italy	**75.00+**
Made in Japan	**50.00+**
Made in Spain	**75.00+**
Martin	**250.00+**
Marx	**100.00+**
Occupied Japan	**50.00+**
Strauss	**150.00+**
Unique Art	**100.00+**
US Zone Germany	**75.00+**
Wolverine	**75.00+**

I've been an avid collector of **Breyer and Hartland animal models** for almost 20 years. I would like to find examples to finish out my collection. I'm also interested in **china horses, dogs, and cats**.

Gay Mahlandt
14971 SW 210th St.
Rose Hill, KS 67133
316-776-2248

I want to buy **toy sewing machines** that really worked by turning crank handle. Prefer ones that have boxes but will consider without. No plastic please. The following prices are for machines in working condition with little wear.

Janet Luedtke
5110-103rd Ave.
Grand Junction, MI 49056
616-434-6884

We Pay

Tin or Metal **15.00-35.00**
Cast Iron **35.00-75.00**

Wanted: **tin toy globes produced by Ohio Art, Chein, Repogle and others.** I prefer globes that are 7" or smaller; these must be in good condition with no rust and minimal dents. Globes with red and yellow oceans, foreign languages, and game bases are particularly wanted as are globes depicting Mars, the moon, or other planets. Banks are okay. I will also pay postage. **Freestanding models of the Eiffel Tower in any material** are also wanted.

Chloe Ross
7553 W Norton Ave. #4
Los Angeles, CA 90046-5523
213-874-3044

We Pay

Tin Toy Globes, ea ....**5.00+**
Eiffel Tower Models, ea ....**5.00+**

I buy **Pound Pur-r-ries (stuffed toy cats) by Tonka in the 12" size only.** I prefer colors other than white. I also buy Pound Pur-r-ries' clothing, especially denim jackets. I'm also interested in **Stays-Stuffed cats by Schaper**, preferably with accessories. **I pay from $1.00 to $10.00** depending on condition, etc.

Linda Toivainen
R.R. 1, Box 128
Waterboro, ME 04087
207-247-3993

I am known for my fair dealings and for paying top prices for **windups, robots, space toys, toys made by TPS, Japanese/German/English motorcycles, Japanese tin cars, clowns, character toys, celluloid, Disney, boats, airplanes, and battery-operated toys**. Of special interest are **pre-1950s holiday items, especially Halloween and Christmas**. On a number of occasions I have paid over $2,000.00 for a single toy. What do you have?

Mark Bergin
P.O. Box 3073
Peterborough, NH 03458-3073
603-924-2079 or fax 603-924-2022

We Pay

Character Toys (any character, any type) ....**up to 15,000.00**
Christmas Items (such as candy containers, Santa figures, old ornaments, figural bulbs, blocks, games, feather trees, figures of any Christmas character, etc.) ....**up to 1,500.00**
Halloween Items (candy containers, diecuts, jack-o'-lanterns, crepe paper goods, figures, etc), vintage only ....**up to 1,500.00**
Robots or Space Toys, tin, Japanese, 1950s, original box ....**up to $24,000.00**
Motorcycles, tin, German or Japanese ....**up to 5,000.00**
Cars, tin, Japanese...**200.00-8,000.00**
Windup Toys, all types wanted...**up to 7,500.00**

I am interested in buying **tin windup toys from the 1950s through the early 1970s** that were made in the U.S., Germany, England, and Japan; **trains** made by Marx, Marklin, and American Flyer; **GI Joes; vintage Barbies and clothes; and Walt Disney items**. Please send detailed description, price, and a photocopy if possible.

D. Lerch
P.O. Box 586
North White Plains, NY 10603

Tramp and Trench Art

We are buyers of **tramp art, most anything made from notched cigar boxes, and trench art, and most anything made from brass cartridge shells.** Feel free to send photos for evaluation.

Sam Kennedy
212 N 4th St.
Coeur d'Alene, ID 83814
208-769-7575

We Pay

Layered Box, 12x6x4"	**50.00-150.00**
Nine-Layered Notched Frame, 2x2"	**50.00-150.00**
Notched Dresser	**200.00-1,000.00**
Bowls of Cigar Sticker Labels	**20.00+**
WWI Shells, w/dates & names	**30.00-100.00**
Shells, w/pictures	**50.00-150.00**
Shell Airplanes	**100.00-200.00**
Shell Lamps	**50.00-200.00**
Shell Ashtrays	**20.00+**

Twin Winton

The Twin Winton name was conceived by twins, Don and Ross Winton. In 1936 (when these 17-year-old twins started a small business making hand-decorated ceramic animal figures and sold them locally in Pasadena, California), Twin Winton became a successful pottery. Don continued to be the only designer for Twin Winton until the pottery closed in 1977. Besides designing for Twin Winton, Don has designed for other companies such as Disney,

Brush-McCoy, Ronald Reagan Foundation, and many others.

Twin Winton made their famed cookie jar collector series, salt and pepper shakers, and many other pieces. They also developed their distinctive woodstain finish. As the author of *Collector's Guide to Don Winton Designs* published by Collector Books, I am interested in researching the company through finding original company correspondence, sales literature and brochures, original pieces, and especially any pre-1963 catalogs. Please let me hear from you regarding Twin Winton.

Mike Ellis
266 Rose Ln.
Costa Mesa, CA 92627
714-646-7112 or fax 714-645-4697

Typewriter Ribbon Tins

I would like to buy typewriter ribbon containers, both tin and cardboard, for my extensive collection. Ribbon tins were made from the 1890s well into the 1970s. Generally, the more graphically appealing a tin is, the more it is worth; however, plain but rare ribbon tins also have value. The best way to find out what you have is to send a photocopy, a photo, or even a hand drawing of your item — or you may telephone me. I will answer all inquiries promptly. Please describe condition and enclose SASE. I also buy **other typewriter-related collectibles** which illustrate secretaries, typewriters, or tins such as blotters, secretarial erasing shields, carbon paper boxes, signs, rulers, tape measures, display cabinets, etc.

Hoby Van Deusen
28 The Green
Watertown, CT 06795
860-945-3456

We Pay

Tins w/Pictures	5.00-50.00+
Tins w/Lettering Only	3.00-20.00+
Wide or Cylindrical Tins	10.00-50.00+
Cardboards	2.00-10.00+
Blotters	4.00-10.00+
Erasing Shields	5.00-15.00+

Carbon Paper Boxes ....**5.00-15.00+**
Signs ....**Call or Write**
Rulers ....**2.00-10.00+**
Tape Measures ....**15.00-30.00+**
Display Cabinets ....**Call or Write**

Typewriters

During the mechanical writing machine's first quarter century (from 1875 to 1900) the biggest manufacturers priced their machines from $100.00 to $125.00. Working men who earned $10.00 a week could not afford these typewriters, so they usually sold to banking and law offices. Because there was demand for a writing machine which was affordable for home use, about 50 manufacturers created small machines without keys or type bars which sold at prices ranging from $1.00 to $15.00. A pointer was used to pick a letter from a row or a line of type, and these primitive devices did slow but adequate work.

I collect these typing devices, called index or indicator typewriters. They are very small and often confused with toys. If you have a machine listed below or other unusual-looking typewriters to offer, please send a photo or begin your inquiry with a telephone call.

Mike Brooks
7335 Skyline Blvd.
Oakland, CA 94611
510-339-1751 (evenings)

We Pay

Automatic **1,000.00**
Blinkenderfer Electric **3,000.00**
Brooks **1,000.00**
Crandall **500.00**
Crown **500.00**
Edison **1,500.00**
Ford **1,000.00**
Fitch **1,500.00**
Jackson **1,000.00**
McCool **1,000.00**
Niagara **2,000.00**
Pearl **1,000.00**

Typewriters

Sun	500.00
Victor	500.00

Nobody pays more! For world's leading collection, I am buying single items or entire collections for top prices! I am especially looking for **early typewriters, ribbon tins, telephones, telegraphs, copying machines, pencil sharpeners, and postcards about the old office.** See my listing under **Adding Machines** in this book. Also wanted is any U.S. Patent model of any of the before-mentioned items. **Magazines, manuals, and books about office equipment** are wanted. **Other interests include:**

Ford Model T Cars
Gramophones
Magic Lanterns
Magazine, *Scientific American*
Movie Cameras
Office Equpment

Optical Toys
Pre-Cinema Material
Sewing Machines (pre-1870)
Toasters
Typesetting Machines

Uwe H. Breker
6731 Ashley Ct.
Sarasota, FL 34241
941-925-0385 or fax 941-925-0487

Typewriters

We Pay

Blick Electric, 1901	20,000.00
Boston, 1886	15,000.00
Brooks, 1885	10,000.00
Coffman, 1902	5,000.00
Cooper, 1852	25,000.00
Crandall, 1879	3,000.00
Edison Mimeograph, 1984	10,000.00
Edland, 1891	10,000.00
Ford, 1893	10,000.00
Hamilton Automatic, 1887	10,000.00
Horton, 1883	10,000.00
Jones Typographer, 1852	20,000.00
Malling Hansen Writing Ball, 1867	30,000.00
Maskelyne, 1893	10,000.00
Morris, 1886	10,000.00
Pearl (Index), 1895	5,000.00
Peeler, 1857	30,000.00

Sholes & Glidden, 1873 ....**15,000.00**
U.S. Typewriter, 1887 ....**20,000.00**
Waverly, 1889 ....**10,000.00**

Vernon Kilns

I collect **Vernon Kilns dinnerware and pottery along with a number of other American dinnerware patterns.** Of particular interest are pieces manufactured from 1930 through the 1950s. Vernon Kilns produced a wide variety of items with distinctive styling. Some of the **Vernon Kilns designers and patterns I collect are:**

Jane F. Bennison — bowls, candlesticks, planters, vases, etc.
Harry Bird — various dinnerware patterns
Don Blanding — Aquarium, Coral Reef & Honolulu patterns; children's pieces or sets
Walt Disney — all dinnerware, figurines & hand-decorated bowls and vases
May & Vieve Hamilton — dinnerware and pottery
Rockwell Kent — Moby Dick, Our America & Salamina patterns
Janice Pettee — Sally Rand & other figurines
Gale Turnbull — various dinnerware patterns
Winchester 73/Frontier Days pattern, most pieces

Please send description, price, and condition of your piece. Photographs are helpful and will be returned. I may be interested in other items also. No phone calls, please. Thank you.

Other wants include: **Brayton Laguna, Catalina Island, and Russel Wright designs in glass, pottery, and wood.**

Ray Vlach, Jr.
5364 N Magnet Ave.
Chicago, IL 60630-1216

We are interested in purchasing **Vernon Kilns pottery by the following designers: Harry Bird, Rockwell Kent, Hamilton Sisters, and Gale Turnball.** We have a special interest in Harry Bird plates with floral, bird, or fish motifs. Please call with sizes and descriptions for prices.

Dave Lusty
Magazine Street Antiques
1829 Magazine St.
New Orleans, LA 70130
504-524-2807

Victorian Collectibles

I purchase **anything from the Victorian era (1845-1900)**. I am especially looking for the unusual, unique items in excellent condition. I can not appraise your items or respond to requests for educational information. Please send picture, written description, and your price.

Gary and Rhonda Hallden
21958 Larkin Dr.
Saugus, CA 91350
805-259-7868

We Pay

Bride's Baskets (also bowls or frames only)	**30.00+**
Books, illustrated children's or color-illustrated bindings	**8.00+**
Boxes, for gloves or collars, usually w/pictures of ladies	**40.00+**
China, hand painted (no decals wanted)	**25.00+**
Clothing, shoes, parasols, etc.	**20.00+**
Cranberry Glass	**20.00+**
Dishes, blue & white floral or historic themes	**20.00+**
Flow Blue	**60.00+**
Paperweights	**15.00+**
Photo Albums, w/pictures on covers	**25.00+**
Pie Birds	**20.00+**
Postcards, unusual	**5.00+**
Purses, beaded, fancy forms or designs	**30.00**
Scrapbooks	**25.00+**
Silver	**35.00+**
Valentines	**25.00+**
Other Old Paper Items, depicting ladies, children or animals	**15.00+**

I have a passion for collecting **all Victorian items**. Nothing is too insignificant. Victorian items with cherubs, animals, children, and flowers are particular favorites. If it's monogrammed or slightly worn, that's okay. Price will depend on the item and its condition. Please send me a list of what you have and the price you are asking. Pictures are sometimes helpful. I buy full estates or individual pieces. Below is a partial listing. Victorians had many special pieces for a single use, and I crave them all — anything that was used by a Victorian man, woman, or child is wanted.

Also wanted are **any items with cherubs (also angels or newts, cherubs without wings)** on them. Items can be almost anything of any material. The price I pay is dependent on the item and its condition. Please send a picture and description of what you have along with your asking price. Below is a partial listing of what I collect.

Cindi Lininger
2205 2nd Ave. W
Seattle, WA 98119

We Pay

Jewelry (cameos, lockets, brooches, pins, hair jewelry, rings, hatpins, hair combs, bracelets, charms, photography pins, hearts, chatelaines), ea **4.00-500.00**
Silverplate or Quadplate (serving pieces, utensils, castor sets, bride's baskets, candlesticks, purses, napkin rings, tea sets, trays, dresser sets, butter dishes, pickle castors, or boxes), ea **2.00-250.00**
Photo Albums, Scrapbooks, or Autograph Books, ea..........................**5.00-50.00**
Pictures or Prints, children, animals, cherubs & flowers, framed or unframed, lg or sm, ea ....**up to 200.00**
Parasols, Purses, or Fans (lace, tapestry, beaded, leather, sequin, or fabric), ea ....**up to 75.00**
Boxes (celluloid, silver, velvet, leather, china), ea ....**up to 75.00**
Baby Items (jewelry, clothes, toys, shoes, rattles, dishes, pictures, furniture), ea ....**up to 50.00**
Card Cases, Match Safes, or Calling Card Receivers, ea ....**up to 75.00**
Dresser Items (combs, brushes, buttonhooks, perfume bottles, hair receivers), ea ....**up to 50.00**
Sewing Items & Accessories (needle cases, scissors, tape measures, thimbles, & seam gauges), ea ....**up to 50.00**
Yard Long Prints, ea...**up to 50.00**
Clothing (camisoles, slips, or hats), ea ....**up to 50.00**
Linens & Lace...**1.00-100.00**
Colored Glass Items (fancy Victorian), ea..**up to 500.00**
China (complete sets or individual pots, tureens, bowls, etc).........**up to 500.00**
Buttons, ea ....**up to 5.00**
Calling Cards or Greeting Cards, old, ea...**up to 5.00**

Items with Angels, Cherubs, or Newts

	We Pay
Candlesticks, porcelain, silver, or gilt, pr	5.00-100.00
Dishes, ea	up to 100.00
Frames, ea	up to 100.00
Jewelry, ea	up to 200.00
Silver Items, ea	up to 200.00
Boxes, ea	up to 50.00
Prints, ea	up to 300.00
Paintings, ea	up to 300.00

Wanted: **elegant and unusual hats of the Victorian era through the 1940s**. I especially collect ones with feather plumes, jewels, or beads. These hats are for my personal collection. Also of interest are **hat stands, hat pins, gloves, cameos, and other accessory pieces**. As I also collect and repair old dolls, I need **antique infants' clothing and accessories** to dress up dolls. Please send a photo or detailed description and SASE. Ship items only after getting approval.

Joyce Andresen
P.O. Box 1
Keystone, IA 52249

	We Pay
Hats, ea	2.00-20.00+
Gloves, pr	1.00+
Hat Stands, ea	3.00+
Hat Pins, ea	5.00+
Cameos, ea	3.00+
Doll or Children's Items, ea	3.00+

I collect **pre-1920s hats, hat pins, hat pin holders, and feathers that may be used on hats, hat boxes, and hair accessories**. Anything that a hat maker would have used is wanted. I'm interested in **any type of hair jewelry** that would have been used prior to the 1920s. Along with these items, **old hair receivers or complete dresser sets** are wanted. Please send information and asking price.

Tiffany Lininger
2205 2nd Ave. W
Seattle, WA 98119

View-Master and Other 3-D Photographica

View-Master, the invention of William Gruber, was first introduced to the public at the 1939-1940 New York World's Fair and at the same time at the Golden Gate Exposition in California. Since then thousands of different reels and packets have been produced on subjects as diverse as life itself. Sawyers View-Master even made two different cameras for the general public, enabling people to make their own personal reels, and then offered a stereo projector to project the pictures they took on a silver screen in full-color 3-D.

View-Master has been owned by five different companies: the original Sawyers Company, G.A.F. (in October 1966), View-Master International (in 1981), Ideal Toy Company, and Tyco Toy Company (the present owners).

Unfortunately, after G.A.F. sold View-Master in 1981, neither View-Master International, Ideal, nor Tyco Toy Company have had any intention of making the products anything but toy items, selling mostly cartoons. This, of course, has made the early non-cartoon single reels and three-reel packets desirable items.

The earlist single reels from 1939-1945 were not white in color but were originally dark blue with a gold sticker in the center and came in attractive gold-colored envelopes. Then they were made in a blue and tan combination. These early reels are more desirable, as the print runs were low.

From 1946-1957 most white single reels are very common, as they were produced in the millions. There are exceptions, however, such as commercial reels promoting a product or obscure scenic attractions, as these would have had smaller print runs. In 1952 a European division of View-Master was established in Belgium. Most reels and items made in Belgium are more valuable to a collector, since they are harder to find in this country.

In 1955 View-Master came up with the novel idea of selling packets of three reels in one colorful envelope with a picture or photo on the front. Many times a story booklet was included. These became very popular and single reels were slowly discontinued. Most three-reel packets are desirable, whether Sawyers or G.A.F., as long as they are in nice condition. Nearly all viewers are common and have little value, except the very early ones, such as Model A and Model B. These viewers had to be opened to insert the reels. The blue and brown versions of the Model B are rare. Another desirable viewer is the Model D, which is the only focusing viewer that View-Master Made.

Condition is very important to the value of all View-Master items, as it is with most collectibles. I buy most all desirable and scarce View-Master material in very good to mint condition.

Also wanted are **Tru-Vue** items. Tru-Vue, a subsiderary of the Rock Island Bridge and Iron Works in Rock Island, Illinois, was first introduced to the public at the 1933 Century of Progress Exposition in Chicago, Illinois. With their popular black and white 3-D filmstrips and viewers, Tru-Vue quickly became the successor to the Stereoscope and stereocards of the 1800s and early 1900s. They made many stereo views of cities, national parks, scenic attractions, and even some foreign countries. They also produced children's stories, some that featured personalities and nightclubs, and many commercial and instructional filmstrips.

By the late 1940s, Sawyers View-Master had become a very strong competitor. Their full-color 7-scene stereo reels were very popular with the public and had cut into Tru-Vue's sales considerably. So it was a tempting offer when Sawyers made a bid to buy out the company in 1951. Sawyers needed Tru-Vue, not only to eliminate competition, but because Tru-Vue owned the rights to photograph Disney characters and the Disneyland theme park in California.

Sawyers View-Master continued to carry Tru-Vue products but ceased production of the 3-D filmstrips and viewers. Instead, they produced a new format of 7-scene 3-D cards with a new viewer to see the pictures in 3-D. These new Tru-Vue cards were sold mostly in toy stores, and today they have little value. All of the pictures used a cheaper Eastman color slide film, which today has mostly faded into a magenta color. Many cards also came apart, as the glue that was used tends to easily separate. The value of these, therefore, is low and many cards were later remade as View-Master reels with better Kodachrome film. When G.A.F. bought View-Master in 1966, they slowly faded out the Tru-Vue format through the next years.

Walter Sigg
P.O. Box 208
Swartswood, NJ 07877

View-Master

We Pay

	We Pay
Camera, Mark II, w/case	100.00
Camera, Personal Stereo, w/case	100.00
Close-Up Lens, for Personal Camera	100.00
Film Cutter, for cameras	100.00
Packet, scenic, 3-reel set	1.00-25.00
Packet, TV or movie, 3-reel set	2.00-50.00
Packet, Addams Family or Munsters, 3-reel set, ea	50.00
Packet, Belgium made, 3-reel set	4.00-35.00
Packet, miscellaneous subject, 3-reel set	3.00-50.00
Projector, Stereo-Matic 500	200.00

Reel, gold center, gold-colored package..**10.00**
Reel, blue..**2.50-10.00**
Reel, Sawyers, white, early ....**25¢-5.00**
Reel, commercial, brand-name product (Coca-Cola, auto makers, etc)...**5.00-50.00**
Reel, 3-D movie preview (House of Wax, Kiss Me Kate, etc).......................**50.00**
Reel, Belgium made **1.00-10.00**
Viewer, Model B, blue or brown, ea..**100.00**
Viewer, Model D, focusing type **30.00**
Any Advertising Literature, Dealer Displays, etc. (items not meant to be sold
   to the public) ....**Write**
Original Factory Items...**Write**

Tru-Vue	We Pay

Card **1.00-3.00**
Filmstrip, children's story..**1.00-3.00**
Filmstrip, commercial (promoting products) **20.00-50.00**
Filmstrip, instructional..**5.00-15.00**
Filmstrip, personality (Sally Rand, Gypsy Rose Lee, etc)..............**15.00-20.00**
Filmstrip, ocean liner **15.00**
Filmstrip, scenic **1.00-5.00**
Filmstrip, World's Fair **7.50**
Viewer **5.00**
Any Advertising Literature, Dealer Displays, etc. (items not meant to be sold
   to the public) ....**Write**

I buy **many kinds of 3-dimensional items.** In the area of **3-D movie memo-rabilia**, any poster, pressbook, lobby card, still, or banner with 3D or 3-Dimensional on it is desired. I pay $100.00 for a one-sheet poster of House of Wax in mint condition. I also buy glass slides that were used in movie theaters. The slides measure 4x3¼". I buy slides from all eras, but prefer pre-1940 slides. I pay $25.00 for any slide with Charlie Chaplin, Lon Chaney, Laurel and Hardy, or Rudolph Valentino. I also buy glass slide projectors.

I want memorabilia on all short films in 3-D and am looking for memorabilia on the following movie titles. There must be '3-D' on the graphics:

Audio Scopiks, 1936
Catwomen on the Moon, 1954
Dangerous Mission, 1954
Faust, 1922
Friese-Green Stereoscopic Films, 1893
Gog, 1954
Gorilla at Large, 1954
Grand Canyon, 1923
Heartbound, 1935

Jesse James Vs. the Daltons, 1954
Jim the Penman, 1915
Jivaro
L'Arrivee Du Train, 1903
Louisana Territoy, 1953
Lumiere Stereoscopic Films, 1935
Lunacy, 1925
M.A.R.S., 1922
Movies of the Future, 1922

New Audioscopiks, 1938
New York City, 1922
Niagara Falls, 1915
Ouch!, 1929
Pathe News, 1929
Plasticons, 1922
Plastigrams, 1922
The Power of Love, 1922
Radio-Mania, 1922

Reve d'Opium (I Dream of Opium), 1921
The Runaway Taxi, 1925
Rural America, 1915
The Ship of Souls, 1925
Southwest Passage
Teleview, 1921
Washington, D.C., 1923
Zigfield Frolic, 1929
Zowie, 1925

Lenticular 3-D posters and displays that actually are 3-D such as Meteor Man, 2001, or Nightmare Before Christmas are wanted. Also wanted are **press-books on all 3-D movies** except:

Gorilla at Large
I, the Jury
It Came From Outer Space
Inferno
Revenge of the Creature
Money From Home

Bwana Devil
The Mask
The Moonlighter
Parisite
Southwest Passage
Sangaree

Any 3-D magazines are wanted. These magazines are viewed with 3-D glasses or some kind of 3-D viewer. The photos look fuzzy and out of focus when seen without a viewing aid. I prefer pre-1960 3-D magazines, but will buy issues from any decade.

I buy **stereoviews** and prefer those from 1920 through 1940. I do not want travelogue or scenery. While most collectors are looking for pre-1890 views, I am not. Photocopies of the stereoviews would be a great help. My favorite subjects are Hollywood, World's Fairs, movie stars, movie theaters, magic and magicians — anything movie related.

I prefer pre-1960 **3-D comic books** but will buy ones from all eras.

Chris Perry, Doctor 3-D
7470 Church St. #A
Yucca Valley, CA 92284
619-365-0475 or fax 619-365-0495

I have been in business since 1981 and I'm the world's largest mail/phone auctioneer of **three-dimensional images in all formats,** from stereo cards ca the 1850s to View-Master reels from the 1970s. I specialize in consignments, but will buy outright if that is preferred. I operate my auctions using U.S. funds, and I buy using U.S. funds.

Note that antique stereo cards can be worth anywhere from 25¢ to hundreds of dollars each; please contact me with listing. Here are some View-

Master wants for purchase if condition is excellent. Thanks for reading this; I look forward to hearing from you!

John Saddy (Jefferson Stereoptics)
50 Foxborough Grove
London, Ontario
Canada N6K 4A8
519-641-4431 or fax 519-641-2899
e-mail: john.saddy.3d@sympatico.ca

View-Master   We Pay

Reel #52, Frontiertown, Adirondack, New York 40.00
Reel #56, Golden Gate Exposition, Foreign Exhibits................................30.00
Reel #57, Golden Gate Exposition, Buildings...30.00
Reel #86, World's Fair, New York, Sculpture..20.00
Reel #87, World's Fair, New York, Foreign Exhibits................................20.00
Reel #94, Storytown, New York 20.00
Reel #1305, President Kennedy's Visit to Ireland, June, 1963.................**200.00**

I am an avid **3-D stereo photo** collector. In the five years I have been seriously collecting, I have amassed a sizable collection. I've paid as much as $2,000.00 for a single collection. Having a great desire to continue building my collection, **all types are of interest but older (prior to 1980) U.S. and foreign-made reels and packets** are wanted. Besides scenics I am especially interested in 'Made in Belgium' reels, military training reels, and medical reels. Personal or amateur-made reels, whatever subject, are wanted also. Please list your collection by reel or packet number when writing me and indicate condition. I am a collector, not a dealer. Your collection will find a good home with me.

I also collect **3-D stereo slides** (4x1⅝"). These are predominately amateur slides made from personal 3-D cameras popular in the 1950s. All subject matter is of interest, but I especially desire scenic and travel topics — U.S. and foreign. I also want stereo viewers and cases. Please write with a brief description of what you have including approximate number of slides and subject matter.

Kyle Spain
620 Brighside Ln.
Pasadena, CA 91107

We Pay

Packet, complete ....3.00+
Made in Belgium Reel...4.00
Military Training Reel 4.00
Medical Reel...4.00
Non-White Reel..2.00+
Personal Reel...1.00
Advertising Reel...5.00

Wacky Package Stickers

I collect **Topp's Wacky package stickers and related items**. They were
made from 1969 through 1976. Reprint series were made after 1976 and I am
not interested in these. Reprint series stickers will have a puzzle on the back. I
am also interested in Wacky ads, Wacky die-cut cards, posters, tatoos, large
posters from 1974 with 77 stickers on them, jigsaw puzzles, beach towels,
cereal boxes that gave away Wackys, inflatable inner tubes, key chains, magnets, Wacky Wall Plaks (Wackys on a piece of wood that hung on the wall),
pogs, can labels, Canadian Wackys (O-Pee-Chee before 1976), and anything
else Wacky! I am **not** interested in any items made by Fleer. I will trade also.
Stickers wanted in excellent or better condition only with the border intact.
Please contact me for an offer!

David Gross
76 Sicard St.
New Brunswick, N.J. 08901
908-246-1589
e-mail: SalandRei@aol.com
Internet: Davidgr@instbbs.camba.com

We Pay

Stickers, Diecuts, Wacky Ads, Patches, Cloth Stickers, tattoos...........25¢-20.00
Ratz Crackers Diecut (#4 or #32) 200.00
Cracked Animals Diecut (#38)..175.00
Good & Empty Wacky Ad (#25)..150.00
Cracker Jerk or Glutton Patch, ea 20.00
Wall Paks, ea 10.00
Cereal Boxes, intact, ea 25.00
Beach Towels, Clothing, Key Chains, Miscellaneous.....................**Call or Write**

Display Boxes, ea 15.00
Can Labels, ea...35.00
Jigsaw Puzzles, complete only, ea..15.00
Original Art 100.00-250.00
Pogs, ea 3.00
Poster, lg 25.00

Watch Fobs

I buy all **authentic advertising watch fobs**. Also wanted are stickpins, pinbacks, mirrors, and **other small advertising items as well as radio premiums, political items, and hunting memorabilia** — especially relating to gunpowder.

David Beck
P.O. Box 435
Mediapolis, IA 52637
319-394-3943

Watch Fobs ....**We Pay**
John Deere, porcelain ....**up to 250.00**
Buggy ....**up to 200.00**
Heavy Equipment ....**up to 150.00**
Gun Powder ....**up to 150.00**

Watches

They say: The 'first' watch made was in the year 1500 A.D. The minute hand did not appear until 1687 A.D. Watches with moveable figures date back to 1790 A.D. There are 195,000 watches sold per day.

We say: Dig out those watches and turn them into money. **Watches need not be working** or in good shape. Our policy is to return your watch that day if you don't like our offer. In all these years, we are proud to say that we haven't returned one watch! Examples of prices are listed below. Depending on condition, gold, diamonds, etc., prices may be much more.

James Lindon
5267 W Cholla St.
Glendale, AZ 85304
602-878-2409

We Pay

Audemars Piquet	350.00
Benrus	20.00
Breitling	100.00
Bucherer	20.00
Bulova	20.00
Cyma	20.00
Ebel	30.00
Gruen	30.00
Hamilton	30.00
Heuer	40.00
Hyde Park	20.00
Illinois	30.00
Le Coultre	100.00
Longines	50.00
Mido	30.00
Movado	80.00
Omega	50.00
Patek Philippe	500.00+
Rolex	300.00
Tiffany	100.00
Ulysse Nardin	80.00
Universal Geneva	100.00
Vacheron Constantin	1,000.00
Wittnauer	30.00
Any Character Watches	Call or Write
Any Advertising Watches	Call or Write
Any Watch-Related Advertising	Call or Write

We have been the advisor for *Schroeder's Antiques Price Guide* for watches for years and have over 33 years experience in the field of **antique pocket watches and vintage wristwatches.** We are a leading authority for watches worldwide. **Watches currently needed include:**

(1) Pocket watches and vintage better wristwatches, both American and European
(2) Especially interested in Patek Philippe, Howard, Illinois, Hamilton, Rolex, railroad (signed railroad dials and railroad movements), keywinds, watches

that chime, up/down winding indicators, chronographs, enamels, calendars, and moon phases

(3) Historial watches, sports-related watches, gold cases, novelty character watches, and unusual watches

(4) Always buying any American pocket watch 21 jewels or higher.

We pay significant finder's fee for leads towards our purchase of large collections, estates, or accumulations. **Watches wanted dead or alive: need not run!** Prices highest for mint condition, original case, dial and movement, and vary according to watch. We are **not** interested in Timex, inexpensive watches made after 1965, nor any lady's wristwatches. We are **serious buyers** of any rare watch. Same day payment. All transactions strictly confidential. Buying prices vary according to condition and originality. Call Today!

Maundy International
P.O. Box 13028-BW
Shawnee Mission, KS 66282
Call Toll Free 1-800-235-2866 When You're Ready to Sell!

We Pay

American Watch Co., 21 jewels & higher	**35.00+**
Ball Official R.R. Standard	**50.00+**
Hamilton, 21 jewels & higher	**50.00+**
Howard (Boston)	**50.00+**
Illinois, 21 jewels & higher	**60.00+**
Jules Jurgensen Copenhagen (pocket)	**250.00+**
Masonic Logo Dial & Movement	**150.00+**
Patek Philippe	**650.00+**
Railroad Watches, 21 jewels & higher	**50.00+**
Repeater (chimes on command)	**150.00+**
Up/Down Winding Indicators (pocket)	**175.00+**

Western Collectibles

We are buyers of old **pre-1930 cowboy Western material — used on the farm or ranch**. We do not buy more modern mass-market pieces but prefer the one-of-a-kind with 'character.' Feel free to send photos.

Sam Kennedy
212 N 4th St.
Coeur d'Alene, ID 83814
208-769-7575

We Pay

Leather Chaps 100.00-800,00
Wooly Chaps...300.00-1,000.00
Spurs 75.00-500.00
Stetson Hats 30.00-100.00
Cowboy Cuffs...50.00-100.00
Six-Guns (need not be working)..50.00-1,000.00
Lever-Action Saddle Guns 100.00-1,000.00
Handcuffs ....50.00+
Badges ....100.00+
Bowie Knives 100.00-500.00
Saddles 100.00-1,000.00
Old Photos ....Call
Original Paintings 100.00-5,000.00

I am a collector and am buying **Western Americana** — the condition of which must be good or better. I pay cash or will horse trade, should you desire.

Other wants include:

Poster of the 1930s oceanliner, *Normandie*
Anything by Jo Mora, especially pictorial maps and posters
Art Deco, cowboy and Indian bookends
Till Goodan artwork and his Bucking Horse statue

T.J. Ahlberg
1000 Irvine Blvd.
Tustin, CA 92780
714-730-1000 or 714-730- 1331
fax 714-730-1752

We Pay

Belt Buckles, Edward Bohlin...200.00+
Bookends, cowboy or Indian, pr ....50.00+
Bookends, Art Deco, pr...50.00+

Catalogs, Indian trade blankets ....**125.00+**
Catalogs, tack before 1950 ....**100.00+**
Magazine, *Cowboy & Indians Magazine*, Summer, July 1993 ....**25.00+**
Movie Poster, John Wayne, Westward Ho ....**100.00+**
Movie Poster, John Wayne, Oregon Trail...**100.00+**
Movie Poster, Bill Pickett, The Bull-Dogger ....**100.00+**
Movie Poster, King Kong, 1933 ....**200.00+**
Poster, Edward Bohlin Belt Buckle, 1939...**100.00+**
Poster, 101 Ranch ....**200.00+**
Posters, Buffalo Bill's Wild West ....**200.00+**

We are actively seeking **pre-1910 paper Western Americana** such as letters, photos, diaries, documents, letterheads, billheads, broadsides, receipts, catalogs, stocks, bonds, and checks. Subjects of interest are lawmen, outlaws, gamblers, nudes, prostitutes, saloons, mining, stage companies, cowboys, western towns, wild west shows, settlers, railroads, army forts, and businesses. Of special interest are items that deal with life in Colorado, but we are interested in items that show early life and struggles from any state or territory in the West.

Single pieces or collections are wanted. Condition and content are important to determine value. Please send a clear photocopy along with SASE. Prices listed are for items in good, clean condition and are only a sample of items of interest. Please let us know what you have.

Gret DeMark
1745 N Main St.
Longmont, CO 80501
303-682-5321

Cabinet Card Photos   We Pay

Buffalo Bill..**100.00+**
Annie Oakley ....**150.00+**
Nudes ....**25.00+**
Identified Western Prostitutes...**50.00+**
Outdoor Town Scene...**15.00+**
Gold Mine Camps ....**35.00+**

Letters Describing   We Pay

Gold or Silver Mining...**15.00+**

Western Collectibles

Cattle Companies .... **10.00+**
Prostitutes.. **20.00+**
Stage Companies .... **20.00+**

Documents & Certificates   **We Pay**

Court Summons, Mining **10.00**
Court Summons, Gambling .... **15.00+**
Court Summons, Use of Guns .... **20.00+**
Mining Assay Certificates... **10.00+**

We are interested in purchasing **cowboy and rodeo memorabilia from the '40s and '50s as well as memorabilia relating to Gene Autry, Roy Rogers, Hoppy, etc. Also wanted are records, autographed photos, banks, plates, and lamps; cowboy vases, planters, and cookie jars are desired.**

Cityslickers Cowboy Collectibles
Richard and Anni Frey
61 Marine St.
Bronx, NY 10464
718-885-0898

                                                             We Pay

Hamilton Classic TV Western Plates.. **20.00**
Royal Doulton Wild West Collector Plates **40.00**
Western-Themed Board Games .... **10.00+**

Whiskey Jugs

I am always on the lookout to buy **'fancy' U.S. ceramic whiskey containers, jugs, or bottles of the pre-prohibition era** for my personal collection (not resale). These are pottery items many whiskey distillers and distributors used to set their products apart from other brands — many of which were merchandised in glass containers. Sometimes they were provided free to special customers; on other occasions, they were meant to enhance a gift of spirits at the holidays. As with all collectibles the condition of the item is of utmost importance. With rare exceptions, I buy only perfect or nearly-perfect items.

Jack Sullivan
4300 Ivanhoe Pl.
Alexandria, VA 22304
703-370-3039

Whiskey Ceramics	We Pay
George Bieler & Sons Rye	100.00+
Minnehaha, w/birds	300.00+
Minnehaha, w/girl in blue	200.00+
Minnesota Weil or Benz Jugs	70.00+
Pullman Bourbon	400.00+
Pullman Rye	400.00+
KT&K-China Jugs	150.00+
Ray's Germacide	80.00+
Quart Jugs w/Gold Lettering	60.00+
Quart Jugs w/Blue & White Stencil	100.00+

Winchester

We are buyers and collectors of Winchester. We are mostly looking for pre-1950 pieces but unusual pieces made after that are also of interest. We are also interested in old ammunition boxes that are bright and undamaged, but not in guns. All pieces must be clearly marked **Winchester**.

Sam Kennedy
212 N 4th St.
Coeur d'Alene, ID 83814
208-769-7575

	We Pay
Advertising Pieces, cardboard	10.00-1,000.00
Ball Bats	75.00+
Chisels	10.00+
Golf Clubs	50.00+
Plains	20.00-200.00
Posters	100.00-1,000.00
Rifle Boxes	1.00-30.00
Screwdrivers	10.00-30.00
Shotgun Shell Boxes	2.00-30.00

Wooden Money

Yes, Norm Boughton takes **wooden money**.

Throughout the United States and Canada, communities have issued wooden nickels and other forms of wooden money to help commemorate civic celebrations. From 1931 when Tenino, Washington, made the first wooden money to 1954, most wooden money was made in rectangular shapes to resemble currency. After 1954 most wooden money was made in round form. Until the 1960s when the government cracked down on the use of wooden money in the celebration area, most wooden money was redeemable for a certain period. The fact that the exchange value of the wood expired and left the wood worthless probably gave birth to the expression 'Don't take no wooden nickels.'

In recent years companies and coin clubs have used wooden nickels for advertising purposes. With the exception of some resturant chains such as McDonald's, Sambos, and Dairy Queens, these are of little or no value.

Norm Boughton
P.O. Box 93262
Rochester, NY 14692
716-292-550 or fax 716-292-6513

We Pay

Tenino WA Flat Issues, 1931 to 1933	**25.00+**
Sambos Resturant Woods, must have city listed	**35¢+**
Civic Celebrations, flat	**1.00-50.00**
Civic Celebrations, Atlantic GA, flat	**10.00**
Civic Celebrations, Olean NY, flat	**3.00**
Civic Celebrations, Vernon TX, flat	**50.00**
Civic Celebrations, Clark Co. VA, flat	**40.00**
Civic Celebrations, round	**50¢-20.00**
Civic Celebrations, Nunda NY, round	**5.00**
Civic Celebrations, Town of Riga NY, round	**17.50**

OTHER INTERESTED BUYERS OF MISCELLANEOUS ITEMS

In this section of the book we have listed buyers of miscellaneous items and related material. When corresponding with these collectors, be sure to enclose a self-addressed stamped envelope if you want a reply. Do not send lists of items for appraisal. If you wish to sell your material, quote the price that you want or send a list of items you think they might be interested in and ask them to make you an offer. If you want the list back, be sure to send a SASE large enough for the listing to be returned.

Advertising

Aunt Jemima
Lynn Burkett
P.O. Box 671
Hillsdale, MI 49242
517-437-2149

Banner Buggies
Richard A. Haussmann
25 Hampton Rd.
Montgomery, IL 60538
708-896-8287

Big Boy
Steve Soelberg
29126 Laro Dr.
Agoura Hills, CA 91301
818-889-9909

Campbell's Soup
Dave and Micki Young
414 Country Ln. Ct.
Wauconda, IL 60084
847-487-4917

Cereal boxes and premiums
Scott Bruce
P.O. Box 481
Cambridge, MA 02140
617-492-5004

Moxie 'Doll House' bottle carton; items relating to mesh purses circa 1920 to 1935
Sherry and Mike Miller
303 Holiday Dr.
Tuscola, IL 61953
217-253-4991

Reddy Kilowatt and Bordon's Elsie
Lee Garmon
1529 Whittier St.
Springfield, IL 62704

Smokey Bear
Glen Brady
P.O. Box 3933
Central Point, OR 97502
503-772-0350

Gasoline globes, pumps, signs and promotional items
Author of book
Scott Benjamin
411 Forest St.
LaGrange, OH 44050
216-355-6608

Motorcycle
Bruce Kiper
2205 Sunset Ln.
Lutz, FL 33549
813-949-5060

Quality porcelain signs and any company catalogs
Mike Bruner
4103 Lotus Dr.
Waterford, MI 48329

Thermometers shaped like old gasoline station pole signs
Peter Cappell
1838 W Grace St.
Chicago, IL 60613-2724
312-871-8735

Jewel Tea products and tins
Bill and Judy Vroman
739 Eastern Ave.
Fostoria, OH 44830
419-435-5443

Old advertising pieces of almost any kind
B.J. Summers
233 Darnell Rd.
Benton, KY 42045

Aluminum

Author of book
Dannie Woodard
P.O. Box 1346
Weatherford, TX 76086
817-594-4680

American Bisque

Author of book
Mary Jane Giacomini
P.O. Box 404
Ferndale, CA 95536-0404
707-786-9464

Animal Dishes

Author of book
Everett Grist
6503 Slater Rd., Ste. H
Chattanooga, TN 37412
615-855-4032
Also aluminum, advertising playing cards, and marbles

Appliances

Jim Barker
Toaster Master General
P.O. Box 41
Bethlehem, PA 10106

Art Glass

All types
The Antique Gallery
8523 Germantown Ave.
Philadelphia, PA 19118
215-248-1700 or
fax 215-247-8411
http://membrane.com/che
stnuthill/antique
_gallery

Especially Boyd,
Summit, and Mosser
Joyce Pringle
3500 S Cooper
Arlington, TX 76015

Art Pottery

All American and Euro-
pean; also ceramics
The Antique Gallery
8523 Germantown Ave.
Philadelphia, PA 19118
215-248-1700 or
fax 215-247-8411
http://membrane.com/che
stnuthill/antique
_gallery

Autograph Albums

Also photograph albums
Sherry and Mike Miller
303 Holiday Dr.
Tuscola, IL 61953
217-253-4991

Autographs

Don and Anne Kier
2022 Marengo St.
Toledo, OH 43614
419-385-8211

Automobilia

All types; also books
L.M.G. Enterprises
9006 Foxland Dr.
San Antonio, TX 78230
phone/fax 210-979-6098

General line; specializing in
Chevrolet
Jim and Nancy Schaut
P.O. Box 10781
Glendale, AZ 85318-0781
602-878-4293

Tire ashtrays; author of book
Jeff McVey
1810 W State St., #427
Boise, ID 83702

Autumn Leaf

Edits newsletter
Gwynneth Harrison
P.O. Box 1
Mira Loma, CA 91752
909-685-5434
Buys and appraises

Aviation

Commercial items from
the 1920s through the
1970s
John R. Joiner
52 Jefferson Pkwy., Apt. D
Newnan, GA 30263
404-502-9565

Airline china, memorabilia,
and chrome ashtrays with
airplanes on pedestals
Dick Wallin
P.O. Box 1794
Springfield, IL 62705
217-498-9279

Avon Collectibles

Author of book
Bud Hastin
P.O. Box 43690
Sal Vegas, NE 89116

Tammy Rodrick
Stacey's Treasures
1509 N 300 St.
Sumner, IL 62466
Also character toys, glasses, cereal boxes and pre-
miums; beer steins, Blue
Willow, head vases, and
trolls

Badges

Pennsylvania drivers
Ed Foley
129 Meadow Vly. Rd. #11
Ephrata, PA 17522
717-738-4183

Banks

Bill Bertoia Auctions
2413 Madison Ave.
Vineland, NJ 08360
609-692-1881 or
fax 609-692-8627

Cast iron or glass
Wayne H. Boyd
11890 Landon Rd.
Richwood, OH 43344

Miniature oil-can banks
Peter Capell
1838 W Grace St.
Chicago, IL 60613-2724
312-871-8735

Marked Ertl
Homestead Collectibles
P.O. Box 173
Mill Hall, PA 17751
Also decanters

Modern mechanical banks
Dan Iannotti
212 W Hickory Grove Rd.
Bloomfield Hills, MI 48302
800-335-5042

Diane Patalano
P.O. Box 144
Saddle River, NJ 07458
201-327-2499

Reynolds Toys

Charlie Reynolds
2836 Monroe St.
Falls Church, VA 22042
703-533-1322

Barb Wire

John Mantz
1023 Baldwin Rd.
Bakersfield, CA 93304
850-397-9572

**Barber Shop
Collectibles**

Burton Handelsman
18 Hotel Dr.
White Plains, NY 10605
914-428-4480

Barware

Especially cocktail shakers
Arlene Lederman Antiques
150 Main St.
Nyack, NY 10960

*Specializing in vintage
cocktail shakers*
Author of book
Stephen Visakay
P.O. Box 1517
W Caldwell, NJ 07707

**Beer Cans and
Breweriana**

Steve Gordon
P.O. Box 632
Olney, MD 20830-0632
301-439-4116

Bells

Unusual; no cow or school
Author of book
Dorothy Malone Anthony
802 S Eddy
Ft. Scott, KS 66701

Birthday Angels

Jim and Denise Atkinson
555 East School St.
Owatonna, MN 55060
507-455-3340

Black Americana

*Buy, sell and trade; lists
available*
Judy Posner
May-October:
R.D. 1, Box 273SC
Effort, PA 18330
717-629-6583 or
November-April:
4195 S Tamiami Trail #183
Venice, FL 34293
914-497-7149
e-mail:
Judyandjef@aol.com

Pre-1950s items
Jan Thalberg
23 Mountain View Dr.
Weston, CT 06883

*Black and golliwog items
of all types*
The Butler Did It!
Catherine Saunders Watson
P.O. Box 302
Greenville, NH 03048
phone or fax 603-878-2171

Black Glass

Author of book
Marlena Toohey
703 S Pratt Pky.
Longmont, CO 80501
303-678-9726

Blade Banks

David Geise
1410 Aquia Dr.
Stafford, VA 22554
703-569-5984

Debbie Gillham
47 Midline Ct.
Gaithersburg, MD 20878
301-977-5727

Blue Ridge

Oscar Hubbert
P.O. Box 1415
Fletcher, NC 28732
704-687-0350

Bobbin' Head Dolls

*Author of newsletter and
guide*
Tim Hunter
1668 Golddust
Sparks, NV 89436
702-626-5029

Bohemian Glass

Tom Bradshaw
325 Carol Dr.
Ventura, CA 93303
805-653-2723 or
310-450-6486

Bookmarks

Joan L. Huegel
1002 W 25th St.
Erie, PA 16502

Books

*Ann Rice, Ann Rampling,
or A.N. Roquelaure hard-
cover first editions*
Vicki Woodrow
2620 W Salem Church Rd.
Covington, IN 47932

Children's illustrated
Noreen Abbott Books
2666 44th Ave.
San Francisco, CA 94116

*Children's illustrated,
Little Golden, etc.*
Ilene Kayne
1308 S Charles St.
Baltimore, MD 21230
410-685-3923

Children's
My Bookhouse
27 S Sandusky St.
Tiffin, OH 44883
419-447-9842

Little Golden Books,
Wonder and Elf
Author of book on
Little Golden Books
Steve Santi
19626 Ricardo Ave.
Hayward, CA 94541

Children's Series
Mr. and Mrs. R.H. Spicer
RD 1, Ashgrove Rd. Box 82
Cambridge, NY 12816

By Jane Holt Giles
B.L. Hornback
707 Sunrise Ln.
Elizabethtown, KY 42701

By Knappen or Hadler
Phoneco
Ron and Mary Knappen
207 E Mill Rd., P.O. Box 70
Galesville, WI 54630

Fine books and antique
toys
Bromer Booksellers, Inc.
607 Boylston St.
Boston, MA 02116

Big Little Books
Ron and Donna Donnelly
P.O. Box 7047
Panama City Beach, FL 32413

Dick and Jane Readers
Wayne H. Boyd
11890 Landon Rd.
Richwood, OH 43344

Bottle Openers

Charlie Reynolds
2836 Monroe St.
Falls Church, VA 22042
703-533-1322

Bottles

Bitters, figurals, inks,
barber, etc.
Steve Ketcham
P.O. Box 24114
Minneapolis, MN 55424
612-920-4205
Also advertising signs,
trays, calendars, etc.

Painted-label sodas
Author of books
Thomas Marsh
914 Franklin Ave.
Youngstown, OH 44502
216-743-8600 or
800-845-7930 (book orders)

Dairy and milk
Author of book
John Tutton
R.R. 4, Box 929
Front Royal, VA 22630
703-635-7058

Sasha Brastoff

Susan N. Cox
Main Street Antique Mall
237 E Main St.
El Cajon, CA 92020
619-447-0800

Brayton Laguna

Susan N. Cox
Main Street
Antique Mall
237 E Main St.
El Cajon, CA 92020
619-447-0800

Breweriana

DLK Nostalgia and Collectibles
P.O. Box 5112
Johnstown, PA 15904
Also Art Deco, novelty
clocks, toys and football
cards

Breyer

Author of book
Carol Karbowiak Gilbert
2193 14 Mile Rd. 206
Sterling Hts., MI 48310

British Royal Commemoratives

Audrey Zeder
6755 Coralite St. S
Long Beach, CA 90808

Brownies by Palmer Cox

Don and Anne Kier
2022 Marengo St.
Toledo, OH 43614
419-385-8211

Brush-McCoy Pottery

Authors of book
Steve and Martha Sanford
230 Harrison Ave.
Campbell, CA 95008
408-978-8408

Bubble Bath
Containers

Matt and Lisa Adams
1234 Harbor Cove
Woodstock, GA 30189
770-516-6874

California Perfume Company

Not common; especially
items marked Goetting Co.
Dick Pardini
3107 N El Dorado St.,
Dept. WTB
Stockton, CA 95204
Also Savoi Et Cie, Hinze
Ambrosia, Gertrude
Recordon, Marvel Electric
Silver Cleaner, and Easy
Day Automatic Clothes
Washer

California Pottery

Pat and Kris Secor
P.O. Box 3367
Rock Island, IL 61204
309-786-4870

Susan N. Cox
Main Street Antique Mall
237 E Main St.
El Cajon, CA 92020
619-447-0800

Camark Pottery

*Author of book, historian
on Arkansas pottery*
David Edwin Gifford
P.O. Box 7617
Little Rock, AR 72217

Cambridge Glass

Debbie Maggard
P.O. Box 211
Chagrin Falls, OH 44022
216-247-5632

Cameras

*Classic, collectible and
usable*
Gene's Cameras
2603 Artie St., SW Ste. 16
Huntsville, AL 35805
205-536-6893
*Wooden, detective and
stereo*
John A. Hess
P.O. Box 3062
Andover, MA 01810
Also old brass lenses

Harry Poster
P.O. Box 1883
S Hackensack, NJ 07606
201-410-7525
Also accessories and 3-D
projectors

Candlewick

Has matching service
Joan Cimini
63680 Centerville-
Warnock Rd.
Belmont, OH 43718

Candy Containers

Glass
Jeff Bradfield
90 Main St.
Dayton, VA 22821
703-879-9961
Also advertising, cast-iron
and tin toys, postcards and
Coca-Cola

Glass
Doug Dezso
864 Paterson Ave.
Maywood, NJ 07607
Also Tonka toys, Shafford
black cats, German bisque
comic character nodders,
Royal Bayreuth creamers,
and Pep pins

Carnival Chalkware

*Radio lamps of plaster;
author of book*
Thomas G. Morris
P.O. Box 8307
Medford, OR 97504
541-779-3164

Carnival Glass

Dave Smith
1142 S Spring St.
Springfield, IL 62704

Cast Iron

*Door knockers, sprin-
klers, figural paper-
weights and marked
cookware*
Craig Dinner
P.O. Box 4399
Sunnyside, NY 11104

Cat Collectibles

Marilyn Dipboye
33161 Wendy Dr.
Sterling Hts., MI 48310
810-264-0285

Cat-tail, by Universal

Ken and Barbara Brooks
4121 Gladstone Ln.
Charlotte, NC 28205
704-568-5716 or
fax 704-375-6508

Ceramic Arts Studio

BA Wellman
88 State Rd. W
P.O. Box 673
Westminster, MA 01473-1435

Character and Personality Collectibles

Author of books
Bill Bruegman
Toy Scouts, Inc.
137 Casterton Ave.
Akron, OH 44303
330-836-0668 or
fax 330-869-8668
e-mail: toyscout@sala-
mander.net
Dealers, publishers and
appraisers of collectible
memorabilia from the '50s
through today

Any and all
Terri Ivers
Terri's Toys
419 S First St.
Ponca City, OK 74601
405-762-8697 or
405-762-5174
fax 405-765-2657
e-mail: ivers@pcok.com

Any and all
John Thurmond
Collector Holics
15006 Fuller
Grandview, MO 64030
816-322-0906

Any and all
Norm Vigue
62 Barley St.
Stoughton, MA 02072
617-344-5441

Batman, Gumby and Marilyn Monroe
Colleen Garmon Barnes
114 E Locust
Chatham, IL 62629

Beatles
Bojo
Bob Gottuso
P.O. Box 1403
Cranberry Twp., PA 16066
phone/fax 412-776-0621

Beatles
Rick Rann, Beatelist
P.O. Box 877
Oak Park, IL 60303
708-442-7907

Betty Boop
Leo A. Mallette
2309 Santa Anita Ave.
Arcadia, CA 91006-5154

Bubble Bath Containers
Matt and Lisa Adams
1234 Harbor Cove
Woodstock, GA 30189
770-516-6874

California Raisins
Larry De Angelo
516 King Arthur Dr.
Virginia Beach, VA 23464

Dick Tracy
Larry Doucet
2351 Sultana Dr.
Yorktown Hts., NY 10598

Disney, Western heroes, Gone With the Wind, character watches ca 1930s to mid-1950s, premiums and games
Ron and Donna Donnelly
Saturday Heroes
P.O. Box 7047
Panama City Beach, FL 32413
904-234-7944

Disney, buy, sell and trade; lists available
Judy Posner
May-October:
R.D. 1, Box 273
Effort, PA 18330
717-629-6583
or November-April:
4195 S Tamiami Trail #183
Venice, FL 34293
941-497-7149
e-mail:
Judyandjef@aol.com

Disney, especially Roger Rabbit
Allen Day
P.O. Box 525
Monroe, NC 28810

Elvis Presley
Author of book
Rosalind Cranor
P.O. Box 859
Blacksburg, VA 24063

Elvis Presley
Lee Garmon
1529 Whittier St.
Springfield, IL 62704

Garfield
Adrienne Warren
1032 Feather Bed Ln.
Edison, NJ 08820
908-381-7083 (EST)
Also Smurfs and other characters, dolls, monsters, premiums; lists available

Gumby
Michael Drollinger
1010 N Walnut
Veedersburg, IN 47987

I Dream of Jeannie,
Barbara Eden
Richard D. Barnes
1520 W 800 N
Salt Lake City, UT 84116
801-521-4400

Li'l Abner
Kenn Norris
P.O. Box 4830
Sanderson, TX 79848

The Lone Ranger
Terry and Kay Klepey
c/o The Silver Bullet
Newsletter
P.O. Box 553
Forks, WA 98331

Peanuts and Schulz Collectibles
Freddi Margolin
P.O. Box 5124P
Bay Shore, NY 11706

Roy Rogers and
Dale Evans
Author of books
Robert W. Phillips
1703 N Aster Pl.
Broken Arrow, OK 74012

Shirley Temple
Gen Jones
294 Park St.
Medford, MA 02155

Smokey Bear
Glen Brady
P.O. Box 3933
Central Point, OR 97502
503-772-0350

Star Trek and
Star Wars
Craig Reid
1911 E Sprague Ave.
Spokane, WA 99202
509-536-8489

Star Wars
Jim and Brenda Roush
739 W Fifth St.
Marion, IN 46953
317-662-6126

Three Stooges
Harry S. Ross
Soitenly Stooges Inc.
P.O. Box 72
Skokie, IL 60076

Tom Mix
Author of book
Merle 'Bud' Norris
1324 N Hague Ave.
Columbus, OH 43204

TV and movie collectibles
TVC Enterprises
P.O. Box 1088
Easton, MA 02334
508-238-1179

Character and Promotional Drinking Glasses

Collector Glass News
P.O. Box 308
Slippery Rock, PA 16057
412-946-2838 or 412-794-2540

Character Mugs

Plastic, also advertising
Cheryl and Lee Brown
7377 Badger Ct.
Indianapolis, IN 46260
317-253-4620

Character Nodders

Matt and Lisa Adams
1234 Harbor Cove
Woodstock, GA 30189
770-516-6874

Children's Play Dishes

Author of book
Lorraine Punchard
8201 Pleasant Ave. South
Bloomington, MN 55420
612-888-1079

Chintz

Marge Geddes
P.O. Box 5875
Aloha, OR 97007
503-649-1041

Mary Jane Hastings
310 West 1st South
Mt. Olive, IL 62069
phone/fax 217-999-7519

Author of book
Joan Welsh
7015 Partridge Pl.
Hyattsville, MD 20782
301-779-6181

Christmas Collectibles

*Especially from before 1920
and decorations made in
Germany*
J.W. and Treva Courter
3935 Kelley Rd.
Kevil, KY 42053
phone/fax 502-488-2116

Cleminson

Robin Stine
P.O. Box 6202
Toledo, OH 43614
419-385-7387

Clocks

All types
Bruce A. Austin
40 Selborne Chase
Fairport, NY 14450
716-223-0711

Comic character; also watches
Author of book
Howard S. Brenner
106 Woodgate Terrace
Rochester, NY 14625

*Novelty animated and
non-animated*
Carole S. Kaifer
P.O. Box 232
Bethania, NC 27010

Clothing

Blue Denim
Clothing Co.
3213 Jeannie Ln.
Muskogee, OK 74453
918-683-1589

Clothes Sprinkler Bottles

Ellen Bercovici
5118 Hampden Ln.
Bethesda, MD 20814
301-652-1140

Coca-Cola

Also Pepsi-Cola
Terri Ivers
419 S First St.
Ponca City, OK 74601
405-762-8697 or
405-762-5174
fax 405-765-2657
e-mail: ivers@pcok.com

*Also Pepsi-Cola and other
brands of soda*
Craig and Donna Stifter
P.O. Box 6514
Naperville, IL 60540
630-717-7949

Coin Silver

Thomas J. Ridley III
MidweSterling
4311 NE Vivion Rd.
Kansas City, MO 64119
816-454-1990 or
fax 816-454-1605
(closed Wed. & Sun.)

Coin-Operated Machines

Ken and Jackie Durham
909 26th St., NW
Washington, D.C. 20037

Mechantiques
Martin Roenigk
26 Barton Hill
E Hampton, CT 06424
860-267-8682 or
fax 860-267-1120

Colorado Pottery (Broadmoor)

Carol and Jim Carlton
8115 S Syracuse St.
Englewood, CO 80112
303-773-8616
Also Coors, Lonhuda, and
Denver White

Comic Books

Avalon Comics
Larry Curcio
P.O. Box 821
Medford, MA 02155
617-391-5614

Comic Strip Art

David H. Begin
4901 Cabrillo Pt.
Byron, CA 94514

Compacts

*Unusual shapes, also
vanities and accessories
Author of book*
Roselyn Gerson
P.O. Box 40
Lynbrook, NY 11563

Cookbooks

*Author of book; also
advertising leaflets*
Col. Bob Allen
P.O. Box 85
St. James, MO 65559

Cookie Cutters

*Author of forthcoming
book*
Rosemary Henry
9610 Greenview Ln.
Manassas, VA 22100

Cookie Jars

Joe Devine
1411 3rd St.
Council Bluffs, IA 51503
712-232-5233 or
712-328-7305

*Buy, sell and trade; lists
available*
Judy Posner
May-October:
R.D. 1, Box 273
Effort, PA 18330
717-629-6583
or
November-April:
4195 S Tamiami Trail, #183
Venice, FL 34293
941-497-7149
e-mail:
Judyandjef@aol.com

Phil and Nyla Thurston
82 Hamlin St.
Cortland, NY 13045
607-753-6770

Corkscrews

Antique and unusual
Paul P. Luchsinger
1126 Wishart Pl.
Hermitage, PA 16148

Cowan

Author of book
Mark Bassett
P.O. Box 771233
Lakewood, OH 44107

Cracker Jack Items

Phil Helley
Old Kilbourn Antiques
629 Indiana Ave.
Wisconsin Dells, WI 53965
Also banks, radio premiums, dexterity puzzles,
pencil sharpeners, and
wind-up toys

Wes Johnson, Sr.
106 Bauer Ave.
Louisville, KY 40207

Crackle Glass

Authors of book
Stan and Arlene Weitman
101 Cypress St.
Massapequa Park, NY 11758
516-799-2619
fax 516-797-3039

Credit Cards and Related Items

Walt Thompson
Box 2541
Yakima, WA 98907

Cuff Links

National Cuff Link Society
Eugene R. Klompus
P.O. Box 346
Prospect Hts., IL 60070
phone/fax 847-816-0035
Also related items

Dakins

Jim Rash
135 Alder Ave.
Pleasantville, NJ 08232
609-646-4125

Decanters

Homestead Collectibles
Art and Judy Turner
R.D. 2, Rte. 150
P.O. Box 173-E
Mill Hall, PA 17751
717-726-3597
fax 717-726-4488

deLee

Joanne and Ralph Schaefer
3182 Williams Rd.
Oroville, CA 95965
916-893-2902

Depression Glass

Elegant glassware
John and Shirley Baker
673 W Township Rd. #118
Tiffin, OH 44883
Also Tiffin glassware

Dinnerware

Blue Bird
Dorothy Crowder
1628 S Stringtown Rd.
Covington, IN 47932

Cat-Tail
Ken and Barbara Brooks
4121 Gladstone Ln.
Charlotte, NC 28205

*Fiesta, Franciscan, Russel
Wright, Lu Ray, and Metlox*
Fiesta Plus
Mick and Lorna Chase
380 Hawkins
Crawford Rd.
Cookeville, TN 38501
615-372-8333
Also other Homer Laugh-
lin patterns

*Homer Laughlin China
Author of book*
Darlene Nossaman
5419 Lake Charles
Waco, TX 76710

Mason's Ironstone
Susan and Larry Hirshman
540 Siskiyou Blvd.
Ashland, OR 97520

*Russel Wright, Eva Zeisel,
Homer Laughlin*
Charles Alexander
221 E 34th St.
Indianapolis, IN 46205
317-924-9665

Dolls

Annalee Motilitee Dolls
Jane's Collectibles
Jane Holt
P.O. Box 115
Derry, NH 03038

*Barbie from 1959 to 1969;
also vintage clothing and
accessories*
Dora Lerch
P.O. Box 245
Garnerville, NY 10923

Boudoir dolls
Bonnie M. Groves
402 N Ave. A
Elgin, TX 78621
512-281-9551

Betsy McCall and friends
Marci Van Ausdall
P.O. Box 946
Quincy, CA 95971
916-283-2770
fax 916-283-4449

*Celebrity and
character dolls*
Henri Yunes
971 Main St., Apt. 2
Hackensack, NJ 07601
201-488-2236

*Chatty Cathy
Author of book*
Don and Kathy Lewis
187 N Marcello Ave.
Thousand Oaks, CA 91360
805-499-7932

*Dolls from the 1960s-70s,
including Liddle Kiddles,
Barbie, Tammy, Tressy,
etc.; co-author of book on
Tammy*
Cindy Sabulis
P.O. Box 642
Shelton, CT 06484
203-926-0176

*Liddle Kiddles and other
small dolls from the late
'60s and early '70s*
Dawn Parrish
9931 Gaynor Ave.
Granada Hills, CA 91343
818-894-8964

Skipper clothing
Sue Wente
115 Marbeth Ave.
Carlisle, PA 17013-1626
717-249-9394

Strawberry Shortcake
Geneva D. Addy
P.O. Box 124
Winterset, IA 50273

Dollhouse Furniture and Accessories

Renwal, Ideal, Marx, etc.
Judith A. Mosholder
R.D. #2, Box 147
Boswell, PA 15531
814-629-9277

Renwal, Plasco, Marx, etc.
Marian Schmuhl
7 Revolutionary Ridge Rd.
Bedford, MA 10730
617-275-2156

Donkey Figurines

Dorothy Crowder
1628 S Stringtown Rd.
Covington, IN 47932

Door Knockers

Craig Dinner
Box 4399
Sunnyside, NY 11104
718-729-3850

Egg Beaters

*Author of Beat This: The
Egg Beater Chronicles*
Don Thornton
Off Beat Books
1345 Poplar Ave.
Sunnyvale, CA 94087

Egg Cups

Joan George, Editor
Egg Cup Collectors Corner
67 Stevens Ave.
Old Bridge, NJ 08857

Egg Timers

Ellen Bercovici
5118 Hampden Ln.
Bethesda, MD 20814
301-652-1140

Jeannie Greenfield
310 Parker Rd.
Stoneboro, PA 16153

Ephemera

Motorcycle
Bruce Kiper
2205 Sunset Ln.
Lutz, FL 33549
813-949-5060

Match holders or match safes
George Sparacio
P.O. Box 791
Malaga, NJ 08328
609-694-4167

Farm Collectibles

Farm Antique News
Gary Van Hoozer, Editor
812 N Third St.
Tarkio, MO 64491
816-736-4528

Fast-Food Collectibles

Author of book
Ken Clee
Box 1142
Philadelphia, PA 19111
215-722-1979

California Raisins
Larry De Angelo
516 King Arthur Dr.
Virginia Beach, VA 23464

Authors of several books
Joyce and Terry Losonsky
7506 Summer Leave Ln.
Columbia, MD 21046
Illustrated Collector's Guide to McDonald's® Happy Meal ® Boxes, Premiums and Promotions ($9 plus $2 postage), McDonald's® Happy Meal (® Toys in the USA and McDonald's® Happy Meal ® Toys Around the World (both full color, $24.95 plus $3 postage), and *Illustrated Collector's Guide to McDonald's® McCAPS®* ($4 plus $2) are available from the authors.

Bill and Pat Poe
220 Dominica Cir. E
Niceville, FL 32578-4068
904-897-4163
fax 904-897-2606
Also cartoon and character glasses, Pez, Smurfs and California Raisins; send $3 (US delivery) for 70-page catalog

Fenton

Before 1980s; prefer hobnail
G. Crinklaw
8188 N State Hwy. AC
Willard, MO 65781
417-742-3940

Figural Ceramics

Ellen Bercovici
5118 Hampden Ln.
Bethesda, MD 20814
301-652-1140

Bobbie Zucker Bryson
1 St. Eleanoras Ln.
Tuckahoe, NY 10707
914-779-1405

Debbie Gillham
47 Midline Ct.
Gaithersburg, MD 20878
301-977-5727

Especially cookie jars, California pottery, Kitchen Prayer Lady, and other imports; also American pottery
Phil and Nyla Thurston
82 Hamlin St.
Cortland, NY 13045
607-753-6770

Especially Kitchen Prayer Lady, Enesco and Holt Howard
April and Larry Tvorak
P.O. Box 126
Canon City, CO 81215
719-269-7230
or
HRC #34, Box 25B
Warren Center, PA 18851
717-395-3775

Fire-King

Authors of book
April and Larry Tvorak
P.O. Box 126
Canon City, CO 81215
719-269-7230
or
HRC #34, Box 25B
Warren Center, PA 18851
717-395-3775

Fishing Collectibles

Cisco's
Sam Kennedy
212 N 4th St.
Couer d'Alene, ID 83814
208-769-7575

Publishes fixed-price catalog
Dave Hoover
1023 Skyview Dr.
New Albany, IN 47150
Also miniature boats and motors

Randy Hilst
1221 Florence #4
Pekin, IL 61554
309-346-2710

Fitz and Floyd

Phil and Nyla Thurston
82 Hamlin St.
Cortland, NY 13045
607-753-6770

Flashlights

Editor of newsletter
Bill Utley
P.O. Box 4095
Tustin, CA 92681
714-730-1252
fax 714-505-4067

Florence

Author of book
Doug Foland
1811 NW Couch #303
Portland, OR 97209
John and Peggy Scott
4640 S Leroy
Springfield, MO 65810

Flower Frogs

Nada Sue Knauss
12111 Potter Rd
Weston, OH 43569
419-669-4735

Debbie Maggard
P.O. Box 211
Chagrin Falls, OH 44022
216-247-5632

Folk Art

Cisco's
Sam Kennedy
212 N 4th St.
Couer d'Alene, ID 83814
208-769-7575

Frank Lloyd Wright

Richard A. Haussmann
25 Hampton Rd.
Montgomery, IL 60538
708-896-8287

Frankoma

Authors of book
Phyllis and Tom Bess
14535 E 13th St.
Tulsa, OK 74108

Author of book
Susan N. Cox
Main Street Antique Mall
237 E Main St.
El Cajon, CA 92020
619-447-0800
Also unsharpened advertising pencils, complete matchbooks, Horlick's advertising, women's magazines from 1900 to 1950

Political donkeys
Dorothy Crowder
1628 S Stringtown Rd.
Covington, IN 47932

Fraternal Collectibles

Masonic and Shriner
David Smies
Box 522
Manhattan, KS 66502
913-776-1433

Odd Fellows
Greg Speiss
230 E Washington
Joliet, IL 60433
815-722-5639

Fruit Jars

Especially old, odd or colored jars
John Hathaway
Rte. 2, Box 220
Bryant Pond, ME 04219
Also old jar lids and closures

Fry Glass

Ron Damaska
738 9th Ave.
New Brighton, PA 15066
412-843-1393
Also cut glass

Fulper

Douglass White
P.O. Box 5400672
Orlando, FL 32854
407-841-6681

Gambling

Cisco's
Sam Kennedy
212 N 4th St.
Couer d'Alene, ID 83814
208-769-7575

Robert Eisenstadt
P.O. Box 020767
Brooklyn, NY 11202

Games

Paul Fink's Fun and Games
P.O. Box 488
59 S Kent Rd.
Kent, CT 06757
203-927-4001

Geisha Girl Porcelain

Author of book
Elyce Litts
P.O. Box 394
Morris Plains, NJ 07950
Also ladies' compacts

Glass Animals

Author of book
Lee Garmon
1529 Whittier St.
Springfield, IL 62704

Glass Knives

Adrienne Escoe
4448 Ironwood Ave.
Seal Beach, CA 90740
e-mail: escoebliss@earth-link.net

Glass Shoes

Author of book
The Shoe Lady
Libby Yalom
P.O. Box 7146
Adelphi, MD 20783

Glassware

Boopies in red
Twila Zackmire
1405 E Bonebrake Rd.
Veedersburg, IN 47987

End of day
Dave Smith
1142 S Spring St.
Springfield, IL 62704

Glidden Pottery

David Pierce
27544 Black Rd.
P.O. Box 248
Danville, OH 43014
614-599-6394

Goebel

Friar Tuck and Cardinals
Carol and Jim Carlton
8115 S Syracuse St.
Englewood, CO 80112
303-773-8616

Grand Army of the Republic

Richard A. Haussmann
25 Hampton Rd.
Montgomery, IL 60538
708-896-8287

Graniteware

Author of books
Helen Greguire
716-392-2704
Also carnival glass and toasters

Greeting Cards

Circa 1920s through 1960s; used okay
Linda and Bruce Cervon
10074 Ashland St.
San Buenaventurea, CA 93004
805-659-4405 or fax 504-659-4776

Griswold

Buying catalogs and research materials only
Author of book
Denise Harned
P.O. Box 330373
Elmwood, CT 06133

Hawaiiana

Eclectic Antiques
Jim and Kaye Whitaker
P.O. Box 475, Dept. WB
Lynwood, WA 98046
206-774-6910

Hallmark Ornaments

Mayor's 1982, 1983, 1984, 1987, 1991, 1993
G. Crinklaw
8118 N State Hwy. AC
Willard, MO 65781
417-742-3940

Halloween

C.J. Russell and
Pamela Apakarian-Russell
Halloween Queen Antiques
P.O. Box 499
Winchester, NH 03470
Also other holidays and postcards

Hartland Plastics, Inc.

Specializing in Western Hartlands
Kerry and Judy's Toys
7370 Eggleston Rd.
Memphis, TN 38125

Head Vases

Jean Griswold
701 Valley Brooks Rd.
Decatur, GA 30033
404-299-6606

Heisey Glass

Debbie Maggard
P.O. Box 211
Chagrin Falls, OH 44022
216-247-5632

Hollow Ware

Thomas J. Ridley III
MidweSterling
4311 NE Vivion Rd.
Kansas City, MO 64119
816-454-1990
fax 816-454-1605
(closed Wed. & Sun.)

Holt Howard

April and Larry Tvorak
P.O. Box 126
Canon City, CO 81215
719-269-7230
or
HRC #34, Box 25B
Warren Center, PA 18851
717-395-3775

Homer Laughlin

Author of book
Darlene Nossaman
5419 Lake Charles
Waco, TX 76710

Horton Ceramics

Darlene Nossaman
5419 Lake Charles
Waco, TX 76710

Hull

Mirror Brown, also Pfaltz-graff Gourmet Royal and other lines
Jo-Ann Bentz
P.O. Box 146 AA, R.R. #3
Birdsboro, PA 19508
610-582-0311

Mirror Brown, also Pfaltzgraff Gourmet Royal
Bill and Connie Sloan
4965 Valley Park Rd.
Doylestown, PA 18901

Imperial Glass

Joan Cimini
63680 Centerville-Warnock Rd.
Belmont, OH 43718
Also has Candlewick matching service

Lee Garmon
1529 Whittier St.
Springfield, IL 62704
Also Fenton plum opalescent

Ruth Grizel
P.O. Box 205
Oakdale, IA 0205

Imperial Porcelain

Geneva D. Addy
P.O. Box 124
Winterset, IA 50273

Indy 500 Memorabilia

Eric Jungnickel
P.O. Box 4674
Naperville, IL 60567
630-983-8339

Insulators

Len Linscott
3557 Nicklaus Dr.
Titusville, FL 32780

Shaun Kotlarsky
2475 W Walton Blvd.
Waterford, MI 48329
810-673-1650
e-mail: HGCo7@aol.com

Irish Belleek

Richard K. Degenhardt
Sugar Hollow Farm
124 Cypress Point
Henderson, NC 28739
704-696-9750

Irons

Author of book
Dave Irons
223 Covered Bridge Rd
Northampton, PA 18067
610-262-9335
Irons by Irons (softcover),
available from the author

Jewel Tea

*Products or boxes only;
no dishes*
Bill and Judy Vroman
739 Eastern Ave.
Fostoria, OH 44830
419-435-5443

Edits newsletter
Gwynneth Harrison
P.O. Box 1
Mira Loma, CA 91752
909-685-5434
Buys and appraises

Jewelry

Marcia Brown (Sparkles)
P.O. Box 2314
White City, OR 97503
503-826-3039

*Enamelled metal daisies,
from 1960s, 2" to 3" dia*
Linda and Bruce Cervon
10074 Ashland St.
San Buenaventurea, CA
93004
805-659-4405 or

fax 504-659-4776
*Bakelite, carved pins and
hinged bracelets*
Sherry and Mike Miller
303 Holiday Dr.
Tuscola, IL 61953
217-253-4991
Also jewelry catalogs and
ephemera circa 1920 to 1935

*Men's accessories and cuff
links only; edits newsletter*
The National Cuff Link Society
Eugene R. Klompus
P.O. Box 346
Prospect Hts., IL 60070
847-816-0035

Josef Originals

Jim and Kaye Whitaker
Eclectic Antiques
P.O. Box 475, Dept. WB
Lynnwood, WA 98046
206-774-6910

Kay Finch

*Animals and birds, espe-
cially in pink with pastel
decoration*
Mike Drollinger
1202 Seventh St.
Covington, IN 47932
765-793-2392

Doris Frizzell
5687 Oakdale Dr.
Springfield, IL 62707

Kentucky Derby and Horse Racing

B.L. Hornback
707 Sunrise Ln.
Elizabethtown, KY 42701

Knives

*Especially Bowie, hunt-
ing, military, and pock-
etknives*
Bill Wright
325 Shady Dr.

New Albany, IN 47150
Knife Rests

Beverly L. Ales
4046 Graham St.
Pleasanton, CA 94566
510-846-5297

Kreiss

Phil and Nyla Thurston
82 Hamlin St.
Cortland, NY 13045
607-753-6770

Labels

Cerebro
P.O. Box 1221
Lancaster, PA 17603
800-695-2235

Lalique

John R. Danis
11028 Raleigh Ct.
Rockford, IL 61111
815-963-0757
fax 815-877-6042

Lamps

Aladdin; author of books
J.W. Courter
3935 Kelley Rd.
Kevil, KY 42053
502-488-2116

*Electric, oil or miniature
Moon & Star pattern by L.G.
Wright or L.E. Smith*
Linda Holycross
109 N Sterling Ave., WTB
Veedersburg, IN 47987

Motion lamps
Eclectic Antiques
Jim and Kaye Whitaker
P.O. Box 475, Dept. WB
Lynwood, WA 98046
206-774-6910

Motion lamps
Will Winn
1147 Rockingham Dr.
Harrisonburg, VA 22801
540-433-3253

Perfume lamps
Tom and Linda Millman
231 S Main St.
Bethel, OH 45106
513-734-6884 (after 9 pm)

Law Enforcement and Crime-Related Memorabilia

Tony Perrin
1401 N Pierce #6
Little Rock, AR 72207
501-868-5005 or
501-666-6493 (after 5 pm)

L.E. Smith

Ruth Grizel
P.O. Box 205
Oakdale, IA 0205

Lefton

Author of book
Loretta De Lozier
1101 Polk St.
Bedford, IA 50833

Liberty Blue Dinnerware

Gary Beegle
92 River St.
Montgomery, NY 12549
914-457-3623
Also most lines of collectible modern American dinnerware as well as character glasses

License Plate Attachments

Edward Foley
129 Meadow Vly. Rd. #11
Ephrata, PA 17522
717-738-4813

License Plates

Richard Diehl
5965 W Colgate Pl.
Denver, CO 80227

Limoges

d' Limoges An' tea'ques
20 Post Office Ave.
Andover, MA 01810
508-420-8773

Lunch Boxes

Norman's Ole and New Store
Philip Norman
126 W Main St.
Washington, NC 27889
919-946-3448

Terri's Toys and Nostalgia
Terri Ivers
419 S First St.
Ponca City, OK 74601
405-762-8697 or
405-762-5174
fax 405-765-2657
e-mail: ivers@pcok.com

MAD Collectibles

Michael Lerner
32862 Springside Ln.
Solon, OH 44139

Magazines

Issues price guides
Denis C. Jackson
Illustrator Collector' News
P.O. Box 1958
Sequim, WA 98382
360-683-2559
fax 360-683-2559

Pre-1950 movie magazines, especially with Ginger Rogers covers
Tom Morris
P.O. Box 8307
Medford, OR 97504
503-779-3164

National Geographic
Author of guide
Don Smith's National
Geographic Magazines
3930 Rankin St.
Louisville, KY 40214
502-366-7504

Marbles

Author of book
Everett Grist
6503 Slater Rd., Ste. H
Chattanooga, TN 37412
615-855-4032

Anthony Niccoli
4220 N Locust #102
Kansas City, MO 64116
phone/fax 816-455-6652

Match Safes

George Sparacio
P.O. Box 791
Malaga, NJ 08328
609-694-4167

Matchcovers

Bill Retskin
P.O. Box 18481
Asheville, NC 22814

McCoy

*Brown Drip Dinnerware;
also Pfaltzgraff Gourmet
Royal and Hall Mirror Brown*
Jo-Ann Bentz
Box 146 AA, Beaver Rd.
R.R. 3
Birdsboro, PA 19508
610-582-0311

Authors of book
Robert and Margaret Hanson
P.O. Box 70426
Bellevue, WA 98005

Milk Glass

Author of book
Ruth Grizel
P.O. Box 205
Oakdale, IA 0205

Moorcroft

Buy and sell
John Harrigan
1900 Hennepin
Minneapolis, MN 55403
612-872-0226

Morgantown

*Ephemera and glass
Author of book; editor of
newsletter*
Jerry Gallagher
420 1st Ave. NW
Plainview, MN 55964
507-534-3511

Motorcycles

*Also related items and
clothing*
Bruce Kiper
Ancient Age Motors
2205 Sunset Ln.
Lutz, FL 33549
813-949-5060

Movie Posters

Movie Poster Service
Cleophas and Lou Ann
 Wooley
Box 517
Canton, OK 73724

Music Boxes

Disc or cylinder
Mechantiques
Martin Roenigk
26 Barton Hill
E Hampton, CT 06424
860-267-8682
fax 860-267-1120

Also monkey organs,
band organs, coin pianos,
organettes, musical clocks
or watches, automated
birds and dolls; anything
antique mechanical music

Napkin Dolls

Bobbie Zucker Bryson
1 St. Eleanoras Ln.
Tuckahoe, NY 10707
914-779-1405

Niloak Pottery

*Author of book; historian
on Arkansas pottery*
David Edwin Gifford
P.O. Box 7617
Little Rock, AR 72217

Nippon

Nippon Philatelics
Frank L. Allard Jr.
Drawer 7300
Carmel, CA 93921
408-625-2843

Non-Sports Cards

Mark and Val Macaluso
3603 Newark Rd.
Marion, NY 14505
315-926-4349
fax 315-926-4853

*Newspaper Collector
Society*
Rick Brown
P.O. Box 19134
Lansing, MI 19134

Novelty Clocks

Carole S. Kaifer
P.O. Box 232
Bethania, NC 27010
Also items of pressed
wood and Syrocco

Sam and Anna Samuelian
P.O. Box 504
Edgmont, PA 19028
610-566-7248
Also motion lamps, transistor and novelty radios

Novelty Radios

Authors of several books
Sue and Marty Bunis
R.R. 1, Box 36
Bradford, NH 03221

Nutcrackers

Earl MacSorley
823 Indian Hill Rd.
Orange, CT 06477

Old MacDonald's Farm

Rick Spencer
3953 S Renault Cir.
W Valley, UT 84119

Open Salts

Marjorie Geddes
P.O. Box 5875
Aloha, OR 97007
503-649-1041

Orientalia and Dragonware

Susie Hibbard
2570 Walnut Blvd. #20
Walnut Creek, CA 94596

Paper Dolls

Author of books
Mary Young
P.O. Box 9244
Wright Bros. Branch
Dayton, OH 45409

Paperweights

Antique and modern; leading artists and Baccarat
George Kamm
24 Townsend Ct.
Lancaster, PA 17603
717-872-7858

Specifically Blue Bell
Author of book
Jackie Linscott
3557 Nicklaus Dr.
Titusville, FL 32780

Pattern Glass

Aurora, aka Diamond Horseshoe
Richard A. Haussmann
25 Hampton Rd.
Montgomery, IL 60538
708-896-8287

Pencil Sharpeners

Phil Helley
629 Indiana Ave.
Wisconsin Dells, WI 53965
608-254-8659

Advertising and figural
Martha Hughes
4128 Ingalls St.
San Diego, CA 92103
619-296-1866

Pennsbury

BA Wellman
88 State Rd. W
P.O. Box 673
Westminster, MA 01473-1435

Joe Devine
1411 3rd St.
Council Bluffs, IA 51503
712-232-5322
712-328-7305

Perfume Bottles

Especially commercial, Czechoslovakian, Lalique, Baccarat, Victorian, crown top, factices, miniatures
Monsen and Baer
Box 529
Vienna, VA 22183
703-242-1357
Buy, sell and accept consignments for auctions

Perfume Lamps

Tom and Linda Millman
231 S Main St.
Bethel, OH 45106
513-734-6884

Pez

Richard Belyski
P.O. Box 124
Sea Cliff, NY 11579
516-676-1183

Pfaltzgraff

Gourmet Royal as well as other dinnerware lines
Jo-Ann Bentz
Box 146 AA, Beaver Rd.
R.R. 3
Birdsboro, PA 19508
610-582-0311

Gourmet, Gourmet Royal
Bill and Connie Sloan
4965 Valley Park Rd.
Doylestown, PA 18901

Phoenix and Consolidated

Author of book; editor of newsletter
Jack D. Wilson
P.O. Box 81974
Chicago, IL 60681-0974

Phoenix Bird Chinaware

Buy and sell; newsletter available
Joan Oates
685 S Washington
Constantine, MI 49042
616-435-8353
Also Erich Stauffer figurines

Phonographs

Parts and accessories
Hart Wessman
600 N 800 W
W Bountiful, UT, 84087
801-298-3499

Photo Albums

Victorian, lithographed print on cover
Sherry and Mike Miller
303 Holiday Dr.
Tuscola, IL 61953
217-253-4991

Photographica

Antique photography and paper
Betty Davis
5291 Ravenna Rd.
Newton Falls, OH 44444
fax 216-872-0386

Circa 1925 of women carrying purses
Sherry and Mike Miller
303 Holiday Dr.
Tuscola, IL 61953
217-253-4991
Also Art Deco picture frames with reverse-painted designs

Any pre-1900
John A. Hess
P.O. Box 3062
Andover, MA 01810

Pie Birds

Also funnels
Lillian M. Cole
14 Harmony School Rd.
Flemington, NJ 08822
908-782-3198
Also old ice cream scoops

Howard Pierce

Susan N. Cox
Main Street Antique Mall
237 E Main St.
El Cajon, CA 92020
619-447-0800

Pin-up Art

Issues price guides
Denis C. Jackson
Illustrator Collector's News
P.O. Box 1958
Sequim, WA 98382
360-683-2559
fax 360-683-2559

Pocket Calculators

Author of book
International Assn. of Calculator Collectors
Guy D. Ball
14561 Livingston St.
Tustin, CA 92680-2618
714-759-2116
fax 714-730-6140

Political

Donkey figurines
Dorothy Crowder
1628 S Stringtown Rd.
Covington, IN 47932

Michael and Polly McQuillen
McQuillen's Collectibles
P.O. Box 11141
Indianapolis, IN 46201
317-322-8518

Before 1960
Michael Engel
29 Groveland St.
Easthampton, MA 01027

Pins, banners, ribbons
Paul Longo Americana
Box 490
Chatham Rd. S Orleans
Cape Cod, MA 02662
508-255-5482

Porcelier

Jim Barker
Toaster Master General
P.O. Box 41
Bethlehem, PA 10106

Author of book
Susan Grindberg
6330 Doffing Ave. E
Inner Grove Hts., MN 55076
612-450-6770
fax 612-450-1895
e-mail: Porcelier@MSN.Com
Specializing in Porcelier China; author of *Collector's Guide to Porcelier China*; autographed copies available from the author for $18.95 + $2.05 postage & handling (Minnesota residents add $1.23 sales tax).

Postcards

C.J. Russell and
Pamela Apakarian-Russell
Halloween Queen Antiques
P.O. Box 499
Winchester, NH 03470
Also Halloween and other holidays

Powder Jars

John and Peggy Scott
4640 S Leroy
Springfield, MO 65810

Sharon Thoerner
15549 Ryon Ave.
Bellflower, CA 90706
310-866-1555

Prints

*Yard Longs, also Long
Ladies*
Author of book
William Keagy
P.O. Box 106
Bloomfield, IN 47424
812-384-3471

Maxfield Parrish
Edward J. Meschi
129 Pinyard Rd.
Monroeville, NJ 08343

Yard Longs
Authors of book
Charles and Joan Rhoden
605 N Main
Georgetown, IL 61846
217-662-8046

*Currier and Ives,
original only*
Rudisill's Alt Print Haus
Barbara and John Rudisill
24305 Waterview Dr.
Worton, MD 21678
410-778-9290

Purinton Pottery

Susan Morris
P.O. Box 656
Panora, IA 50216
515-755-3161

Purses

Beaded glass
Sherry and Mike Miller
303 Holiday Dr.
Tuscola, IL 61953
217-253-4991

Veronica Trainer
P.O. Box 40443
Cleveland, OH 44140

Puzzles

*Wood jigsaw type from
before 1950*
Bob Armstrong
15 Monadnock Rd.
Worcester, MA 01609

before 1950
Mr. and Mrs. R.H. Spicer
RD 1, Ashgrove Rd.
Box 82
Cambridge, NY 12816

Norm Vigue
62 Bailey St.
Stoughton, MA 02072
617-344-5441

Radio Premiums

Bill Campbell
1221 Littlebrook Ln.
Birmingham, AL 35235
205-853-8227
fax 405-658-6986

Radios

Antique Radio Labs
James Fred
Rte. 1, Box 41
Cutler, IN 46920
Buy, sell and trade; repairs
radio equipment using vac-
cuum tubes

*Authors of several books
on antique, novelty and
transistor radios*
Sue and Marty Bunis
R.R. 1, Box 36
Bradford, NH 03221

Author of book
Harry Poster
P.O. Box 1883
S Hackensack, NJ 07606
201-410-7525
Also televisions, related
advertising items, old
tubes, cameras, 3-D view-
ers and projectors, View-
Master and Tru-View reels
and accessories

Railroadiana

*Any item; especially
china and silver*
John White, 'Grandpa'
Grandpa's Depot
1616 17th St., Ste. 267
Denver, CO 80202
303-628-5590
fax 303-628-5547
Also related items; cata-
logs available

*Colorado Railroad,
D.&R.G.RR., R.G.S.R.R.,
R.G.W.Ry., Uintah Ry.,
Colo.- Midland R.R.*
Daniel E. Price
627 Ox Bow Rd.
Grand Junction, CO 81504

*Also steamship and other
transportation memora-
bilia*
Fred and Lila Shrader
Shrader Antiques
2025 Hwy. 199
Crescent City, CA 95531
707-458-3525
Also Buffalo, Shelley,
Niloak and Hummels

Records

45 rpm and LP's
Mason's Bookstore, Rare
Books, and Record Albums
Dave Torzillo
115 S Main St.
Chambersburg, PA 17201
717-261-0541

*Picture and 78 rpm kid-
die records*
Peter Muldavin
173 W 78th St.
New York, NY 10024
212-362-9606

Especially 78 rpms
L.R. 'Les' Docks
Box 691035
San Antonio, TX 78269
Write for want list

LP's, 45 rpms; '50s-'60s
rock 'n roll
Mr. and Mrs. R.H. Spicer
RD 1, Ashgrove Rd.
Box 82
Cambridge, NY 12816

Red Wing Artware

Wendy and Leo Frese
Three Rivers Collectibles
P.O. Box 551542
Dallas, TX 75355
214-341-515
Internet: rumrill@ix.net-
com.com

Regal China

Van Telligen, Bendel, Old
MacDonald's Farm
Rick Spencer
3953 S Renault Cir.
West Valley, UT 84119
801-973-0805

Road Maps

Also National Geographic
Society supplements
Charles R. Neuschafer
New World Maps, Inc.
1123 S Broadway
Lantana, FL 33462-4522
407-586-8723

Noel Levy
P.O. Box 595699
Dallas, TX 75359-5699

Rooster and Roses

Jacki Elliott
9790 Twin Cities Rd.
Galt, CA 95632
209-745-3860

Roselane Sparklers

Lee Garmon
1529 Whittier St.
Springfield, IL 62704

Rosemeade

NDSU research specialist
Bryce Farnsworth
1334 14½ St. S
Fargo, ND 58103
701-237-3597

Roseville

Andrew E. Thomas
4681 N 84th Way
Scottsdale, AZ 85251
602-947-5693
fax 602-994-4382

Rowland and Marsellus

David Ringering
Salem, OR 97301
503-585-8253
Also other souvenir and
historical china with
scenes of tourist attrac-
tions from 1890 through
the 1930s

Royal Bayreuth

Don and Anne Kier
2022 Marengo St.
Toledo, OH 43614
419-385-8211

Royal China

BA Wellman
88 State Rd. W
P.O. Box 673
Westminster, MA 01473-1435

Royal Copley

Author of book
Joe Devine
1411 3rd St.
Council Bluffs, IA 51503

712-323-5233
712-328-7305
Buy, sell or trade; also pie
birds

Royal Doulton Tobies

John Harrigan
1900 Hennepin
Minneapolis, MN 55403
612-872-0226
Buy and sell

Royal Haeger

Toe-Tapper musicians
Dorothy Crowder
1628 S Stringtown Rd.
Covington, IN 47932

RumRill

Wendy and Leo Frese
Three Rivers Collectibles
P.O. Box 551542
Dallas, TX 7535
214-341-5165; internet:
rumrill@ix.netcom.com

Ruby Glass

Author of book
Naomi L. Over
8909 Sharon Ln.
Arvada, CO 80002
303-424-5922

Russel Wright

Author of book
Ann Kerr
P.O. Box 437
Sidney, OH 45365

Salt and Pepper Shakers

Plastic gasoline pumps
Peter Capell
1838 W Grace St.
Chicago, IL 60613-2724
312-871-8735

Joe Devine
1411 3rd St.
Council Bluffs, IA 51503
712-232-5233 or
712-328-7305

Pattern glass
Authors of book
Mildred and Ralph Lechner
P.O. Box 554
Mechanicsville, VA 23111

Figural or novelty; buy, sell
and trade; lists available
Judy Posner
May-October: R.D. 1,
Box 273
Effort, PA 18330
717-629-6583 or
November-April:
4195 S Tamiami Trail #183
Venice, FL 34293
941-497-7149
e-mail:
Judyandjef@aol.com

Schoenhut

Publishers of Inside Col-
lector and Antique Doll
World
Keith & Donna Kaonis
60 Cherry Ln.
Huntington, NY 11743
516-261-8337
fax 516-261-8235

Schoolhouse
Collectibles

Kenn Norris
P.O. Box 4830
Sanderson, TX 79848

Scottie Dog Collectibles

Donna Palmer
2446 215th Ave. SE
Issaquah, WA 98027

Scouting Collectibles

Author of book
R.J. Sayers
P.O. Box 629
Brevard, NC 28712
Book available by sending
$24.94 plus $4 for shipping
and handling

Buy, sell, trade
Tim Warner
509-11 Margaret Ave.
Kitchener, Ont.
Canada N2H 6M4
519-745-7947

Sebastians

Blossom Shop Collectibles
Jim Waite
112 N Main St.
Farmer City, IL 61842
800-842-2593

Sewing Collectibles

Marge Geddes
P.O. Box 5875
Aloha, OR 97007
503-649-1041

Sewing Machines

Toy only; authors of book
Darryl and Roxana Matter
P.O. Box 65
Portis, KS 67474-0065

Shawnee

Rick Spencer
3953 S Renault Cir.
West Valley, UT 84119
801-973-0805

Corn King and Corn
Queen
Rebecca S. Thomas
4681 N 84th Way
Scottsdale, AZ 85251
602-947-5693
fax 602-994-4382

Shot Glasses

Author of book
Mark Pickvet
P.O. Box 90404
Flint, MI 48509

Silhouette Pictures
(20th Century)

Author of book
Shirley Mace
Shadow Enterprises
P.O. Box 1602
Mesilla Park, NM 88047
505-524-6717 or
505-523-0940
e-mail:
shmace@nmsu.edu

Silver Plate

Especially grape patterns;
also sterling
Rick Spencer
3953 S Renault Cir.
W Valley, UT 84119
801-973-0805

Silverware

Thomas J. Ridley III
MidweSterling
4311 NE Vivion Rd.
Kansas City, MO 64119
816-454-1990 or fax 816-
454-1605 (closed Wed. &
Sun.)

Slag Glass

Author of book
Ruth Grizel
P.O. Box 205
Oakdale, IA 52319

Sharon Thoerner
15549 Ryon Ave.
Bellflower, CA 90706
310-866-1555

Snow domes

Author of book and newsletter
Nancy McMichael, Editor
P.O. Box 53310
Washington, DC 20009

Soda Fountain Collectibles

Harold and Joyce Screen
2804 Munster Rd.
Baltimore, MD 21234
410-661-6765

Soda-Pop Memorabilia

Craig and Donna Stifter
P.O. Box 6514
Naperville, IL 60540
630-717-7949

Painted-label soda bottles
Author of books
Thomas Marsh
914 Franklin Ave.
Youngstown, OH 44502
216-743-8600 or
800-845-7930 (order line)

Sports Collectibles

Equipment and player-used items
Don and Anne Kier
2022 Marengo St.
Toledo, OH 43614
419-385-8211

Bobbin' head sports figures
Author of guide
Tim Hunter
1668 Golddust
Sparks, NV 89436
702-626-5029

Paul Longo Americana
Box 490
Chatham Rd., S Orleans
Cape Cod, MA 02662
508-255-5482
Also stocks and bonds

Golf collectibles
Pat Romano
32 Sterling Dr.
Lake Grove, NY 11202

Sports Pins

Tony George
22431-B160 Antonio
Parkway #252
Rancho Santa Margarita,
CA 92688
714-589-6075

Souvenir Spoons

Thomas J. Ridley III
MidweSterling
4311 NE Vivion Rd.
Kansas City, MO 64119
816-454-1990
fax 816-454-1605
(closed Wed. & Sun.)

Stangl

Birds, dinnerware, artware
Popkorn Antiques
Bob and Nancy Perzel
P.O. Box 1057
4 Mine St.
Flemington, NJ 08822
908-782-9631

Statue of Liberty

Mike Brooks
7335 Skyline
Oakland, CA 94611

Stauffer (Erich) Figures

Joan Oates
685 S Washington
Constantine, MI 49042

String Holders

Ellen Bercovici
5118 Hampden Ln.
Bethesda, MD 20814
301-652-1140

Syroco and Similar Products

Carole S. Kaifer
P.O. Box 232
Bethania, NC 27010

Doris J. Gibbs
3837 Cuming #1
Omaha, NE 68131
402-556-4300

Teapots and Tea-Related Items

Author of book
Tina Carter
882 S Mollison
El Cajon, CA 92020

Telephones

Antique to modern; also parts
Phoneco
207 E Mill Rd.
P.O. Box 70
Galesville, WI 54630

Tire Ashtrays

Author of book
Jeff McVey
1810 W State St., #427
Boise, ID 83702

Toothbrush Holders

Author of book
Marilyn Cooper
8408 Lofland Dr.
Houston, TX 77055
713-465-7773

Torquay Pottery

Jerry and Gerry Kline
604 Orchard View Dr.
Maumee, OH 43539
419-893-1226

Toys

Aurora model kits, and especially toys from 1948-1972
Author of books
Bill Bruegman
137 Casterton Dr.
Akron, OH 44303
330-836-0668
fax 330-869-8668
e-mail: toyscout@sala-mander.net
Dealers, publishers and appraisers of collectible memorabilia from the '50s through today

Building blocks and construction toys
Arlan Coffman
1223 Wilshire Blvd.,
Ste. 275
Santa Monica, CA 90403
310-453-2507

Die-cast vehicles
Mark Giles
P.O. Box 821
Ogallala, NE 69153

Games and general line
Phil McEntee
Where the Toys Are
45 W Pike St.
Canonsburg, PA 15317

Hot Wheels
D.W. (Steve) Stephenson
11117 NE 164th Pl.
Bothell, WA 98011

Model kits other than Aurora; edits publications
Gordy Dutt
Box 201
Sharon Center, OH 42274

Paper-lithographed and paper on wood toys
Mark and Lynda Suozzi
P.O. Box 102
Ashfield, MA 01330
phone/fax 413-628-3241

Puppets and marionettes
Steven Meltzer
670 San Juan Ave. #B
Venice, CA 90291
310-396-6007

Renwal toys in original box and Renwal policemen
Mary Soelberg
29126 Laro Dr.
Agoura Hills, CA 91301
818-889-9909

Sand toys
Authors of book
Carole and Richard Smyth
Carole Smyth Antiques
P.O. Box 2068
Huntington, NY 11743

Slot race cars from '60s-'70s
Gary T. Pollastro
4156 Beach Dr. SW
Seattle, WA 98116
206-935-0245

Tin litho, paper on wood, comic character, penny toys and Schoenhut
Wes Johnson, Sr.
106 Bauer Ave.
Louisville, KY 40207

Tootsietoys
Author of books
David E. Richter
6817 Sutherland
Mentor, OH 44060
216-255-6537

Tops and Spinning Toys
Bruce Middleton
5 Lloyd Rd.
Newburgh, NY 12550
914-564-2556

Toy soldiers, figures and playsets
Phoenix Toy Soldier Co.
Bob Wilson
P.O. Box 26365
Phoenix, AZ 85068
602-863-2891

Transformers and robots
David Kolodny-Nagy
3701 Connecticut Ave.
NW #500
Washington, DC 20008
202-364-8753

Trolls
Roger Inouye
765 E Franklin Ave.
Pomona, CA 91766
909-623-1368

All windup and battery-ops, working or not
Leo E. Rishty
The Toy Doc
77 Alan Loop
Staten Island, NY 10304
712-727-9477
fax 718-727-2151

Walkers, ramp-walkers, and wind-ups
Randy Welch
Raven'tiques
27965 Peach Orchard Dr.
Easton, MD 21601-8203
410-822-5441

TV Guides

TV Guide Specialists
Jeff Kadet
P.O. Box 20
Macomb, IL 61455

Twin Winton

Joe Devine
1411 3rd St.
Council Bluffs, IA 51503
712-232-5233 or
712-328-7305

*Author of book due out
by mid-1998 through Col-
lector Books*
Mike Ellis
266 Rose Ln.
Costa Mesa, CA 92627
714-645-4697
fax 714-645-4697

Typewriter Ribbon Tins

*Also related items; edits
newsletter*
Hobart D. Van Deusen
28 The Green
Watertown, CT 06795
203-945-3456

Valentines

Author of book
Katherine Kreider
Kingsbury Productions
P.O. Box 7957
Lancaster, PA 17604
717-892-3001
or
4555 N Pershing Ave.
Ste. 33-138
Stockton, CA 95207
209-467-8438

Vallona Starr

Author of book
Bernice Stamper
7516 Elay Ave.
Bakersfield, CA 93308
805-393-2900

Van Briggle

Dated examples
Author of book
Scott H. Nelson
Box 6081
Santa Fe, NM 87502
505-986-1176
Also UND (University of
North Dakota) and other
American potteries

Dave Smith
1142 S Spring St.
Springfield, IL 62704

Vandor

Lois Wildman
175 Chick Rd.
Camano Island, WA 98282

Vaseline Glass

Terry Fedosky
Rte. 1, Box 118
Symsonia, KY 42082

Vernon Kilns

Maxine Nelson
873 Marigold Ct.
Carlsbad, CA 92009

View-Master and Tru-View

Harry Poster
P.O. Box 1883
S Hackensack, NJ 07606
201-410-7525

Walter Sigg
3-D Entertainment
P.O. Box 208
Swartswood, NJ 07877

Wade

Author of book
Ian Warner
P.O. Box 93022
Brampton, Ontario
Canada L6Y 4V8

Walking Sticks and Canes

Bruce Thalberg
23 Mountain View Dr.
Weston, CT 06883

Warwick

*Any item or research
materials*
Authors of book
Pat and Don Hoffman Sr.
1291 N Elmwood Dr.
Aurora, IL 60506
708-859-3435

Watches

Character and personality
Author of book
Howard S. Brenner
106 Woodgate Terrace
Rochester, NY 14625

All brands and character
James Lindon
5267 W Cholla St.
Glendale, AZ 85304
602-878-2409

*Antique pocket watches
and vintage wristwatches*
Maundy International
P.O. Box 13028-BW
Shawnee Mission, KS 66282
800-235-2866

Watt Pottery

Author of book
Susan Morris
P.O. Box 656
Panora, IA 50216
515-755-3161

Rick Spencer
3953 S Renault Cir.
W Valley, UT 84119

Western Americana

Author of book
Warren R. Anderson
American West Archives
P.O. Box 100
Cedar City, UT 84720
801-586-9497
Also documents, autographs, stocks and bonds, and other ephemera

Especially Civil War items
K.C. Owings, Jr.
P.O. Box 19
N Abington, MA 02351
Also autographs and paper items

Western Heroes

Author of books, ardent researcher and guest columnist
Robert W. Phillips
Phillips Archives of
Western Memorabilia
1703 N Aster Pl.
Broken Arrow, OK 74012
918-254-8205
fax 918-252-9363

Westmoreland

Author of books, edits newsletter
Ruth Grizel
P.O. Box 205
Oakdale, IA 52319-0205

Winchester

Cisco's
Sam Kennedy
212 N 4th. St.
Coeur d'Alene, ID 83814
208-769-7575

World's Fairs and Expositions

D.D. Woollard, Jr.
11614 Old St. Charles Rd.
Bridgeton, MO 63044
314-739-4662

Index